JACK KEROUAC
THE BUDDHIST YEARS

JACK KEROUAC
THE BUDDHIST YEARS

COLLECTED WRITINGS

EDITED BY CHARLES SHUTTLEWORTH

SAL PARADISE PRESS
LOWELL, MA

RARE BIRD
LOS ANGELES, CALIF.

THIS IS A GENUINE RARE BIRD & SAL PARADISE PRESS BOOK

Rare Bird Books | Sal Paradise Press
6044 North Figueroa Street
Los Angeles, CA 90042
rarebirdbooks.com

Copyright © 2025 by Jim Sampas, Literary Executor, the Estate of Jack Kerouac

FIRST HARDCOVER EDITION

All rights reserved, including the right to reproduce this book
or portions thereof in any form whatsoever, including
but not limited to print, audio, and electronic.

For more information, address:
Rare Bird Books Subsidiary Rights Department
6044 North Figueroa Street
Los Angeles, CA 90042

Set in Minion/Janson
Printed in the United States

Art by Schae Koteles
Cover Design by Schae Koteles and Robert Schlofferman
Interior Design by Hailie Johnson

10 9 8 7 6 5 4 3 2 1

Publisher's Cataloging-in-Publication Data available upon request.
Library of Congress Control Number: 2024951847

Contents

7   In-Text Citation Abbreviations and Additional Works Cited

10   Transcription Notes

12   Introduction

35   My Sad Sunset Birth (1941)

37   The Story Just Begins (1949)

39   "I Was Born at Five in the Afternoon" (May 1954)

44   Reflections on Birth (from Dharma Notebooks) (1954)

46   "Morning March 12 1922" (1954)

47   Confessions of the Father (December 1954)

51   First Memories (1954)

55   The Heart of the World: The Legend of Duluoz (April 1954)

81   The Legend of Three Houses (June 1954)

149   The Long Night of Life (December 1954)

162   A Dream Already Ended (Two Versions) (1954)

173   "The Universe is empty …" (1954?)

175   Dharma Fragments (1954)

180   Ascetic Plans for the Future (1954)

186   The City and the Path (April 1955)

195   On The Path (August 1955)

208   The Little Sutra (1955)

211   The Blessedness Surely To Be Believed (Two Versions) (1955, 1956)

217   Beat Generation (March 1957)

227   Avalokitesvara (May 1957)

236   Two 1957 Fragments (1957)

238   Northport Sutra (September 1958)

240   Four Poems

         Tao (Mexico 1957)

         God (Orlando 1957)

         The Chinese Poet (1958)

         Untitled "Paradise is the blissful smile" (1958)

245 Letters to Myself (November 1960)

253 Bed Thoughts at 3 A.M. (January 1962)

257 Sources

261 Acknowledgments

264 Images and Figures

In-Text Citation Abbreviations

By Jack Kerouac

AU = *Atop an Underwood.* Viking Penguin, 1999.

BOD = *Book of Dreams.* City Lights Publishers, 2001.

BS = *Big Sur.* Penguin Books, 2011.

DB = *The Dharma Bums.* Penguin Classics Deluxe Edition, 2006.

DP = *Desolation Peak: Collected Writings.* Rare Bird Books, 2022.

DS = *Doctor Sax.* Grove Press First Black Cat Edition, 1975.

GB = *Good Blonde & Others.* City Lights / Grey Fox Press, 1993.

LT = *Lonesome Traveler.* Grove Press First Black Cat Edition, 1970.

MCB = *Mexico City Blues.* Grove Press First Evergreen Edition, 1959.

OTR = *On the Road.* Penguin Books (Penguin Great Books of the 20th Century), 1999.

OTROS = *On the Road: The Original Scroll.* Penguin Books, 2007.

PAS = *Pomes All Sizes.* City Lights Books, 1992.

S = *The Subterraneans.* Grove Press, 1958.

SGE = *The Scripture of the Golden Eternity.* City Lights Pocket Poets Series, 2001.

SL1 = *Jack Kerouac: Selected Letters, Volume 1, 1940–1956*, ed. by Ann Charters. Penguin Books, 1995.

SOD = *Some of the Dharma.* Viking Penguin, 1997.

S-P = *Self-Portrait.* Rare Bird Books, 2024.

TC = *The Town and the City.* Harcourt Brace & Company Harvest Book Edition, 1983.

UK = *The Unknown Kerouac: Rare, Unpublished & Newly Translated Writings*, ed. by Todd Tietchen; trans. by Jean-Christophe Cloutier. Library of America, 2016.

VOC = *Visions of Cody*. Penguin Books, 1993.

VOD = *Vanity of Duluoz*. Paragon Books, 1979.

VOG = *Visions of Gerard*. Penguin Books, 1991.

WU = *Wake Up: A Life of the Buddha*. Penguin Classics, 2009.

WW = *Windblown World: The Journals of Jack Kerouac 1947–1954*, ed. by Douglas Brinkley. Viking Penguin, 2004.

By Others

BB = *A Buddhist Bible*, ed. by Dwight Goddard. Beacon Press, 1970.

BIT = *Buddhism in Translations,* trans. by Henry Clarke Warren. Atheneum Edition 1963, originally published by Harvard University Press, 1922.

LOB = *Sacred Books of the East, Volume 19: The Fo-Sho-Hing-Tsan-King: A Life of Buddha*, trans. by Samuel Beal. Motillal Banarsidass Publishers, 2010, originally published by Oxford University Press, 1883. (Commonly referred to as the Buddha Charita or Life of Buddha.

SBE = *Sacred Books of the East, Volume 10: India and Buddhism*. Kessinger Publishing, LLC reprint edition, originally published by Oxford University Press, 1881.

TCB = *The Teachings of the Compassionate Buddha*, ed. by E. A. Burtt. Mentor Books, 1955.

WCI = *The Wisdom of China and India*, ed. by Yin Yutang. Random House / The Modern Library, 1942.

Additional Works Cited
By Jack Kerouac

The Sea Is My Brother: The Lost Novel. Da Capo Press, 2012.

The Haunted Life and Other Writings. Da Capo Press, 2014.

By Others

Burroughs, William, *The Letters of William S. Burroughs: 1945–1959*. Viking, 1993.

Proust, Marcel, *Swann's Way*, trans. by Linda Davis. Penguin Books, 2002.

Thoreau, Henry David, *Walden and Civil Disobedience*. Barnes and Noble, 2005.

Transcription Notes

IN REGARD TO FORMATTING (paragraphing, punctuation, capitalization, etc.), I've striven to present the material in a manner that's respectful of the originals and reflective of Kerouac's style. That said, the originals vary widely, and in three cases there are both the original handwritten drafts and portions that Kerouac typed to try to publish or share with friends: part of chapter 2 of "The Legend of Three Houses" entitled "The Tragedy of Old Bull Balloon," the opening section of version 2 of "A Dream Already Ended," and the opening section of "Beat Generation." These have instructed my choices as, when typing, he often changed ampersands to "and"s, for instance, and spelled out words he'd originally abbreviated like "shd." Thus, I've also spelled out such abbreviated words (and, in most cases, numbers less than 10) with the exception of (a) ampersands in Kerouac's poetry and (b) words such as "tho," "thot," and in some cases "yr," which constitute eye dialect and reflect the author's preference. As for spelling, I've fixed obvious errors and preserved Jack's use of chiefly British variants ("tranquillity," "arbour," etc.) as well as antiquated spellings ("Porto Rico" and "Rumania").

Regarding the typewritten documents, while most of the time Kerouac's typing is extremely precise, there are others where it's messy, either because he was drunk or the typewriter was defective (having spaces, for instance, where an apostrophe should be). A certain amount of regularization was necessary, therefore, to give this book a more cohesive look where too precise a reproduction would be distracting. While I admire what was done with *Some of the Dharma* and the 2001 edition of *Book of Dreams*, I am following Ann Charters' lead with her two volumes of *Selected Letters* except, of course, that all of the material herein is being presented unabridged. In a few cases I have inserted a word in brackets where it seemed an obvious, inadvertent omission; and in a few other cases where the words were indecipherable, I have inserted bracketed ellipses.

As for interpreting Kerouac's handwriting, which in some cases is challenging, especially when the writing is expressionistic, full of sound words and unconventional spellings (chapter 3 of "The Legend of Three Houses" in particular), I've taken great pains to get the words right, and I've added notations where that was impossible. Overall, I have used my best judgment, and wherever I felt ninety percent certain of a word, I've gone ahead and included it rather than resorting to blanks, question marks, or ellipses.

Introduction

THE PURPOSE OF THIS volume is to share the wealth of previously unpublished writings reflecting Jack Kerouac's Buddhist thinking, to show how Buddhism influenced his work primarily from 1954–'56 and to a lesser extent thereafter, giving him a new vocabulary to discuss spiritual questions that he'd been asking himself all along. From a young age Kerouac was a spiritual thinker and questioner, and he always considered himself a spiritual writer. This statement might come as a surprise to people who only know him as the author of *On the Road*, but if that's the case, they didn't read it closely enough. Gilbert Milstein recognized it in his rave *New York Times* review on the day it was published, writing that Sal and Dean's "excesses" in their "frenzied pursuit of every possible sensory impression" are "made to serve a spiritual purpose [...] The 'Beat Generation' [...] does not know what refuge it is seeking, but it is seeking."[1] And in his journals, amid his two-and-a-half-year struggle to write *On the Road*, Kerouac stated that his purpose was "my own personal salvation and the salvation and treasuring of human life" (WW 223). That was in October 1949, when he was twenty-seven. Five months later he went further, writing on March 1, 1950, "I want to become, and pray to be, an earthly prophet" (WW 275). And in a letter to Neal Cassady in August of that year, he wrote about his conception of a "Celestial Wheel" in heaven consisting of "crazy steel structures":

> My calling is to find out the shape & form of these things so I can know what I'm doing in heaven in my place on the Wheel. I don't have to know "how it works," like Bill B[urroughs] strives to know, only the shape, the form, the final action. [...] I don't write for artistic reasons at all, because I was made by the sky, no part of this lettuce nature, no part of Western Civ. either, and sent as an emissary among many emissaries (many are chosen, few come) to study the shape of the world and most the shape of the poor mind here. All's in a mind, mind is all. Not born of

---

1   *The New York Times*, "The 'Beat' Bear Stigmata Those Who Burn, Burn, Burn" (September 5, 1957).

the apple womb but risen from a blind in graves of salt and sand to pipe the message of the dead.[2]

The root of Kerouac's spirituality began much earlier. Raised in a deeply Catholic French-Canadian neighborhood in Lowell, Massachusetts, Jack was steeped in religion, which was radically intensified when, at age four, his older brother, Gerard, died at age nine of rheumatic fever. Jack's parents reacted to this tragedy in a way that was typical of French-Canadian families—by declaring Gerard a saint who had been called back to Heaven, one who was too good, too pure for this world. Jack grew up hearing stories about Gerard's saintliness, stories he recounted repeatedly in his writing, most notably in his letters to his "blood brother"[3] Neal Cassady three months before the scroll draft of *On the Road*, and in *Visions of Gerard* five years later. Jack attended Catholic schools until he was eleven, receiving First Holy Communion, attending Confession, and serving as an altar boy. There was always a crucifix hanging in his home; he'd visit Lowell's Franco-American Grotto to view the Stations of the Cross, where the story of Jesus's Passion was vividly depicted; and he also had visions, seeing the family's statue of Ste. Thérèse "turn its head at me [...] I knew I was haunted but said nothing" (DS 4–5).

At age nineteen, in a piece entitled "On the Porch, Remembering," Kerouac states that at age six he was asking himself, "What is there to life [...] Is there nothing but death to assuage this?" declaring, "I was a morbid child" and "wondering whether it wouldn't have been better not [to] be born" (AU 98). In the same piece he writes that, while looking at the night sky, "the mystery of the universe began to augment before me" (97). And sprinkled through *Atop an Underwood*, the collection of Jack's earliest writings, are many of the ideas that he'd repeat throughout his career—on the one hand about "the wound of living" (188), life's lack of meaning, and the emptiness of existence (26, 40, 187), and on the other that life is "brief and lovely" and "strange and beautiful, yea as a dream" (192) and that within every being is a spark of the divine. In "Concentration" the young narrator, high on beer, declares one night to a group of men in a bar, "you too are God. All of you are, but you do not realize it" (31).

---

2   Berg Collection 74.7, Kerouac, Jack to Cassady, Neal, August 19, 1950 (Photocopied autograph and typed letters).

3   See SL1 323, 323, and especially 472, where he states, "I'm not too sure that maybe you aren't my brother Gerard reborn..."

The Buddhist Years

In all of Kerouac's early works there's an earnest desire for meaning. In 1943's *The Sea Is My Brother*, George Everhart complains, "My knowledge of life is negative only: I know what's wrong, but I don't know what's good [...] I'm not saying there is no good. You see, good means perfection to me..." (13–14). George, who is an academic (representing one side of twenty-two-year old Jack's personality), states, "I want a life with purpose" (33), while Wesley Martin, an experienced merchant seaman (representing Jack's adventurous, wanderlusty side), feels "a thrill of anticipation" as he's setting off once again, relishing "A simple life! A serious life! To make the sea your own [...] to brood your very soul into it" while giving "thanks to a God more a God than any to be found in book-bound, altar-bound Religion" (54–55). In *The Haunted Life*, Garabed Tourian (a.k.a. Sebastian "Sammy" Sampas) argues to the somewhat more jaded, directionless Peter Martin that "life is lovely and fragile" (52), comparing it to a rose, just as Jack would later call the world "an ethereal flower."[4] But then in *The Town and the City*, Peter becomes the primary searcher after meaning. His belief in God wavers, as at one point he "suddenly believed" (308) but soon after writes to his brother Francis, "I've been cheated, I've been cheated! I wish with all my might there is a God!" (317). Later in the novel, he becomes deeply reflective about God as well as himself:

> What was all the excitement and mystery and sadness in his soul? [...] And what of himself, Peter Martin, his own nature: why was it so vast, false, complex, shifting, treacherous, saddened by the mere sight of life. Something complete, and wise, and brutal too, had dreamed this world into existence, this world in which he wandered haunted. Something silent, beautiful, inscrutable had made all this for sure, and he was in the middle of it, among the children of the earth. And he was glad (360–61).

The Kerouac family dynamic and the friendships Jack developed were factors in the schism that existed within himself. After Gerard's death, while Jack's mother, Gabrielle, doubled-down on religion, becoming even more devout, his father, Leo, left the Church. In his late teens Jack went through an atheistic period alongside Sammy Sampas's fervently socialist ideology; and then in his

---

4   The term "ethereal flower" appears in the *Lankavatara Scripture*: "As thou reviewest the world with thy perfect intelligence and compassion, it must seem to thee like an ethereal flower of which one cannot say: it is born, it is destroyed, for the terms being and non-being do not apply to it" (BB 278). See also SOD 41 et seq., VOG 49 et seq., SGE verse 35, DB 104.

early twenties, amid the backdrop of World War II, having met Lucien Carr, Allen Ginsberg, and William Burroughs, he entered a period of decadence in which the focus was on individual spiritual perceptions—visions largely drawn from the use of narcotics[5]—as well as socially transgressive behavior to investigate the gamut of human experience. Another shift occurred with Leo's death of spleen cancer in 1946. In Leo's final months, twenty-four-year-old Jack became his nurse and was with him when he died; and the loss had a profound effect, being further evidence of the horror of existence while also increasing his family loyalty. On his deathbed, Leo asked Jack to take care of Gabrielle; and in the aftermath Jack wrestled with his mixed emotions for his father, who had been an overweight, heavy-drinking, inveterate gambler and bigot with particular hatred for the New Deal, Blacks, and Jews. In a letter to Neal Cassady a year after Leo's death, Jack wrote of "[t]he hatred I had for his face!" while also asserting "I really and actually believe now that, while my father was alive, I loved him more than any son ever loved his father" (SL1 117–18). Leo's illness and death also coincided with Jack's decision to write *The Town and the City*, which would become his first published novel. It was a massive undertaking, ultimately an 1,100-page manuscript that took more than two years of effort before it was edited, cut by half. In his journals while writing it, Jack wrote of his need for spiritual belief and guidance. As a child he had looked to Leo as the person who "knows everything, knows what should be done at all times and how one should live always." Having grown up to recognize his father's many flaws, he felt that "there must be a way, an authority, a great knowledge, a vision, a view of life, a proper manner, a 'seemliness' in all the disorder and sorrow of the world" and then wrote, "*That there should be something to turn to for advice* is God—God is the 'should-be' in our souls" (WW 144).

In the years following his completion of *The Town and the City*, Kerouac's spiritual yearnings accelerated. Amid the hopeful period after its sale and before publication, he wrote in his journals about resolving "the final questions of life" and about "the consolation of the mortal enigma by means of a recognition of the State of Gratitude" (WW 193). "I insist that life is holy," he wrote in August 1949. "[I]t is not a lonely accident. Therefore [...] we must love and be reverent of one another, till the day when we are all angels looking back" (WW 205, 211). And in September, in an incomplete story entitled "The Hip Generation," Red

---

5   In his 1963 written responses to interview questions posed by John Clellon Holmes, Kerouac stated that a motive behind his narcotics use (primarily Benzedrine during that period) was the "*derangement of the senses*," which "has to be undergone at least once in a lifetime or the artist has not seen the other side of consciousness" (UK 311).

The Buddhist Years

Moultrie, musing in his jail cell, thinks to himself "that beatitude is really ours, that everything is actually all right [...] and that the Saviour has really saved us already."[6] But in 1950, his hope for a lucrative writing career faded. Amid mediocre reviews, the novel didn't sell well. There were no reprints, paperback editions, or a movie sale; and he was struggling to follow it up with a next book, working on ideas for two novels, *Doctor Sax* and *On the Road*, the latter a story about "two guys hitch-hiking to California in search of something they don't *really* find, and losing themselves on the road, and coming all the way back hopeful of something *else*" (WW 123). He spent two-and-a-half years until coming upon the right approach, a semi-fictional account of his actual travels typed up in a rush of words without paragraphing or page breaks on a continuous sheet of paper (sliced to fit his typewriter and with sections taped together) that could stretch out like the road itself. It took enormous faith to take the final product to editor Robert Giroux, unroll it in his office, and believe Giroux would embrace it; and over the next six-and-a-half years, amid personal attacks, professional rejections, and his own self-destructive behavior, his faith was tested again and again.

In 1951 *On the Road* was considered too outlandish for publication both in style and substance. Then came more blows: his eight-month marriage to Joan Haverty dissolved, and he was hospitalized with another bout of thrombophlebitis, the doctor warning him that, if untreated, he could die. This experience proved to be pivotal, as "bothered by the spectre of death" (UK 105), he decided that, regardless of the lack of commercial success, writing was his calling and mission in life: "It may sound vain, but the act of writing seems holy to me [...] Holy... sacred...to use the written word in honor of life, in defense of life against the forces of death and despair" (UK 101). Kerouac reiterated this sentiment many times, calling it "my duty on earth to tell the story of what happened to some of the people I knew," adding, "that like Dostoevsky I was doomed to suffer out all my life to 'draw breath in pain' and tell their stories [...] that my father might gladly look back from his grave at what I had decided to do with his legacy, that my brother Gerard also would bless me, that there was nothing nobler in the world for me to do with my lifetime" (UK 328). It was then that he first devised his sketching technique of writing: "[I]n the Vet hospital [... I] unfolded my secret desire in writing at last:—to tell exactly what happened and not worry about style but only worry about completeness of detail and the hell with what

---

6   Berg Collection 4.22 Typescript, revised. "The hip generation. I. Early appurtenances, September 1949."

anybody thinks" (UK 312). Before he left the hospital, he also had a vision, "a face in my window, saying 'Write what you want.' I thought it was Faulkner, I think it was really Dr. Sax" (UK 170). In retrospect, "I didnt dream any of it would ever be published except in the madhouse [...] but I was ashamed that I was not going to help my mother" (UK 312–13).

Kerouac's first sketches form the opening pages of *Visions of Cody*, kicking off another prolific period of writing where within a year he wrote that novel as well as *Doctor Sax* and "October in the Railroad Earth" while also commencing work on *Book of Sketches* and *Book of Dreams*. But the prospects for publication were virtually nil. He received a $250 advance from Ace Books for *Cody* (which he was calling *On the Road*), but when Carl Solomon read it, he turned it down flat, and even Allen, who was acting as Jack's agent, was dismissive, calling *Cody* "great but crazy in a bad way," mocking its aural language as at times unintelligible, and saying, "I don't see how it will ever be published" (SL1 372–73). The next year, 1953, was psychologically even worse. Jack began it by writing *Maggie Cassidy*, thinking it more commercially viable as a love story amid a young man's coming of age, but with his freewheeling writing style, it fared no better. Meanwhile his personal life continued to deteriorate. In late May he signed onto the SS *William H. Carruth* sailing out of San Francisco, his first job on a merchant ship since 1944. The trip was supposed to last four months, destined for Korea, but while working aboard, he was morbidly uncommunicative and unable to conform, considering himself, as a waiter in the officers' mess, a "whitejacketed sudden-waiter-slave of scows" and the ship "a floating prison" (LT 93,100).[7] He sailed south to the Panama Canal and then up through the Caribbean, the Gulf of Yucatan, and the Gulf of Mexico, but in Mobile he got drunk overnight, missed his morning duty, and was seen walking on the street, still drunk and shirtless, with a prostitute. So, fired from the ship, he collected his pay in New Orleans and made his way back to New York.

By this time Kerouac was clearly alcoholic. It may well have been an inherited condition: both of his parents were heavy drinkers, as was Jack's paternal grandfather, Jean-Baptiste, who purportedly died at age 58 of the potato-peel vodka that he made himself. As Jack chronicles in several of his books, his alcoholism was also socially induced: as a teenager and young adult, getting

---

7   See also S 2: "I'd just come off a ship in New York, paid off before the trip to Kobe Japan because of trouble with the steward and my inability to be gracious and in fact human and like an ordinary guy while performing my chores…"

The Buddhist Years

drunk was equated with manliness, and so by 1953, at age 31, he'd been drinking to excess for more than a decade. In New York that fall, becoming involved with a new lover, Alene Lee, his drinking was a major factor in destroying their relationship, as he would drag her through drunken late-night revels or else abandon her to keep partying himself, unable to resist the fever of the moment. Jack relished rowdy, all-male bull sessions with friends, wanting ecstasy and escape from mundane existence as well as all the demons that plagued him—his paranoid insecurities, feelings of failure, and anger toward the publishing industry, incensed in particular by the commercial success of John Clellon Holmes's beat novel *Go*, which included many of the same characters as *On the Road*.[8] By his own account, he also wanted to break up with Alene, realizing that Gabrielle, who was as racist as Leo, would never accept Jack's relationship with a Black woman. But in the aftermath, according to him, he was devastated and suicidal.[9]

This is where most of the work within this volume begins—in late 1953, when Kerouac, seeking solace and wanting to retreat from the world, first turned to Thoreau and then, through him, to Eastern religion. *Walden* had long been an inspiration to him; in a letter to Allen in June of '49, he wrote of having "decided someday to become a Thoreau of the Mountains. To live like Jesus and Thoreau [… a]nd go away in the mountains forever" (SL1 193). Now, four-and-a-half years later, Jack, despondent and broke, was inspired by Thoreau's praise in *Walden* of Eastern asceticism:

> Most of the luxuries, and many of the so called comforts of life, are not only not indispensable, but positive hinderances to the elevation of mankind. With respect to luxuries and comforts, the wisest have ever lived a more simple and meagre life than the poor. The ancient philosophers, Chinese, Hindoo, Persian, and Greek, were a class than which none has been poorer in outward riches, none so rich in inward. We know not much about them. It is remarkable that *we* know so much of them as we do. The same is true of the more modern reformers and benefactors of their race. None can be an impartial or wise observer

---

8   In *Go*, Kerouac is a major character (Gene Pasternak), as is Allen Ginsberg (David Stofsky) and Neal Cassady (Hart Kennedy) along with Luanne Henderson (Dinah) and Al Hinkle (Ed Schindel). The novel details the latter three's visit to New York that is more briefly covered in part 2 of OTR. For several years Jack's anger stifled their friendship, as Jack felt *Road* was superior and Holmes had stolen his thunder.

9   See pp. 195 and 228 herein.

of human life but from the vantage ground of what *we* should call voluntary poverty (15–16).

As Jack relates in two of the stories in this volume, "On the Path" (1955) and "Avalokitesvara" (1957), Thoreau's references to "Hindoo" philosophy led him to start investigating Eastern religious texts: "At home at night in my sweet and quiet room I perused the news about the Indian Bhagavad heroes, the *Zendavesta*, the *Koran*, till I came to Asvaghosha's *Life of Buddha* (translated by Samuel Beal) and there I stopped" (see p. 196 herein). In the story of the Buddha, Jack saw himself; it validated his despair and gave him a course of action. As a young man Siddhartha Gautama, having grown dissatisfied, abandoned his family and swore off earthly pleasures to understand the reason behind the world's miseries—"The pain of birth, old age, disease, and death"—and to try to transcend them, to

> search for the happiness of something that decays not, that never perishes, that never knows beginning, that looks with equal mind on enemy and friend, that heeds not wealth nor beauty, The happiness of one who finds repose alone in solitude, in some unfrequented dell, free from molestation, all thoughts about the world destroyed, dwelling in some lonely hermitage, untouched by any worldly source of pollution, begging for food sufficient for the body.[10]

The future Buddha became an ascetic wanderer. Then, after achieving complete enlightenment while meditating in the shade of the Bodhi tree, he became a teacher, educating disciples about the way to nirvana—by following his precepts and the Eightfold Path.

For the next three years, Kerouac immersed himself in the study primarily of Buddhist and Taoist texts, seeking personal salvation while also attempting to share what he learned in an effort to educate and emancipate others. In the short term the former effort was the more successful: Buddhism did offer him some psychic relief during an exceedingly painful period—the second half of the six-and-a-half-year stretch between writing *On the Road* and its publication. But when he talked about Buddhism, few people listened. The irony is that in the long term the opposite occurred: he, unable to live up to Buddhist precepts, re-embraced Christianity, and died alcoholic; whereas, through the influence of *The Dharma Bums* in particular, he had a major effect in exposing people to Buddhism, ushering in a new consciousness that took hold in the Sixties.

---

10   LOB 46, 49–50.

The Buddhist Years

People well-versed in Kerouac's writings will recognize 1954 as the one of the few years that, while in his prime (1951–'61), he did not produce a major work. But in fact Kerouac was always writing, and amid his Buddhist study, there was certainly no letup. The majority of this volume was written in 1954, and there was a plethora of other work that year. One of his activities, as he poured through Buddhist texts, was to type large sections verbatim, seemingly for his own edification. At some point he culled them into a manuscript entitled "Bodhi (Indian for 'Wisdom')" that today resides in the New York Public Library's Kerouac archive—122 single-spaced pages totaling more than 70,000 words and that likely was even larger: his typed section of the Buddha Charita, which begins on page thirty-three of the "Bodhi" manuscript (Jack hand-wrote the page numbers) has a typed page number of 86. Meanwhile he was writing in and typing up his Dharma journals—work eventually published as *Some of the Dharma*; he wrote his *San Francisco Blues* poems, the story "cityCityCITY," and entries for *Book of Sketches* and *Book of Dreams*. In all of his work that year, the Buddhist influence is evident. In *Book of Dreams*, the first reference appears in his commentary at the end of the "LIVID LIPS OF TELEVISION" dream which in his notebook was dated December 11, 1953, and there are frequent references thereafter, many of them complaints about "the infinite never-ceasing painful karma-activity of the discriminating brain" (221), "all the forms the Dharmakaya One-Essence assumes, in these raving human dreams—this raving human Dream this world" (226), etc. Even "cityCityCITY," a science fiction tale inspired by that summer's Army-McCarthy Hearings, which Jack watched on television in Gabrielle's Richmond Hill apartment, ends with a Buddhistic message, as thirteen-year-old M-80, rocketing away, escaping cityCityCITY, reads a letter from his adopted father, T-3, which tells him to

> pray—pray—for I believe that our reward is without end, we just dont know it, OUR REWARD IS WITHOUT END, and it comes to us in some ghostly afterway that must have something to do with the common essence of all things and has to do with what we were before we thought we were born…it's ONE THING, ONE perfect emptiness of light without end.[11]

Kerouac was particularly drawn to Mahayana Buddhism: known as "the greater vehicle," it more closely resembles Catholicism, as it believes in the divinity

11   GB 213.

of the Buddha and emphasizes the cultivation of love and compassion for all living beings; as well as Pure Land Buddhism, a Mahayana branch that focuses on an afterlife in a Heaven-like Buddhaland. Avalokitesvara, the bodhisattva of infinite compassion and mercy, was Kerouac's favorite deity, to whom he prayed and sought to emulate. A bodhisattva by definition is a buddha-to-be, one who delays reaching nirvana in order to assist others by showing them the way. This gave more meaning to Kerouac's work as a writer: he was striving not for personal accomplishment and glory but to ease human suffering. And Buddhism justified his lifestyle: with its vision of the material world as empty and illusory, he was free to do what he wanted.

Buddhist teachings gave voice and credence to feelings that Kerouac claimed he'd had since childhood. In version 2 of "A Dream Already Ended" herein, he states that his central text, the *Diamond Sutra*, was "in agreement with my own infant suspicions, that life is only a dream. A short vague dream encompass't round by flesh and tears." And in "Avalokitesvara" he writes of himself as a "young Buddhist [...] fascinated by the teaching that everything is emptiness which is something he's suspected ever since he was 16 years old (he thinks) but actually since baby crib wise."

$\sim$

I'VE ALWAYS BEEN DRAWN to Kerouac's more spiritual writing, first in reading *The Dharma Bums* and later *Visions of Gerard* and *The Scripture of the Golden Eternity*. Then in the 2000s I tackled *Some of the Dharma*, a vast, rich text that opened my eyes wider. It led me to re-read *Mexico City Blues*, enabling me to penetrate and appreciate it more deeply. And there's much more that's been published over the years, scattered within his books of poetry and prose. Kerouac's readings of Eastern texts enriched his vocabulary, added to his poetic expression, and softened his outlook: yes, all life is suffering, but he became more expressive of the wonders of existence, especially the beauty and sentience of nature.

The years 1954–'57 are routinely classified as Kerouac's Buddhist phase, although as the later pieces included here reveal, Buddhism remained enmeshed in his spiritual thinking; after 1956 he stopped studying Buddhism save for re-readings of the *Diamond Sutra*, but he never fully relinquished its ideas and imagery. To be clear, though, Kerouac was never strictly a Buddhist; he was drawn to Taoism also, especially the writings of Chuangtse (Zhuangzi), which he encountered in *The Wisdom of India and China*, and he never abandoned

The Buddhist Years

Christianity, especially his love of Jesus. His goal was always syncretic, an effort to mix all religions into a single universalist vision.

These years were also difficult, as so much of his life was; he had few people with whom he could share his beliefs. Around the house Gabrielle started calling him "Mahatma,"[12] and Lucien Carr was dismissive, as was William Burroughs, who wrote to Jack that "Buddhism is only for the West to study as history, that is, it is a subject for understanding"; it was "not A Solution" but "a form of psychic junk."[13] Allen left in December 1953 for Cuba and Mexico and didn't return to the States until July. Jack's typing of *Some of the Dharma* was specifically to share with him, hoping for a disciple, but he had no such luck with the Cassadys, with whom he went to stay in San Jose in February 1954. They had become devotees of Edgar Cayce, an American spiritualist whose Christian beliefs included subjects such as reincarnation, psychic healing, the lost world of Atlantis, access to Akashic records, etc. The result was that they argued, and Jack left in March, staying at the Cameo Hotel, a favorite San Francisco flophouse, before returning to Richmond Hill and Gabrielle in April, where he wrote two of the longer pieces in this volume: "Heart of the World: The Legend of Duluoz," begun April 19, and "The Legend of Three Houses" begun June 22. It's clear that he wasn't happy, as in his journals he was contemplating becoming a hermit, living in a cave in the Mexican desert or else in the woods in Northern California, going so far as to write out directions and draw a map of Pomo Indian trails east of Ukiah, CA, and to study the native flora, learning the difference between edible and poisonous plants and mushrooms[14] as well as how to make maple sugar and how to subsist on acorns, mashing them into cakes and roasting them to make coffee. On a positive note, sometime that summer he had an experience that he recounts in *The Scripture of the Golden Eternity* (verse 64) and twice more in this volume:[15] while working in the garden behind the Richmond Hill apartment house, he passed out and, for what felt like five minutes, he believed he perceived and experienced the golden eternity—the soothing emptiness of perfect bliss and tranquility, happiness and peace.

12   Berg 49.2 Holograph notebook "Dharma (1)." (Begins: "Memory Babe Dec 9, 53").

13   Burroughs 226–27.

14   See figs. 3–12.

15   See pp. 239, 249 herein. See also "Coda: Jack Kerouac's Dream" in *Big Sky Mind: Buddhism and the Beat Generation* (Riverhead Books, 1995).

In October Kerouac took a break from New York City, traveling by bus to Lowell, where he stayed in a cheap hotel, walked around the old neighborhoods, and had an awkward visit with his first love, Mary Carney. The trip to Lowell stimulated his writing "The Long Night of Life," a fascinating precursor to *Visions of Gerard*. By the end of the year, though, he was despondent, being among other things pressed by ex-wife Joan for support of their now-two-year-old daughter Jan (Jack, denying paternity, was fearing arrest). Writing in his Dharma journal on December 19, the end of what he called a "pivotal year," he stated,

> I am at the lowest beatest ebb of my life, trapped by the police, "retained in dismal places," scorned and "cheated" by my friends (plagiarists), misunderstood by my family, meanwhile mutilating myself (burning hands, benzedrine, smoking, goofballs), also full of alcoholic sorrow and dragged down by the obligations of others, considered a criminal and insane and a sinner and an imbecile, myself self-disappointed & endlessly sad because I'm not doing what I knew should be done a whole year ago when the Buddha's printed words showed me the path…a year's delay, a deepening of the sea of troubles, sickness, old age creeping around my tired eyes, decrepitude and dismay, loss of solitude & purity—I must exert my intelligence now to secure the release of this Bodhisattva from the chains of the City.

> WHAT is the advice of the Buddhas concerning the effectuation of the release of this Bodhisattva so that he may freely enter his desert hermitage of solitude, purity & Dhyana? (SOD 185).

His life improved in 1955, mostly professionally, as his writing output caught fire. While this volume will show that he wrote well in '54, nearly everything was unfinished; he couldn't find his direction, becoming bored with writing projects and/or searching for the right approach to convey his deepening spirituality. He began by writing what he eventually titled *Wake Up*,[16] re-telling the life of the Buddha through the scripture he'd read and his own sensibility, while also continuing *Some of the Dharma*. Then in a magnificent outburst while in Mexico City in August, after attempting "On the Path," a story of his discovery of Buddhism included herein, he wrote his *Mexico City Blues* poems and the first half of *Tristessa*. He traveled up to California in mid-September, and after three

---

16 Kerouac considered numerous titles, including "Awake Beyond Existence," "Stop and Wake Up," "The Tathagata Is Awake," "Essential Mind: The Story of the Buddha," and "Buddha Tells Us."

The Buddhist Years

months there returned to North Carolina, where on December 27 he started *Visions of Gerard*, finishing the handwritten draft on January 16, 1956. He also had growing support for his writing: Malcolm Cowley became an influential advocate, aiding in the publication of two *On the Road* excerpts: "Jazz and the Beat Generation" in the *New World Writing 7th Mentor Edition* (under the pseudonym Jean-Louis), published January 1, 1955, and "The Mexican Girl" in the Winter 1955 issue of *The Paris Review*. Cowley was also instrumental in Kerouac's receiving a $300 grant from the National Institute of Arts and Letters and, as an editorial consultant for Viking Press, paving the way for *On the Road*'s publication. Jack was also on hand for the Six Gallery reading which launched the San Francisco Poetry Renaissance, creating national publicity for the burgeoning Beat movement. It was there than Allen first read "Howl." He'd encouraged Jack to read also, but due to shyness he'd refused.

Kerouac's personal life was more up and down. Gabrielle retired from her job as a skiving machine operator in a Brooklyn shoe factory and moved down to Rocky Mount, NC, to live with her daughter, Nin, Nin's husband, Paul Blake, and six-year-old Paul Blake Jr. Although Jack was able to live there rent-free, the situation was uncomfortable, as the Blakes were also struggling financially, and they resented his refusal to work. His discomfort likely inspired "The City and the Path," a story in which Peter Martin lives as a hermit in Mexico practicing Buddhist meditation away from family and friends; and Kerouac also made two attempts at drafting "The Blessedness Surely to Be Believed" to spread "The Happy Truth" that life is an illusion, a view which his relatives summarily dismissed. He left North Carolina at the end of July and had a better time in Mexico City and especially Berkeley, where he stayed with Allen and made great new friends in the poets Gary Snyder and Philip Whalen. But in late November he and Allen had a drunken argument over Buddhism, causing Jack to leave in a huff, retreat to the Cameo Hotel, and spend Thanksgiving alone. Days later Natalie Jackson, Neal's girlfriend, committed suicide, and after another uneasy stay with the Cassadys, Jack reluctantly headed east for Christmas, hopping a freight and then hitchhiking, feeling himself to be homeless.

The climax of Kerouac's Buddhist phase came in 1956 with his upbeat conclusion to *Some of the Dharma* on March 15 followed in April by *The Scripture of the Golden Eternity*, which is ultimately a syncretic merging of all religions:

"[W]hat's in a name?" asked Shakespeare. The golden eternity by another name would be as sweet. A Tathagata, a God, a Buddha by another name, an Allah, a Sri Krishna, a Coyote, a Brahma, a Mazda, a Messiah, an Amida, an Aremedeia, a Maitreya, a Palalakonuh, 1 2 3 4 5 6 7 8 would be as sweet. (28)

The turning point proved to be Kerouac's experience that summer as a fire lookout on Desolation Peak. His two months alone on the mountaintop was the kind of retreat from the world that he'd always longed for, and as he wrote to Philip Whalen in February, he "hoped [to] be able to do that work every single year from now on" (SL1 547). The reality proved too much for him, however; rather than achieving ultimate enlightenment, he suffered extreme bouts of boredom and depression and in the aftermath never reapplied. Instead he continued his itinerant lifestyle, traveling to Mexico City in September; New York in late November, where he stayed with a new girlfriend, Helen Weaver, until she threw him out; Christmas in Orlando, FL, where the Blakes and Gabrielle had moved; New York again in January 1957 with his newest girlfriend, Joyce Glassman (later Johnson); across the Atlantic in February by Yugoslavian freighter first to Tangier, where he helped Burroughs type *Naked Lunch* and gave it its title; then France and England in April before a return to New York (back with Joyce) and Orlando; and in May a bus trip across the country with Gabrielle in what was supposed to be a permanent move to Berkeley that lasted only two months: in July she returned to Orlando and Jack went briefly back to Mexico City, then was in New York in time for *On the Road*'s September fifth publication.

Following 1955's "On the Path," 1957's "Avalokitesvara" was Kerouac's second attempt to tell the story of his discovery of Buddhism, but again he abandoned it, perhaps because of the turmoil while with Gabrielle in Berkeley but more likely because he needed a more interesting approach. Six months later he found it, writing in medias res: rather than starting from the beginning—December 1953—*The Dharma Bums* opens in September '55 and quickly shifts the focus onto Japhy Ryder (Gary Snyder).

The first two entries in this volume, "My Sad Sunset Birth" and "The Story Just Begins," are the only ones included before Kerouac's Buddhist phase begins, and they serve to demonstrate how his immersion in Buddhism reinforced ideas that he'd had all along. Written most likely in late 1941, "My Sad Sunset Birth" shows the nineteen-year-old Kerouac questioning the meaning of his

The Buddhist Years

existence as, at age six, he felt an awakening of consciousness. It reveals him as introspective and something of a depressive; and it contrasts interestingly with the pieces that follow, beginning with "I Was Born at Five in the Afternoon"—a series of meditations on his actual birth and his first memories, depictions closely linked to William Wordsworth's in "Ode: Intimations of Immortality" (i.e., the sense that before birth, people were in Heaven (a.k.a. the golden eternity) and to there shall return, "safe in heaven dead"[17]):

> Our birth is but a sleep and a forgetting:
> The Soul that rises with us, our life's Star,
> > Hath had elsewhere its setting,
> > And cometh from afar:
> > Not in entire forgetfulness,
> > And not in utter nakedness,
> But trailing clouds of glory do we come
> > From God, who is our home:
> Heaven lies about us in our infancy!
> Shades of the prison-house begin to close
> > Upon the growing Boy,
> But he beholds the light, and whence it flows,
> > He sees it in his joy;

Next, in "The Story Just Begins," written in 1949 while Kerouac was struggling to write his second novel, to be called *On the Road*, the main character, Red Moultrie, expresses the same ideas that predominate Jack's Buddhist writing: "everything is […] all right," "nothing that happened really matters," reality is "merely a silly game he was playing," and "the Saviour has really saved us already."

~

THIS COLLECTION SHOWS JACK at his earnest, soulful best. The writing is consistently and wonderfully Kerouacian: it is honest, reflective, heartfelt, and revealing, with great characterizations amid his self-exploration as he wrestles with his consciousness, desperate for belief. Even when speaking of prenatal memories, there can be no doubt that he is sincere.

Readers can make up their own minds about this material, having their own takeaways and identifying favorites, but I'll offer some further notes here:

---

17   See MCB's 211th Chorus. See also VOG 44: "'Why did God leave us sick and cold? Why didnt he leave us in Heaven?'"

- "Heart of the World: The Legend of Duluoz" is fascinating for Kerouac's portrayal of his family members at the time of his birth: the sweet innocence of five-year-old Gerard and three-year-old Nin in chapter 3; the earthy, somewhat sexualized description of Gabrielle (called Evangeline) in chapter 5; and especially the portrayal of Leo (Eno), which also includes some sexual detail (we learn he's soon to be impotent), creating Oedipal overtones. In his conversation with his friend Charley in chapter 4, Leo both resents and pities Jack's birth, and he's absent for it, choosing to stay away from home and up all night playing poker with some railroad hands and Old Bull Baloon, a fictionalized version of W. C. Fields. (According to Jack, Leo played poker with W. C. Fields on at least one occasion.)[18] Contrastingly, chapter 11's portrait of Leo is much more poignant and elegiac.

People familiar with *Visions of Gerard* will recognize the two scenes including Eno and Bull (chapters 6 & 7), as they're very similar to the version in that novel written a year and a half later. Jack clearly utilized this one in writing the latter, the difference being that in *Visions of Gerard* the game is played on the night Gerard dies. In both cases Leo is absent, indulging himself during a crucial family event.

Chapter 9 is adapted from a prose piece Kerouac wrote in San Luis Obispo in 1953 while working for the Southern Pacific railroad. Jack also used the first half of the chapter in *Book of Sketches* (248–54), breaking the lines into his poem-like sketch form. In this typed version (the original was handwritten) he made numerous edits, most significantly deleting the opening sentence, which read, "THERE IS A MEMORY so deep, so beautiful, in the memory of this world, right or wrong—" Jack's decision to insert this as a chapter has a powerful effect on the whole, as it further smashes chronological time, being set both the month before Jack's birth and in the summer of 1950 near Mexico City, while also including references contemporaneous with its drafting. Also notable is the piece's original title, "Death of Gerard," included in *Book of Sketches* but not here, suggesting that Jack associated his birth with Gerard's death four years later, as if the one precipitated the other.

- "The Legend of Three Houses" is the longest piece in this collection. Begun on June 22, 1954, it is the start of what would have been an epic novel involving many characters of the three extended families but focusing on

18   See UK 314.

The Buddhist Years

three main ones: nine-year-old Ray Smith (the stand-in for Jack), eight-year-old Cody Deaver Jr. (young Neal Cassady), and, once again, Old Bull Baloon. There is a similar plot element from an earlier work, "Old Bull in the Bowery," written two years earlier, as both Ray and Cody Jr. travel to New York City with their fathers, who've arranged to rendezvous with each other; and in chapter 3 Kerouac borrows from that earlier work in telling elements of Cody Jr.'s backstory and arrival in New York. In this version Jack once again demonstrates deep sympathy for the experiences Neal suffered in Depression-era Denver, growing up destitute with an alcoholic father. The differences, though, are striking, and many are indicative of Kerouac's increasingly spiritual bent.

Most significant are the changes to Ray's and Bull's circumstances, as Kerouac reimagined these characters. In this story Old Bull most closely resembles William Burroughs with elements of W. C. Fields and Leo thrown in; and where in "Old Bull in the Bowery" he was Cody's father's alcoholic cohort, here he is Ray's father, and he demonstrates far more love, sentimentality, and compassion. When Ray was a newborn, Bull had abandoned him, devastated after his wife had died giving birth. Ray has been raised in an orphanage, but now Bull returns, rescuing him and taking him on the drive to New York City. Along the way he also plans for a much longer journey that will include stops in North Carolina, Texas, Mexico, San Francisco, and finally Denver, each destination involving an act of charity or repayment of a debt. This Old Bull Baloon is still a heavy drinker, but he's actively seeking to help others, seemingly to make amends. He also at one point particularly reflects Leo when he brushes cigar ashes off his thick thighs (see pp. 61, 78 & 172 herein and VOG 99).

That Kerouac chooses to portray himself as an orphan is, of course, psychologically revealing. In a 1951 letter to Neal, he wrote, "I always felt like an orphan because my brother, who came before me, died to 'save me,' as it were, for my mother's arms (here I'm acquiescing to the pre-established musings of any Freudian mysterious-reader)" (SL1 281). In this story, however, Bull is both father and mother, dispenser of paternal instruction and maternal affection, saying while on their journey together, "Don't ever cry about life, Raymond—And anyway this old man loves ya." Meanwhile, despite his young age and strict Catholic upbringing, Ray is filled with

Buddhist perceptions such as, while "brooding at his Catechism desk [...] suddenly his mind roamed into a vision of the dreamlikeness of existence and he saw everything as visionary flowers in the air."[19]

In imagining "The Legend of Three Houses" as an epic, Kerouac drew upon locations that he knew well. Riverville, ME, is a stand-in for Lowell with its mill canal and "grotto and the cross"; Big Kincaide, NC, represents Nin's home in Rocky Mount; over the years Jack spent extended time in Denver, Mexico City, and San Francisco; visited Burrough in Texas; and had a memorable stopover in Butte, MT, on a bus ride east from San Francisco (depicted at the end of part 2 of the *On the Road* scroll version only):

> In Butte Montana I got involved with drunken Indians; spent all night in a big wild saloon that was the answer to Bill Burroughs' quest for the ideal bar; I made a few bets on the wall, got drunk; I saw an old card dealer who looked exactly like W. C. Fields and made me cry thinking of my father (OTROS 278).[20]

Arguably, "The Legend of Three Houses" is marred by too much exposition—in particular most of chapter 1, where a vast cast of characters is introduced—but the writing flows nicely, a mood is established reflecting a blue-collar American Buddhist-Taoist viewpoint, and the narrative sings with earthy dialogue and eccentric turns of phrase. The action doesn't begin until chapter 2, when the story switches to Ray, and Bull arrives at the orphanage. Along the way Kerouac seemingly became aware of this problem, writing in his notebook, "It's all style, no story," and changing its title to "On the Road" (clearly liking the title and intent on making use of it amid the completed novel's continuing rejection by publishers). The highlight is Ray and Bull's road trip, which, once it reaches Lowell becomes a ghostly tour through Kerouac's past: first there's a great baseball scene; then Bull goes to locate his friend Eno Duluoz (i.e. Leo) by visiting his printing shop. Eno isn't there, having gone to the racetrack, but Ray meets his slightly older self: Hunky (Henri-Michel) Duluoz "(a very strange boy) (whom Ray would

---

19   The term "visionary flowers in the air" comes from the *Surangama Sutra*: "The Tathagatas...regard all of the perceptions of sight, their causes and conditions, and of all conceptions of phenomena, as being visionary flowers in the air, having no true nature of existence within themselves. But they regard the perceiving of sight as belonging to the Essence of the wonderful, pure, enlightening Mind (Bodhi)" (BB 145). See also SOD 43 et seq., WU 92.

20   See also MCB's 1st Chorus, which begins, "Butte Magic of Ignorance."

The Buddhist Years

meet again in his haunted travels in this haunted life)" is Jack at age twelve. Then, after Lowell, with Ray asleep in the car, Bull drives past a castle (shades of *Doctor Sax*) and an old man with long white hair walking along the road, reminiscent of both *On the Road*'s Ghost of the Susquehanna and "old man with white hair [...] walking toward us with the Word" (49).

- "The Long Night of Life," written in late 1954 after Kerouac's October trip back to Lowell, is another precursor to *Visions of Gerard*, written a year later. Chapter 1, "My Discovery of the Dharma," is wonderfully evocative, mixing family history with an overarching, *Genesis*-like sense of world history and world-as-illusion based on Buddhist beliefs. It's also memorable for its concise, sympathetic depictions of both Leo and Gabrielle. Chapter 2, "Birth," continuing the rich, spiritual focus, also repeats some elements from "Heart of the World: The Legend of Duluoz," i.e., the litany of Jack's childish nicknames and a lengthy discussion of Gerard and Nin based on a family photo of them near the time of Jack's birth (see fig. 1). Chapter 3, "The Castle," discusses the origin of his invention of *Doctor Sax,* leading to a poignant memory of Gerard's being injured while sledding. Jack's memory of Nin's kindness toward him in the aftermath amid his irrational sense of guilt is heartbreaking. And Chapter 4, "Gerard," tells a story of Gerard's bringing home a hungry boy named Beaupré and compassionately asking Gabrielle to feed him. It's a story Jack repeats in *Visions of Gerard*, and other stories mentioned here he elaborates on in the novel. My sense is that Kerouac gave up on "The Long Night of Life" because he was still searching for a better approach to writing this first part of the Duluoz Legend, and a year later he found it by taking the focus off of himself and putting it more squarely on his older brother.

- Version 2 of "A Dream Already Ended" has two known drafts. The first is a longer, handwritten ms. that takes twenty-eight pages of a 1954 notebook that also includes entries for *Book of Dreams*; and the second is a typed version that repeats the first ten pages of the handwritten draft. For me the latter portion is the most interesting, as it tells two detailed stories, the first showing Kerouac's compassion for a poor young Mexican boy being overworked by his disabled farther, and the second, set in New York, where he witnesses an obese man eating an elaborate meal while he himself is broke, hungover, and starving. The man is a clear precursor to "fat Mr. Groscorp" in *Visions of Gerard* (written a year later), who eats "his necessitous Samsara dinner" while observing Gerard's funeral from his apartment across the street from the church (121–23), although that seed was planted much earlier, as Jack also mentions a story he wrote at age nineteen about a 300-pound man, Mr. Gross, eating a huge meal in a local restaurant.

- The lists that Kerouac drew up in the section entitled "Ascetic Plans for the Future," written in 1954 on "Twentieth Century-Fox Film Corporation" inter-office memo stationery (see fig. 3; Jack had worked as a script synopsizer), reveal much about his mindset during this period. What's most telling are the "Fears" listed in "Elements of the Basic Deceit," which reveal that he couldn't really be happy anywhere and that he wasn't cut out for the solitary existence he liked to imagine. His fears are even more pronounced in an unpublished entry in his Dharma notebook in which he modifies his plans, imagining instead a nomadic life on the road:

> In this Western world I cant delude myself that I can go live in solitude in the desert "in a rain shelter"—what about the law? what about snakes, scorpions, & lizards? what about great rains? how can I carry enough food let alone water on my back to last more than a week at a crack? in other words how can I travel light like a Buddhist ascetic if I cant beg my food and water in towns? Clearly, to practice Buddhism in the West with its laws, customs, ideas of property, proprieties, overpopulation and development of outlying areas, its general coverage of the face of the earth here, you've got to have a *front*, or device. Mine is going to be a rolling hut, a hermitage on wheels, a panel truck with food supplies, water in cans, sleeping bag, in which I'll travel from desert to mountain to sea to city and back to desert—dry from rain, safe off the rattlesnake ground, apparently within legal rights tho homeless on the western world road.
>
> I've got to work for this truck & will have to do some work to keep it in repair, like Thoreau and his lovely 19th Century hut at Walden Pond Massachusetts—
>
> I can just see myself, a Bhikshu, hiking thru some Indiana town at the height of some panic over a child sex killing. This isnt India. I can just see myself making my regular round of meal-begging in Georgia or Alabama. I cant even see myself boiling greens over a wood fire in

The Buddhist Years

the Appalachians, the Fire Rangers would spot my smoke & put me in jail for lack of fine.[21]

- "The City and the Path" also reveals Kerouac's desire to live a life of solitude in the desert, as he envisions alter ego Peter Martin "living the life of a religious hermit in a hollow in the hills outside of Tenancingo, Mexico, a tiny village at the end of the road." In *Some of the Dharma*, Jack discusses his plans for "THE CITY & THE PATH," writing that in it Peter Martin "goes from agape of Town & City (the original ms.) to Karuna" (161), i.e., from the Christian sense of Christ's love for humankind to the Buddhist universal compassion of a Bodhisattva. He also states that it is "My duty to become a Bodhisattva Teacher & teach the Path from my desert hut---no other duty" (160). By the end of the piece, however, Peter grows bored and yearns to return to civilization—New York and San Francisco—to be with his friends.

- In telling the tale of Kerouac's initial study of Buddhism, both "On the Path" and "Avalokitesvara" serve to correct the multiple biographies that date its beginning as in early 1954. In both of these pieces, Jack states it began in November 1953 (although in "The Long Night of Life," he says it was December), the impetus being the devastation he felt after his breakup with Alene Lee. He also reveals in "On the Path" that he stole his copy of *A Buddhist Bible* from the Richmond Hill branch of the New York Public Library.

A title page that appears separately in the Kerouac archive reveals that Jack had planned "On the Path" to be a major work. Dated January 5, 1955 (whereas the actual text is dated August 19), it reads as follows (written in dark pencil suggesting bold print):

On the Path

Being an Explanation to his Mother of his Discovery of the Path of the Buddhas of Old, Consisting of Three Parts, 1) Discovery of the Path of the Buddhas of Old, 2) Progress on the Path of the Buddhas of Old, 3) his Most Fervent Final Wish.

by

Jean-Louis[22]

---

21   Berg Collection 49.4: Holograph notebook "Dharma (3)" (dated from July 29 1954). See SOD 143: Kerouac radically amended this entry.

22   Berg Collection 3.22: Holograph fragment (one page).

- Version 1 of "The Blessedness Surely-to-be-Believed" is the first draft of what Kerouac ultimately called his "Emptiness Prayer." See *Some of the Dharma* 401 for the draft labelled "PRAYER OF THE THREE INEXISTENCIES." The next draft, beginning "Three ways in which things are empty," appears on 407–08; and another draft, labeled "PRAYER OF THE THREE EMPTINESSES," follows on 408–09. Yet another version appears in the letter to Carolyn Cassady of March 2, 1956 (this letter is located in the Neal Cassady Collection Box 2.6 at the Harry Ransom Center, The University of Texas at Austin). Thus "Emptiness Prayer," written in April 1956 on the first two pages of the notebook that contains the handwritten draft of *The Scripture of the Golden Eternity*, is at least a sixth draft, and an abbreviated version of the prayer appears in *The Scripture*'s forty-sixth verse.[23]

- "Beat Generation" focuses on Kerouac's monthlong hospital stay from August to September, 1951, when he was suffering from thrombophlebitis. It's an interesting supplement to his 1951 Journal, included in *The Unknown Kerouac*, as in the journal Jack is mostly introspective, making critical decisions about the future direction of his writing. In this piece, while it's colored by his Buddhist spirituality, it's more outward-looking, including compassionate portraits of his fellow patients amid the excitement of the New York Giants' baseball season (a year when they won the National League pennant before losing the World Series to the New York Yankees).

- "Avalokitesvara" shows Kerouac in more boisterous form. It's particularly notable for what it reveals about his life with Gabrielle at the time, the two sharing a small one-bedroom apartment.

In his journal, he wrote:

> "Tonight, May 27 [1957], I begin AVALOKITESVARA
> Wish me luck—
>> big Chinese confession adventure of an American Buddhist
>> Dharma Bum—
>> How I discovered Avalokitesvara and grew in understanding of
>> Him, and roamed,
>> and climbed mountain;

---

23   Ann Charters' detailed examination of the differences between the April 1956 notebook version of the Emptiness Prayer and *The Scripture*'s forty-sixth verse appears in *Kerouac at the "Wild Boar,"* ed. by John Montgomery (Fels & Firn Press, 1986) 139–41.

and argued with Bishops,
and had laughs, and sufferings,
and triumphed in that I could live
and write a book about it—
HEE!
Wrote seven chapters long and short,
4000 words and on the way!
—Thank you, Lord[24]

It is the last entry in that particular journal, and on its back inside cover he drew a picture of "Buddha Laughing on Mt. Lanka!" (see fig. 2). But by June 4, he'd become disenchanted with the project, writing that "Avalokitesvara is bogged down in generalities 'discussing' the Dharma and such crap—"[25]

• Regarding "Northport Sutra," Kerouac wrote in his journal on September 11, 1958: "Just wrote my funny NORTHPORT SUTRA—I'd gone out in yard to decide everything, under tree—The answer is always the same—but I wrote it better tonight."[26]

—Charles Shuttleworth

24   Berg Collection 56.3: Diary # 3. Holograph diary "Feb. - May '57."

25   Berg Collection 56.5: Diary # 5. Holograph diary "Berk / 1957."

26   Berg Collection 56.12: Diary # 12. Holograph diary "Fall / 1958."

My Sad Sunset Birth

MY SAD SUNSET BIRTH[27]

The day I was born, there was snow on the ground and the descending sun colored westwise windows with an old red melancholia, as of dream.

I was walking home with my sled, aged six.

Suddenly I stopped in my tracks and stared, standing quietly on the sidewalk in Centralville.

"What is this?" I asked myself, noticing the sudden swoop of a sad moment as it flew across our rooftops. "What is this strange thing I see?"

In that manner, I was born to the world, February 1929, just before supper.

How can I adequately describe this birth of mine with words? It was something strange, something intensely haunting. The wisp of winter's dusk caught hold of me—for the first time in my little life I was puzzled by the sound of children's voices, the smell of snow at sunset, the vapors which puffed from my mouth with every icy exhalation, and above all, that fleeting old sadness which hung tenderly over the crimsoning houses of Centralville.

"Well I'll be damned," I said to myself. "I'll be damned."

That year, 1929, was the year of the great Stock Market crash; the year, they tell me, which saw the crumbling of paper institutions, the inevitable end of ever-rising business, the soaring aloft from windows of broken business men, Clyde Van Dusen winning the Derby down in Kentucky,[28] the Athletics winning the World Series, and as for myself, the introduction of Popeye to America's vast funny-page audience. "By Segar," I used to say, "Copyright 1929, Popeye and the Thimble Theatre, by Segar, All Rights Reserved, King Features Syndicate."[29]

---

27   Another version of this story, written around the same time, is "Sadness at Six" in AU 182–83.

28   In 1929 Clyde Van Dusen was the name of both the horse and the horse's trainer. The horse, a son of Man o' War, won the Kentucky Derby by two lengths on a sloppy track. The trainer, a former jockey, was one of the nation's leading trainers during the 1930s and the top trainer at Santa Anita during the 1941 season while working for the California stable of MGM studio boss Louis B. Mayer.

29   The character Popeye first appeared in 1929 in E. C. Segar's *Thimble Theatre* comic strip.

The Buddhist Years

From that day of my birth onward, I began to wonder about things as I had never done before. When the Stock Market crashed, I ignored it completely, being quite busy wondering, and finding more food for thought in Popeye and the Thimble Theatre, second to the last page of the *Boston Evening American*. My father was a small business man, and he was not affected by the crash. The night of the stock market crash, my father took my mother out to a movie. My sister and I stood on the back porch singing 'Pierre et Jacques' right out into the night. We sang and sang, and our French words echoed through around that part of Centralville—know what? I would like to fly out into space this very moment and catch up with the scientific sound waves of our song that night in 1929—I imagine the words are somewhere beyond Uranus by now, but I would love to go up there and listen to them as they advance on through space, singing and echoing in the blackness, "Pierre et Jacques, Pierre et Jac-ques, dormez vous, dormez vous?…"[30] and so forth. It is a very amazing thing to know this.

And so, I was walking along the sidewalk with my sled, unborn, and suddenly I saw everything, the old glow of dying sun, chimneys stringing off mournful smoke upward, snowbanks in the street being pink and sadly hunched—and I was born. "Pourquois?" I asked myself. "Pourquois?" Which is exactly what I ask myself even today. Centralville was gleaming redly, quietly; I heard a dog barking, and the children coasting on the hill were making plenty of swell noise; it was February, and all over the neighborhood the strange old color grew older and older and I was born, amid radiant glowings, born into the world to get in line with other men, for better or for worse, and with a sweep of wonderment, I began to live—a man on this earth, his relation to all things, to himself, to his fellow man, to society, and above all to the universe. I was born and the music began to filter into my being, the colors accentuated deeply, and weird flutings as of Joyce could be heard emanating from my lips; and the windows of the houses grew sadder and sadder, and are getting sadder every day.

30　According to Prof. Jean-Christophe Cloutier, who has translated and written extensively on Kerouac's writings in French, "Pierre et Jacques" is referred to several more times in the Kerouac archive and is likely a regional (or maybe even strictly Lowellian) version of the famous song. He adds that "In parts of New England, racist jokes making fun of French Canadians are called 'Pierre et Jacques jokes.'"

The Story Just Begins

I The Story Just Begins   '49

Earl John Moultrie, known as Red, decided many things when he suddenly stood transfixed in the cafeteria that winter night in New York with his gaunt, bony, melancholy face that was always turned aside and down in pensiveness; as now, over a cool and contemplative jaw; and his smooth auburn hair that combed close to his head and gave him a burnished, rocky look, and brown eyes that sometimes were red in the light of bulbs: standing there, fairly tall and wiry-strong, with the look of a man who might walk as if in white sneakers across a tennis court in the afternoon, with motionless arms hanging, knuckly hands touched with pale freckles; a soft brown spot like a dark signature on his cheek, and a part at the back of his head where his hair always stuck up so gently, a mild yet severe young man in an overcoat. He decided many things in a flash because his mind was on fire, but mainly, and finally, he decided, "The only wrong I've ever done is believe that wrong exists and to go around with that idea in my head and look at everybody through such eyes. But when I am dead I will look back on life only with love, as though nothing that happened really mattered, and therefore I will see that everything was right after all, and holy and reverent, and so strangely dear. Why is it that we forget from one moment to another what we did before? Why aren't we serious? Do we really want to be crass? When I am dead I will look back and the rounder will be gone, and all the rounding is done; the whore will be gone, and all the whoring is done; the thief will be gone, and all the thieving is done; the tease will be gone, and all the teasing is done; and the lover will be gone, and all the loving is done. So it is necessary to believe even right now on earth that nothing is wrong, this moment, and to do this I must overlook this moment of dumb existence when everything seems to [be] wrong in my head, and begin to go about as if looking back from my death with gladness and sorry joy that I no longer exist and with all these knowledges. To do this, and to realize that the joys of life elude the angry man, and that the joys of life are infinite and happen every day, every minute, maybe almost every second for all I know, that the joys of life are

The Buddhist Years

really here, that everything is actually all right, and all is poor innocence under the skies after all, and that the Saviour has really saved us already, I must forgive myself for past sins of impatience and complaint and go on and become shrouded in the vision of an angel that has died, *no matter what.*

"And also I must have the body of an angel for this—this which is the only possible and the only impossible idea, the first and the last—and take care of myself someway, till the day when I won't have to any more. I must do this whether it's all prearranged or not, because of course I don't know what's prearranged across these spaces, and I don't care about that. And in any case I need a new mind and now I am innocent. Also I want my soul back."

Whereupon Red looked around and tried to see the cafeteria through the eyes of an angel that had died, and it was almost merely a silly game he was playing with what he had heard called reality.

But he knew he was right.[31]

---

31   The incomplete manuscript contains three more paragraphs, omitted here because they merely provide background on Red's father Wade, the unnamed narrator, and the narrator's father Smiley.

"I Was Born at Five in the Afternoon"

I was born at five in the afternoon when the sun was red on the rooftops of March and snow was melting in the warm mysterious air. Pisces, the 12th, 1922, Lowell, Massachusetts, Jean Louis Kerouac. The soul fell sighing into the fault sour sea of suffering wondering instantly on sight of the grainy makeup of the portals of the world, *Why?* The Infinite had woven itself a new limited wonderer trapped inside a burden of flesh at the dissolution of which years later in the sweet hour of the death it would re-admit to its imageless ecstasy which is not only eternal like "God" but I am "God" as you are who am me as I am you. The babe is pure but only bearer of mind in a body of dung; chastised, evilized and wrinkled and all done with the already completed journey that began at my pink toe-tips, the other end of "my life" would present "me" with the proper grave to lap the husk in, released, a sweet escapee. Death is Truth. Death is the Golden Age. Life is not worth living.[32] All sentient life is tormented. Each being from bud to god is the Messiah deceived in a limited hassle of body, the intrinsic nature of which is eternal silence and infinite emptiness smilingly flowing to accommodate a mold of condition. The world is ever deceived, unreal and does everything wrong anyway; why ever give it any further consideration? My task is now to undo the world thread by thread till I have accomplished the rope trick of Magadha.[33] Every word, line, concept and chapter of this book is intrinsically the emptiness flowing freely and perfectly from its smile in the womb of timelessness to serve my anxious terrestrial striving to discuss the undiscussable; from inborn ecstasy it manifests according to Ignorance directly thru the lead of my pencil to the better unborn page.

Mindfall created the world. It was an original mistake full of torment and now remorse. Nothingness was moved and potentialized, phenomena appeared, and because phenomena is subject to a beginning and an end,

---

32   Jack repeats these three sentences in version 2 of "A Dream Already Ended" (see p. 163).

33   Magadha was a region in ancient India sacred to both Buddhists and Jains, as it was the birth-place of Siddhartha Gautama and the area where Mahavira preached. The Indian rope trick is a magic trick in which a rope in a basket levitates without external support and is then climbed, often by a boy, the magician's assistant.

The Buddhist Years

the arbitrary conception of Time appeared, and with it, past, present, and future of all phenomena. Remembrance, or memory, is the future aspect or the future tense of that phenomena that because we now have seen it and speak of it, has had its past tense, its appearance; in the brain are filed all the slides that when selected from the filing cabinet therein by some jolt of concurrence and combination, are slipped into the illuminated projector and thrown on the screen we call Memory, and yet these poor slides are in themselves phantasmal and unreal negatives pressed postulating from the original illusion received by the eyeball coming into contact with a piece of phenomena which is all of two things: inner perception of sight perceiving a projection of itself which is emptiness potentializing and accommodating to order, and it is the world equipped with eyeballs looking at itself in free dispassionate unbroken flow perfectly imitating the complete everywhereness of unbeginning unending emptiness. Therefore Memory is the future tense of a false appearance, the mindsore of false birth, the phantom of a phantom in a phantom world, and, perfectly fittingly, it is all we have to work with in relating our lives.

Because all my life bemused by red sunsets, and haunted by Thomas Wolfe's formal recognition of them as discriminated individualized units of eternity meaning, I wonder if I remember on my pristine screen that first high moment of head emerging blind from the mother's womb into a redlight world. "*Le soleil eta rouge rouge!*" my mother Gabrielle Kerouac says, "The sun was red red!"—more than usual its redness soaked deepened in the waters of the Merrimack as seen from the windows of the hilltop house where my birth took place, at No. 9 (my lucky number) Lupine Road, in the Centralville section of Lowell; fantastically it flamed in the rearward east windows beyond Lupine Road (a name denoting *wolf* but phonetically sounding off *pines*, of which there were many and also all reddened in my birth hour on the hill); and in the eyes of glancers in the opposite west Pawtucketville side of the river it flashed reflecting from these windows of Centralville houses so disposed in conjunction with the watcher's momentary position as if, as I later thought at the age of 10 when my family moved to Pawtucketville and I'd sunset see, a certain window of a certain house had been selected as manifestor of the votive flame in the sacred hour, by which it secretly seemed to me the family was blessed though these occupiers of the sanctified bungalow couldnt know because they werent in Pawtucketville and in my spectating position to see and realize that radiating red fire signaling to heaven off their humble upstairs windowpane, in which understanding there came to me the realization that because "God" was manifesting this phenomena in secret for secret me without letting the family know or anyone else in the world except some co-idiot saint in Pawtucketville like me sunset-hung (a distinct possibility vaguely acceptable in the multiple world of worlds where facts are not so surprising as possibilities because of the infinity in the tininess of things) I was let into the secret of divinity not only because divinity was everywhere and so was I but I was that divinity itself, from any position, I was "God" himself. Sometimes I wondered if I-circumstanced and the sun had selected the window of my birth bedroom on Lupine Hill Road as holy fireburner for the sacred departing hour, because I never could tell or tried to make sure from that distance of over a mile across, whether 9 Lupine was visible, but if so I could take it as a sure sign of family blessing and my being God anyway. The fire radiating from the little windowpane made an aureola big as the house itself and visible by fiery nature at a distance from which the house itself was out of sight, thus the impressiveness, offset only by the fact that several windows not just one were selected by sunset. Had I been certain of the relative visibility of 9 Lupine Road I would have been certain only of its *conforming* hence the failure to attach any importance to spotting it and watching its sun windows. At the moment of my birth a red flame emanated from the windows to the front of the house and dazzled that spot on the opposite shore of the river from which today, since the house still stands, if the spot exists, i.e., if 9 Lupine is visible there (otherwise it would have to be some treetop in Centralville itself) I could to great advantage get high some sunset eve on the actual scarlet romance burning silently in the vast Organo of the world from the very pitiful window where all this heartrending violence began that has been named for me, "Your life," "It's your life and it's up to you to decide what to do with it," this birth, decay, disease, old age and death so universal and so brutalized that did it really belong to an actual me rather than being but a hideous consequence of birth, of origin, I would have buried it like treasure long ago in my happy cave of gold and seen to it that it did not mold; just as, if God had made me, or had I been the "God that made the world," no such unhappiness would have been the result, no such cold materialistic spite and Philistine scorn of self would have been allowed, no pain and utter abandoning to the dogs of

The Buddhist Years

mortality, since everything I made to live, because issuing from my image of myself, would be piece and living extension of myself, angel of my heart, unless I am the Devil.

Far better to be unborn, and never in any red light of sunset, as if the world was on fire somewhere and men mistook it for the rosy outlook of things, have labored out sweatheaded and glued to come positiving in this glarous bulb globe in flames called earth.

Field mice sleeping in the cold ground mist of night must wear that same pout of innocence as my midwife Doctor Simpson wore in his secret pillow that melting March Twelfth night in 1922, and for the same proud, ignorant, pathetically exhausted reasons, fuming with anxiety in big and little snore.[34]

Oh to show how the Tranquil and Eternal Mind from its Golden Oneness Dream came and emanated its pure compassion, pity and love into this world full of us dolls that are nothing but aggregate atomic balls generally known as "clay" by our soddier forebears tormented into molds of ball-grouping and pushed to flow into forms and motions (actor of the prime with your purple mask!); how the Eternal and Tranquil Mind came and illumined our dark antlike stupid existence with the Mind Essence Goldenness for the sake of reneging on and undoing the Ignorance which was the Fall and Beginning of it all and which has to be wished and concentrated out of existence like the ropetrick among the Magi Screamers when the boy rises into void like a vineclimber and at SARTOR! he vanishes, back into the Infinite Emptiness again when sun's fury fires and gases'll have stopped such throbbing vibration for balance and merely fall, for what goes up must come down; when our orgones[35] shall cease appearing as they do now in this universe of lights flashing everywhere, of electric prickling, the sun wheeling and sawing around its malleable sometimes oval core, the balance shifts racing hysterically to hold the system up, the solar sorrow; man the forward sprout that from the lowest once-orgone sunstuff vibratory rock came via chlorophyll vegetable moss re-beginnings and is the first of sentient

---

34 See DB 25: "I heard a mouse snoring in the garden weeds."

35 "Orgones" are a reputed form of energy radiating throughout nature proposed by the Austrian psychologist Wilhelm Reich (1897–1957). William Burroughs was an adherent of Reich's theories and in his life built several "orgone energy accumulators," which were reputed to improve health and vitality, especially sexual energy and potency.

mistake life to have been reached by Mind Essence[36] regathering itself back to essence vibration soon essence non-vibration; pitiful man a solar system of flesh molecules flailing against the receiving air of emptiness and getting what he puts in, back. These just ruins, dead planets left and the orgones of the world gone, and life shall have taken a flyer.

Leo Kerouac was in his easy chair dozing to the monotone of his home. "Then the wind will erode the rest," he woke up thinking, not knowing why, and got up to make the toilet. Blam, he was on his hands, he never felt it when his dead foot made contact with the floor. He kneeled stunned as wife and son assimilated blood shocks in the heart from the hearing of the gigantic fall of the 230-pound man on the linoleum carpet. "What's the matter?" they shouted in and out of their minds. Leo, like Oliver Hardy when something utterly unforeseen and completely disagreeable interrupts everything, pressed his lips together and turned his head in exasperation away and opened his mouth and went "tsk" and sighed elaborately and shook his head and said "Good God Christ" and gathered up his leg, grunting like a football guard about to rhinoceros into the line off one hand, and hopped hugely shaking the house two hops to the sofa, where he fell sitting sprawled in a haggard trance, like some old flabbergasted whore.

"*Mende moi donc*, ask me not!"

I said in French out loud, "—what did you do?"

"H-h-h-h-h-a-a-a-a!" came the final releasing exacerbated sigh. "I just fell asleep on my foot, that's all."

---

36   "Mind Essence" and the equivalent terms "Essence of Mind" and "Essential Mind" appear frequently in Buddhist scripture, contrasting "true Essence of Mind and its self-purifying brightness" with "deluding and transient thoughts which are nothing but falsity and vanity" (BB 112).

The Buddhist Years

Reflections on Birth (from Dharma Notebooks)

1.

Bells—noon—San Jose 2-10-54

I was born into the fault sour sea of suffering at five o'clock in the afternoon when the sun was blood red on the rooftops of Centralville, March, snow thawing, whoever I was, coming prepared and freighted with brain body, moist eyeballs fresh for sight, mouth & nose, & butter flesh made to melt in the transient forge of life time, and family name, Kerouac, and equipment for defense, aggression, withdrawal, & grave, wondering instantly on sight of the grainy makeup of the portals of the world: why?

WHY is the only question

—The Infinite had woven itself a new limited wonderer trap & inside a burden of flesh at the dissolution of which years later on the sweet hour of my death the Infinite would re-admit to its own formless ecstasy which I suddenly realize is not only eternal, like "God," but I myself am "God," as you are who am me and I you.

2.

It wasnt that the red light was of any importance at that time, in fact it was a yellow orange light and it reflecting from more than one windowpane from those of the same house due to immodifiable position of the sun, the pane, the watcher; rather it was the vast awe of the light that flamed, as if the world was on fire somewhere and men mistook it for the rosy outlook of things, that amazed me, since finally my whole life is said to be taking place in the dying sun whenever nowadays in distant unrestful cities far from the sitbanks of home rivers I look and there it is flaming in windows of warehouses or automobiles and the votive holy motionless burn stops there, just as newspapers continue to disappoint one throughout life because history has taken its turns its own way and the matter is settled there: the bleakness that we will have to bear with us on our road to painful death. All arising from birth.

Far better to be unborn, to never have been born, to never in any red light of sunset have labored out sweat headed and glued to come positiving in this glarous bulb ball globe in flames called earth. But the doctor attending my birth was well pleased with his work and complimented himself to his extent where guilt did not interfere in normal nightcap retirement on the night of March 12, 1922, as some William Carlos Williams doctor of poetry giving expression to some private doubt as to the validity of the *value* of this birth of "mine," or just going to sleep to pout with that same innocence of field mice in the misty night watches when I watch.

"Morning March 12 1922"

MORNING MARCH 12 1922, the fields are still brown where the snow has melted, the leaves of Autumn 1921 are still piled beneath the sad trees but have begun to mush and mingle in a fragrant rot predicting Spring. The sun is up and bright red at 6:30 rising from behind the hill on Lupine Road where my little brother Gerard stands, hand to brow, surveying the pristine beginning of the world. I am not yet born; eleven hours to go. My mother lies abed in the bedroom of the second floor flat on Lupine Road in Centralville, shades drawn, breathing sweetly, warmly on her pillow. My father Leo Duluoz peeks in with a worried frown. "A-brap!" he coughs, returning to the kitchen tying his suspenders. "Gerard!" he calls. He opens the hall door and calls again. He looks out the window and sees his little son motionless and mystical in the road surveying sunrise.

Poor little angel, he thinks in French (Pauvre tit' ange), "and to think," he mutters to add in English, "that now I got another one comin and the coal bill this year the highest in history." Sigh. "Ah ma mere, ah my mother," he thinks sitting before the stove and suddenly remembering his own mother.

In the bedroom little Caroline child stirs in her bed and mutters through fumbly lips some dream language as yet unrecorded by holy writers of the future.

In my mother's womb I stare happily into the transcendental holy milk of eternity, not dreaming what's about to happen to me when I am ejected into the cold and loveless bleak air of human life.

Crystal silence Shhhs in the ears of little Gerard on the road. "What is that noise?" he wonders. "Shhh. I hear it in my room, in the schoolroom, in the air, in my ears, everywhere. It's God."

Across the sere meadow above Burnaby Street he sees the clustered pines of Dracut turn gold in the sun-tip's touch. A little boy is standing alone in the field with his long shadow cast. It's my ghost, about to be born, the first morning of the world.

* * *

A BIRD IS SAILING in the saffron sky as though the Holy Ghost wanted it.

Confessions of the Father

CONFESSIONS OF THE FATHER   Dec. 29, 1954

These are the confessions of Father Duluoz that were found in his hermitage, as elaborated and arranged into a story by his most fervent disciple, Young Jean-Louis.

In time to come causes and conditions will unite and give the illusion of a sentient being forming in a womb, and this being will be born and grow and suffer and decay and die and vanish. In time past, in the same way, causes and conditions united and gave the illusion of a sentient being forming in a womb, and Father Duluoz was born and grew and suffered and decayed and died and vanished.

It was a beautiful pure day, cloudless, when he was born. You looked at the perfect emptiness of the sky where there was nothing but invisible particles of dust reflecting the sunlight and saw only the blue illusion, and because of the morbidity of the perception of sight through your mortal eyeballs you saw a few imaginary blossoms in the air,[37] and the cosmic particles swarming like electricities winking on and off as if benign winks that all is well, and you wondered "Can this nothingness be the origin of all created things, to which all created things return?"

It was 1922. Below the crystal emptiness the earth was like a stain. Mill stacks of the city poured black smoke into the sky, like ink spilling on a mirror yet not affecting the purity of the mirror's reflection. A great river, the Merrimack, swarmed around the town in its valley bed and rolled without gaps in the current towards the sea. Now it was the Merrimack; tomorrow in the sea the water could no longer be called the water of the Merrimack. The city was Lowell, Massachusetts; the country the United States of America. A selfbelieving butcher stood in his doorway at pure blue dawn, aproned, stroking his huge moustache with satisfaction among the

---

37   This term comes from the *Surangama Sutra*. In "Manjusri's Summation," it refers to "the falsity of all sense perceptions," declaring them "all alike illusive and delusive visions of unreality, and all the three great realms of existence [i.e., the Desire Realm, the Form Realm, and the Formless Realm] are seen to be what they truly are, imaginary blossoms in the air" (BB 259). See also SOD 78 et seq., VOG 49, 118.

The Buddhist Years

charnels of his own making. Men like ghosts swam in the sea of sidewalks inside mind, full of human hope, every one of them a sentimental realist. Counting and calculating their advantages whether large or small, looking furtively into the eyes of what they took to be other selves, they appeared to be moving around under the enormous emptiness. They never looked up; and they had yet to remove the veil of ignorant angry greed to gaze upon their own true, bright, blissful, mysterious Essence of Mind, discarding the body as so much froth on the ocean of suffering, and dwelling on the contemplation of that wonderful shining suchness, like the empty sky, that is our own Mind Essence that never dies.

Father Duluoz spent most of the day in the womb of his mother Evangeline Duluoz, clinging to his warm comforts. At five when the sun was low and red and the snow was melting everywhere, he was forced out into what there was inevitable, also because of causes and conditions, the bleak and ghastly dream of this world. His eyes shut tight against the arbitrary conception of the brightness of light, he wailed; he was cold. Everything that touched him hurt, as though he was suddenly cast in a valley of darts.[38] "Come now, come now, coo, coo, it's not so bad," said the kindly doctor whacking him upside down. He was pampered and pummeled and washed and swaddled in. He was a blue baby, something was wrong with his blood. Gradually he turned pink. Gradually he opened his eyes. But because he was a little angel straight from heaven, as the old folk say in French Canada, he didn't know how to be mad. He stared through things at the snowy nothingness; he saw mothswarms of heaven permeating throughout.[39] The light was on in the bedroom of the upstairs flat on Lupine Road but you could see red shadows of the sailing sun behind the windowshade. A kind of coo of thaw rippled outside; dogs barked in it, sending sound vibrations against the little ear in the sea of mind. Great gnashing phantoms inside

---

38   Kerouac repeats the phrase "valley of darts" first in SOD in March 1954 and later in WU: "This valley of darts, which we call life, a nightmare" (31). See also p. 163 herein.

39   Kerouac in many texts refers to "mothswarms" and like phrases to suggest life's unreality and/ or a divine presence. See, e.g., pp. 57 & 73 herein. See also S 63: "nameless events of the millionfold mothswarms"; VOC 328: "this skeletal earth and billion particled gray moth void"; VOG 110: "suddenly a great swarming mass of roe-like fiery whitenesses, as if a curtain had opened, […] innumerably revealed the scene behind the scene […] the central entire essence of which is dazzling radiant blissful ecstasy unending"; BS 187: "suddenly […] there's the golden swarming peace of Heaven in my eyelids," etc.

mind flailed around the bright room. Father Duluoz took it all to be a new dream now.

For aeons before that he had dwelt in a peaceful emptiness neither waiting nor not-waiting to come to this dream; the sound had been like the seething salt sea receding in the sand, unceasing; the sight had been like the Milky Way, neither dark nor bright throughout. Now there were all kinds of contrasts of bright and dark being forced on him, as it were, making for shapes that he discriminated and picked out as separate from one another; and his crystal mind became confused. Besides his body was too heavy, it weighed him down, he wished to cast it off and return to his origin in bliss. But it was too late. Causes and conditions had united, his mother and father had united and conditions of nature had ignorantly and systematically done their work, and here he was. But just for a moment he realized in his pristine mind that it was only a dream and therefore just hallucination, not really there, and all he had to do was ignore it, which he did, in mind, and everything truly vanished.

So as like the little kitten when you first see him quiet down from play, and suddenly he's sitting with his little paws folded under him, meditating with slitted eyes, undisturbable, ignoring your call, ignoring your touch, so Father Duluoz entered on the infantly Samadhi and refused to respond to the ripples of the dream around his body.

"He's so quiet, he ought to cry a little more."

"Y waite awright mon ti n'ange," said the mother satisfied. "Y dor." Which means, "He'll be alright, my little angel, he's sleeping."

* * *

BURBLE OF COOKPOTS fascinated the thinking-mind of Father Duluoz as he woke from long naps in his crib. What was that inexpressibly peaceful warm bubbling going on?—and the smells of steamy peace that floated around and made the windows mist and sweat? He stared through the long afternoon at the amazing shadowy shapes of the room. He couldnt make out Mish from Mash when it came to people but he had already begun to discriminate and understand his own hand as not being the same as empty space; his career in worldly ignorance was well begun. He even closed his fist on space and failed to catch some. He knew that was because his fist was neither a thing nor a no-thing, and he didnt believe in it; nor did he believe in space being either a thing or a no-thing, and didnt believe in it either.

The Buddhist Years

He just goofed with his hand and pouted fatly and smelt of rancid milk. He burped and urged and gave his body right back to the world, a dream for a dream. Besides he didnt care. And at night he dreamt his rosy dreams, holy void.

Because he got fat they nicknamed him Ti Pousse, Little Thumb. They also called him "Tourlipi," "Ti Choux," "Ti Loup," "Ti Rard," "Ti N'ange," "Ti Pette," "Ti Cul," "Ti Mechant," and all kinds of "Littles" to fit the occasion whenever he was like tourlipi , like cabbage, like a wolf, like Gerard (his name), like an angel, like a phart, like an ass, like a bad, and sometimes they called him "Ti Ti," or, Lil Little.

"OO Ti Fou," said his sister Cecile seeing him grurk his little mouth, which means, "Little Crazy."

April came, and the nations of birds; syrupy pines, and softness, a pinkness in the clouds, and the soft plap of snowpiles off roofs and trees. Purling musics came from the meadows of the world without, blew in with the ballooning curtains, brought noises of rare, remote, unsatisfied doings on the vast Rubens landscape with all its chickens and children and dogbarks and reprimands, the screams and hammerslammings, voices of men and great motor-yawks of mindless bleak machines. The baby received it all, imprints on his liquid eardrum, without perceiving differences. In this world of appearances, full of imaginary effects, he tried hard to remember his original mind. Later they told him it was real and sent him to school to convince him that things were real. He hated school because of an intrinsic distrust of the ignorance of the world.

[On a separate page is the following alternate version of the first two paragraphs]

These are the confessions of Father Duluoz found in his hermitage, as elaborated and arranged in story-form by his most fervent disciple, young Jean-Louis.

Father Duluoz, like all of us, would never have appeared in the world except for causes and conditions that united to give the illusion of his being. In time to come, causes and conditions will unite and some other human being will make his appearance in the world, suffer, grow old and die and vanish.

First Memories

1.

My first memory is of being in my mother's arms in a rocking chair in the air, the street is somehow Boisvert Street in Lowell Mass. and it is a gray-mist day, she's wearing the old brown bathrobe that was later worn I think by my father in one of his numerous illnesses. Behind us is all the Church with its snowy mystery, its angels and saints, its mists of Valkyrian love,[40] its niches for statues. I have my face buried in my mother's shoulder and altho the air is cold and gray, the brown bathrobe is warm and deep and brown.[41] The chair is a rocking chair and it is situated above the lawn of an old house (later occupied by my old buddy Mike's family)[42] on the corner of Boisvert and West Sixth. The river is not far away, there is mist on the river, in the woodyard nearby. It is old and old—If I were really Memory Babe, the name given me by my boyhood chums owing to my insane memory for details everybody'd long forgotten, I could remember whether this was a memory or just a thought, or even if it were really the first memory of my life.... Not long after I was in a crib and it was gray outside the window and I stared at it through beaded curtains of some kind, out on Lakeview Avenue and again the river. Always rain, rain in my dreams and memories, maybe the rain of my baptism when the good kindly priest sprinkled me and intoned the Latin words that say that the water gives life. Rain and rivers. In fact the day I was born they tell me the snow was melting so rapidly that there were regular rivers of rivulets flowing down from under steep snowbanks, downhill to the river, which received it with a rush onward. Then there was that rainy

---

40 In Norse mythology, a Valkyrie is one of the maidens of Odin who choose which heroes will be slain in battle and then guide their souls to Valhalla.

41 See DS 18–19: "my mother's robe sends auras of warm brown (the brown of my family)—so now when I bundle my chin in a warm scarf in a wet gale—I think on that comfort in the brown bathrobe."

42 Michael Fournier, Jr. (1921–'91) was a close friend when he and Jack were growing up in Lowell. Gabrielle and Leo were friends with Marie Fournier and Mike, Sr., and Jack enjoyed sleepovers at the Fourniers' with Mike, Jr. and his many siblings: brothers Paul and Robert and sisters Claire, Laurette, Rita, and Jeanette.

The Buddhist Years

morning when my brother Gerard was putting on his rubbers in the kitchen, outside you could hear the splatter of the rain, 8 AM, he was on his way to school I guess: from the ceiling of the kitchen hung the bare bulb that was all golden mysterious electricity in the wetness. And lying in my crib listening to the thunder.... And the time my mother took me in the baby carriage to the local shoe repair shop and it was dark in there, gloomy shelves, thousands of dark rainy shoes, and then we went out and I saw a little man in a slanted hat walking off towards the rainy mists of the river, up a long sad boulevard sadder than life of ancient Russia, I saw it all. It was my first and last view of the gray rain hat man.[43] Grit on the sidewalks of Centralville as my carriage wheels were propelled along. What tender milk is the rain! It was 1922 in New England and I was born for better or worse. I was married to life whether I liked it or not.[44]

2. [45]

my first memory is so obscure I dont even remember if it was a memory or just a dream which I dreamed one night either in childhood, or later— strange dream-memory of being in my mother's arms—but O the pine trees beyond the last strange memory of the hill of the street, the vistas of Ottawa, this poem—the abadkabadra of good batted out the woesome child flesh pot called ti jean kerouac on march 12 1922 and for what? in the red sun with snow melting down the lupine sides of the world, following rivulets to the greater rivulet of the river where it dissolved in the big sea-going tide and went god knows where any mor'n you should expect me (or I should expect you) to remember, know, learn, appreciate, pray to know or even understand one iota of, why we were born—well, because god wanted somebody to appreciate Heaven again, I guess we did fall—and did you see the way that hill ran off (forget the name of it), how all the snows of death grit girl did melt and come running down (coldspot pink conscience on the ice), and

---

43   See VOG 125–26 for another version of this memory of the shoe repair store and the man in the gray hat.

44   There are two apparent typos in these last sentences, which I've chosen to correct. Jack's typed text reads "sadder than life *or* ancient Russia," and "What tender milk *in* the rain!" (italics mine).

45   Kerouac's typing of this ms. was extremely messy, so I've done my best to preserve its style (esp. its inconsistent capitalization) while making necessary corrections. In cases where he was either making up a word or I couldn't discern the word he intended, I have left it as is, i.e., "thujrman," "mourfloing," and "rectivk."

the sliders all slided, and all done and washed in the river away, we come to the high pine tree in the march night racked by high winds, the howling moon, the raving dog, the mail—In my mother's arms in the sky, on a drizzly day above boisvert woodyard felling logs with zzzzzzzzzes of time—and how if fhy did the candle racks flicker in the baptismal church, wow, the way I was baptized was with rain and there was grit on lakeview avenue as the thujrman came walking the thunder man and the man of the wall and the high parties in the dream hotel and all the castles on the hill and that eventual solitudinous halo of the snake making a rack of candleflickers in the church of st. jean baptiste, where else would you have jean baptized? In poufter cell? And high above the street in my mother's arms, she was wearing the brown bathrobe of the family sicknesses, how warm the brown bathrobe with the little woolen dots and how cold the gray drizzle in the air as we sat there rocking in god's white heaven waiting for certainty to make our eyes close again, and how we did rock above the street (boisvert) only a block from st. louis de france church (louis my middle name) and the name of the section of lowell is centerville (name of the place in avignon where de popes did quail about the advancing tartar of the south)[46]—how winds do blow grit dust in the back alleys of aiken and west sixth, ugh, and how they did get to be drowsy alleys of mystery and fellaheen housewife washlines and children mourfloing in the sand and even I got to play in the dump and got to learn hail and drizzle and saw the all awesome bridge leading away to the rectivk mysteries of downtown lowell where leo my father went waddling along selling insurance, I was blessed by the fact that my father in heaven gave me a good and kind father on earth, gold bless it all, and a good mother, a sweet, smart mother, a mother who knows the ropes, and an ingenuous sister and a saintly brother who protected me—but the death grit girl did have a hill leading though to the eternal schoolteacher who stood in a valley in the red october morning of all time and held my hand and pointed to a gray schoolhouse but me my mind was on the way that valley led to all the world and africa and never would end till the man in the white shirt chased me that way for good and all, aye—and what can little boys born in scotland say different about their prenatal memories? So obscure that first memory it must not be a memory at all but a dream, or a premonition of the buddha

---

46   The Lowell neighborhood was Centralville, but Centre-ville d'Avignon is the ancient part of the French city.

The Buddhist Years

charita[47] as I too had long golden hair in heaven and when I was ejected from my white cottage to come bring down the message of Heaven for Everybody Sinners and All No Matter What You Do and I was set sailing in this misery sea, here I am, trying by allhuman artistic means to tell the truth and not just a story.........the red schoolteacher had later fields where the shadows were long and old john chalifoux drove the ford, and the pine trees on the hill were strange indeed and as if unreal which of course they are, unreal...What was the meaning of the first memory of the world when it roused itself from ripple and went from worse to worse till eggs began to stir in the bottom of the mind slime and poof: people...well people are good enough and they suffer so here we are.

---

47   See SOD 9, where Jack lists as part of his "Bibliography" of spiritual texts, "LIFE OF BUDDHA , or BUDDHA CHARITA, by Asvaghosha, trans. S.Beal (Sacred Books of the East Vol 19)."

The Heart of the World: The Legend of Duluoz

The Heart of the World

THE LEGEND OF DULUOZ   Apr. 19, 1954
1—Run On, Little Ghost
Finding My Well Full of Shadow

(1)

SLEEPING IN A GOLDEN DREAM, deep in the womb of mind.
I REMEMBER ETERNITY when the womb of mind surrounded he who was God.
I REMEMBER THE AEONS of smileless, vast and God-like regard when mankind came about. Man is God.

We shall sleep in golden light again, deep within the womb of mind.

I remember the smile of peace and satisfaction I wore in my mother's womb, the noises without, the clattering dishes and beginnings and morning of life in the world.

I remember the horrible nightmare of the moment of birth, when I was forced headlong out of the warm happiness into the cold unhappiness. I was jarred and stunned, slapped out of sleep, chastised for being lazy and sleepy, kissed, handled everywhere, tumbled into sheets. We just think that we're being born, when we're born. We just think that we're dying, when we die.

I remember the slivers of the slats of my brown wicker basket baby carriage, and inexpressibly peaceful the afternoon sun pouring in through the slid down dome to edify my rest.

I do not remember the little pink woven stuffs I wore tight around my head and over pudgy wrists I see in an old original photograph of me in the baby carriage on a dirt road among the houses of Lowell Massachusetts sometime in 1922.

The Buddhist Years

They named me Michel Henri Duluoz and had me baptized in the Catholic church, St. Louis de France was the name of the parish, in French *la paroisse*. The difference is as if infinite, when you hear said la paroisse, instead of the parish, and make your first imaginary pictures of what the others are talking about with those words, those sounds. I saw la paroisse as some kind of vast field, almost as of battle, of knights clashing with lances, in the first grayday hours when I became conscious of my being in the world with people who evidently loved me and were taking care of me anyhow, bending over my crib, calling me Ti Michel, giving me what I wanted, leaving me alone, and going "A BWA A BWA" all day long with others in other parts of the house, pieces of which after the several eternity-years of babyhood I began to pick out, among them la paroisse, always spoken with angry authority that made me sad, because I wanted my world to be completely understandable to me. La Paroisse as far as I was concerned was like the vision I now have of French Canada, now that I am a grownup man in America which has infolded me in a strange security I instantly can see in the look of rainy trees on the horizon of New York State the moment I travel south of the Canadian border; La Paroisse was like what's north of that border, farmers in boots in the mud, farmers with bleak roofs, dark angry faces, the contemptuous faces of the beautiful French girls on Ste. Catherine Street in Montreal, the ancient redbrick English backstreets of Montreal huddling like Medieval Europe under tall iron churchsteeples forlorn as France in heavens of cannon iron; something under imperial flags, oppressive, gloomy, hopeless; which, on sight of the rainy trees of America, vanishes back across the border; the long hope of America, like a thinker whittling in the woods. La Paroisse in my mind was angry, silly, a gloomy large unlighted hall on a rainy day and you imagine you see bats in the swarming dark of the corner beams. It was funerals, the smoke from waxen musical pots wielded by a mysterious bishop of snow lace bending his head solemnly at lollytonguing sinners in rumpled clothes made more rumpled at the kneeling rail with an eagerness belying their sins; the lowering of the host to their tongues, and how they rushed back up the main aisle in a hurry for overtime with looks of downcast piety barely concealing the package of butts in the suitcoat pocket. Everybody looking everywhere in an enormous restless shuffle of knees, feet, elbows, rosaries and adjustments of cloth and coat as if judgment day refused to come and they knew it and had the burden of time and the thorns and prickles of discrimination in the world to bear. The looks of astonishment on the mouths of adventurous boys digging all this for the first few times at the ages of 5 or 6—like the blond boy whose eyes were too close together, who, in the seat next to mine at table in the first grade, used to whistle under his breath and chew his eraser and blow me breathsmells that were like unclean wood, that I didnt like, that made me form my first frowns of social dissatisfaction; in church, kneeling, he looked everywhere as though he wanted to start making a lot of noise and rush up and talk to everybody, all the people in the church, end up sprinting through the crowd shouting "STA RA BA, STA RA MA NE LE RA!!!!" or words to that effect, meaning, "I dont care about you people, my name is Picard! Try to catch Picard! Assezyes a poignez Picard! Bleu-aaaaaah!" jamming [in] his mouth fistful of hosts and chewing maniacally up the cloth of thought because it is forbidden to chew the host with your teeth, you must let it melt majestically and as it were, heavenly, in your mouth of mouths. In my imagination the church was in a turmoil all the time; these my thoughts were the thoughts of a little boy who couldnt speak English, just baby French, "J ai tombez sur l planfer" (I fell on the foor).

* * *

(2)

MY BABY CARRIAGE had thin wheels on thin rubber tires rolling on thin axles, and the whole thing dipped softly throughout, like a basket, when I was pushed drowsily thru the humming as-if-Fellaheen streets of downtown Centralville, the east bank hill community of Lowell, traditionally French in population around the corners of Lakeview and Aiken and Lilley. I see these names written in dull red letters in my dreams, painted by some Rembrandt against a brown shroud of myriad cosmic moths swarming, like Tathagata radiance, or orgones, the living substance that flashes on and off, gleaming like spermatozoa, throughout the world, as if winks from a benign and secret lover in the universe; little prickly lights that might well be taken for compassion, signs of safety and ecstasy in store for us all on the other side of our fear by some future Buddha. Lilley came down from the green humps of hills that lazed in the sun up the Centralville valleyslope, and joined Aiken and Lakeview at groups of wooden tenements teeming with life like the Lower East Side of New York. Markets, some pushcarts, shoe repairs, barbers' poles, laughter of talkers in the sidewalk entrances, the smell of dung and old wood soaked with ice on icewagons already mingling in the century with the new city smells of gasoline and gas exhaust. In my little carriage, clinging to the sides with my fingernails clutching unconsciously tense, open faced to look at everyone because I had learned that people had spiritual intelligence, as my mother shopped for cabbage and carrot, I dug the streets for the first time, thinking them to be a waking dream materializing before my cherubic inability to feel the responsibility to have to cope; just descended from some thoughtful post in heaven, I was an innocent beginner in the darker dream down here in the coliseum of ignorance we've dared to call real and sell and swear by. Papier mache canals flowed in downtown Lowell, men smoking cigars stood by the rail spitting in the waters that reflected lost hope clouds of 1922; to their way of thinking, the money in their pocket was real and was about to buy an actual porkchop which, though it has since disappeared, the hunger with it, the hungerer to boot, can still be called real, though it neither was not, nor was, but beyond such consideration anyway, like a reflection of a porkchop on water: this was the way I saw the streets, reflections in my pure orb unborn. But already that spiritual intelligence of men and women had been put to work on me, and I already'd Latah-like[48] begun to respond to their ootchykoo tricks with smiley tricks of my own based on a previous estimate of what I could get from doing this. Already I was defiled enough to cling to, and cherish, "favors," where only 12 months before, in that smile inside the mother's womb, the only "favors" I was aware of were being fed me silently through the navel tube in uteral deeps of the sea of fault sour suffering's organic egg, unready to move, too frail and too refined to cry, still an angel but invested with the properties of the fish, the lizard, the snake and the mammal rat. So the streets were not Arabian mysteries yet, but figures on a surrealist screen like old movies made in the Twenties in Germany by impressionists high on cocaine; shadows in the jazz age filing by.

* * *

(3)

THE AFTERNOON OF MY BIRTH the whole world is red, warm, snows are melting and falling "ploff" off the pines to the soft snow under which melts run ringing and singing to the river; pitch gums stink the fragrant thaw; tree trunks are as black as stove polish; clouds mass huge and whorly

---

48   "Latah" is a Malay term for an uncontrollable startle reaction due to outside stimulus causing, among other possibilities, an involuntary immediate obedience to commands.

and majestically muff on by, white as angels, mysterious as snow, sad as divers off high divingboards just leaving.

The house is in an uproar, my mother's in the bedroom with Doctor Ouellette, neighbors run in and out, so my little brother Gerard and little sister Caroline go out on the second story porch of the Lupine Road house and sit on the woodplank railing. The sun goes red and deep over the river as five o'clock nears, hour of my birth. Gerard has a soft fall of hair over his brow, a wistful and almost unnaturally sad expression in the eyes, pathetic little black stockings running up into his little shorty pants, highbutton shoes, a Russian like holy like shirt with collar buttoned at the neck. He's five. My sister Nin has a soft bob of hair and little navy dress so impossibly lost in eternity and so French, with similar black socks, similar highbutton shoes,[49] it's as though the scene wasnt America but provincial France. But the next house has burntwood rainboards and white pillar porch and is bleakly American.

Nin, three, talking to her only brother, speaking her little voice in the void three years has claimed her now and still she does not understand, "Why they got that, those boards?" meaning the weatherslats next door.

Gerard, who doesnt know, and holding her hand in his tightly, "She pa, dunno, it's God figured and put that there because he never comes to ask us and doesnt want us to botder his things."

"Are we going to play this afternoon?"

They'd been playing a series of new games that were so amazing to the little girl, the world had changed, wherein he was as the solemn inevitable Son of God.

"Wont be able today because they's too many people in the house and we got a baby."

"Where's the baby?"

"He's gonna come down the chimbley (la chumbnez) and he's gonna ask for bread."

This I heard in my womb, and remember grayly.

"Well we put him a boat in the sink?"

"Like us he's gonna have one."

"How old is he, him?"

---

49 The details that Kerouac describes here are based on a photograph of Gerard and Nin specifical-ly discussed in "The Long Night of Life" (see fig. 1 and pp. 154–155 herein).

The Buddhist Years

"Same as us."

"What we gonna call him?"

"Artzimidee??? Semanedee, Karamenee, Pastafoulee."

"Kerabidou, Barstonrinfou."

"Moudou le fou."

"Sicai le gram."

"Partou partouffe ha ha ha ha ha ha ha ah!"

Behind them the red afternoon projected its strange visage of sorrow upon the air.

Simultaneously they lose themselves in a reverie facing in the same direction hand in hand, the light throws a long shadow across their shirts. Their eyes become lost in the gritty scene of the world, but softened in late light for some reason like votive candles lit in the earth, the sundown of tired day, afterfires of the sad and weary world, mementos of day, hushers of fret noise, lamp for tired fathers tramping with coats overarm to the beer foam saloon, big red ball of fire in the western hill sinking to find the other side of things, reflector in brownly crimson mystery of fate's sad decidings among the unsad hopes, hymnal slow march to the peace. Little Nin squints to watch it, turns her head a little convulsively aside, fearing the ball, the wonder, the mystery; Gerard, bigger, holding a littler hand, gaining courage from his courage, faces straightin sad the mortal sun with its solar sorrow; sees faintly through hurting eyes the faint vibration of the sun-edge where fires a million miles in dimension race to hold its balance up or the world will fall.

"If the sun wasnt beatin like that we'd all fall down the world."

"It hits on the wall?"

"Sure it hits the wall."

He sees the mysterious inner gray ball of the sun within the red orbit, the furious distant fires flagellating around the rim, insane angers of the void, anxieties of karma racing back and forth with equally tormented interest.

"God's gone," he says mournfully, and Nin feels his hand slacken.

"Who's that God?"

"He didnt come."

"You waited for him?"

The sea swims in his face as she looks at his handsome pale mask blankly buried in puzzlement of agony, and as though swirls in his eyeballs of a myriad snow, and the sight of his long grim cheek pains her little feminine human heartbroken recognition, and her hand squeezes his, childlike crumpled inside his palm she but squeezes his thumb but he understands the mystery of intelligence and the insoluble, unlocatable misery of time and flesh.

"Pa peur, ti Nin, dont be scared, Lil Nin, look the moon it's gonna come out early and be big and blue before we eat."

Not yet the sorrowed big bulb atoning moonface will blear on them, but at nightfall.

* * *

(4)

MY FATHER BIG 230 pound Eno Duluoz was being driven home by an ex-insurance salesman friend of his and they'd stopped a moment at 4:30 on the dump on the banks of the Merrimack at Lakeview Avenue and West Street, to take a quick shot out of the pint and get out and "lookat the sun" and be philosophical, having just made friends the night before with a big bunch of railroad men in a poker game in a Boston & Maine switchman's shanty, scheduled to continue the game tonight, and Eno with a kid being born, swapping the bottle back and forth.

"So you're gonna have another kid, but look at that old sun, red and same as ever."

My father with straw hat in big gnarled veiny hands, collar bursting out soft and unstylish over his coat lapels from folds of thick muscular neck, frown dark on his brow, hair curly, dark, crisp, nose bulbous, mouth grim but sentimental, kneeling on one knee, examining the sunset with serious and exact and ponderous officialness, nodding slowly, "I'll tell ya Charley, there aint never been a mystery of this world I didnt stand in awe of, when standin in front of it, or kneelin on one knee as I am now." Strangely, rockily, the redness shows on the ridges of his face. His head is held slightly on one side, a little like Gerard looks at the sun, but in this case, the father's, the sadness is held inside a manly grace, or rather, a manly brace, the philosophicalness abides higher in the cranium than it does in the recentness of the angel child; experience has made a man of Eno, birth and tender years an angel of Gerard. Lips pressed together to make the whole face storm, Breton, hot, worried, Eno Duluoz leaned his big arms on thick knees, thick thighs, brushed the cigar smoke from the pants of his thigh, fixed his face in the setting sun of March 12, 1922, like some Medieval wallguard waiting for the Jesus Child,

The Buddhist Years

nodding, "I'll be goldanged…aint it a strange world, Charley…here we are, by the side of the river, two men, we have families, somehow or other we got the notion we were romeos and gave up our little suspender streetfights and our Saturday night popcorn dates and made googoo eyes at the girls at basketball games and hit hero homeruns and then got married to prove everything about ourselves and developed these big endless holes to throw our money in—Do you realize how much money it's costing me to keep up that family?—Does any young guy ever know how much it's gonna cost him, when he thinks of getting married?—It's like throwing ten dollar bills in the gal dang ocean, Charley"——Charley passed the bottle, wishing the theme to be expanded upon—and Eno swigged, swallowed, capped, expanded—"an ocean, they have *this* they need, *that* they need, this week, next week, Caesar never had it so good I'm tellin you, Charley"—the meaninglessness of the statement makes them grow solemn and serious—"It's a hell of a world to have to take care of yr self even alone, lest you dont run out there and try to run a FAMILY, why, hell, a man can stand upright long's he has no debts, but what's his future if he has a wife, a woman who wants dresses, scissors, meat, do you blame her?—who wants socks for the kiddies, rent, heat in the winter…when it gets below zero who's gonna stock up that coalbin?—ha?"

"I dunno, Eno, why any of us ever gets married, but we all seem to do."

"It's a durn purple shame, an American shame, why, a man would be a hell of a lot better if in his youth he went off and be Babe Ruth or Tarzan or some Earl Sande[50] of the country, but go get himself hung upside down by the hook of marriage…marriage is bad enuf, but I have a new kid comin, boy or girl what happiness can it ever know, the world bein as it is."

"I dunno, Eno, sometimes the world is happy."

"Dont give me that stuff. The world is everywhere ever unhappy and you know it and he knows it and she knows it and everybody knows it as well as I do, uff, phooey, I'm gonna do my best but I'm not promising anything, I'm not promising the moon to MY children, I'll try, I'll do all I can, and everything I know, even [if] I dont have to, for why the hell should I have to, really? Come on, forget, let's finish this bottle; I predict one thing: if it's a boy, he'll be unhappy as I am, and when he kneels on one knee, to look

---

50   Earl Sande was a Hall of Fame Thoroughbred horse jockey and trainer. As a jockey he was the leading money winner in 1921, 1923, and 1927 and won the Triple Crown aboard Gallant Fox in 1930. After retiring in 1932, he was the top trainer in the US in 1938, and in the 1940s he owned and operated his own stable.

at the sunset or the sea, I wager he'll be like me, unhappy, uncertain, it'll hurt his heart and break his skin and bones in two and wide apart and make mush of im in the end, but hole hat or no hole hat and happy sand holes of infancy or not, I predict it, seawave breezes once in a while, sand most of the time…" (slup, a slug)—"Let the women wash it, I'm thru, I'm the culprit, officer, o offi sair, sir, but take me away not now, some other time, Offi ser Charley," as he and Charley dance and gesture Cop and Arrest of Innocent Civilian on the red haunted banksides of 4:45 Lowell in the mud and molten snow, "Take me away peaceably, I want to play one more game of poker and that's tonight with those boys in Chelmsford, O Lord. Ha ha ha."—Harsh laughter, lighting of cigars, pulling up of thigh pants, clearings of throat, popping of eye bulge doubt, staring into the blank to wait for further time as they drive off, heads motionless in the passing whirring car like cut off heads of puppets made serious by an evil smiling puppeteer hiding behind the Saturday afternoon Germanic drapes with little masks painted at intervals leering.

* * *

(5)

MY MOTHER Evangeline Duluoz had posed only about three years ago at Hampton Beach on the spectral snow white sands of a lost summer afternoon, with little Gerard in front of her also snow white and with little dark eye slits like a cute cartoon, his soft yellow hair luirssant in the sun. How trim, slim of waist, full breasted and majestically voluptuous my mother is in her skirt of New Look length (the year is 1919), with long sleeved blouse and kerchief around neck, and bonnet with flower at front like miners' lamps or firemen's emblazoes; behind them, on the low tide Atlantic slick, Atlantican and lost, slide swimmers running but looking like modernistic Holiday Magazine thingirl ads running over the mirror of some magic perfume to some lavender poem underneath, but it's a real longpanted swimmer of 1919 hurrying with refreshed feet across the little sands and gurglets of the beach; noble Indian like cowboys in huge bathingsuits standing, like cigar store Indians rather, waiting for the ball to be thrown. But there stands Evangeline Duluoz ("Eve" my father called her, simply) ("Say, Eve, where the hell's my shirt?"). Her hair is bunned back hard and slick towards the back of her head, over her ears, making her look in the oldfashionedness like an Indian; her face is youthful but in the picture sun-stern; you can see she is not frivolous,

The Buddhist Years

probably not sensual, more interested in duty, serious, ageless, ungirl-like, but handsome, feminine, soft.

Now she's having her third, lies in the bedroom on Lupine Road as the doctor ministers her manifestation from the Essential Mind, the child, that cometh glue headed and sugarlipped from untold karmas of commingling parents, unnumberable the karmaic[51] kingdoms that came before to build the architectures of this deed, to suffer in the world, to grow old, decay and die, lost in the swirl of birth and rebirth unfigurable. "Pauve ti t ange doree," she says on seeing me, having me laid little and brown like a little turd in a snowy blanket in her arms, "poor little golden Angel," for which the Heavens on high did bless her.

"Ti Pousse," they called me after a few months of fatty milk and sucking at the world larder and my own thumb probably, "lil thumb," my nickname that stuck for life; in French this is; in English I became known at first as Mickey, then Mike.

Outdoors my father walked the kids around, frowning in thought, manly, sad; on the hill top were the white haunted[52] birch.

"Poor gal," he thought of Evangeline, genuinely hit by the pain and evil, which wasnt going to last long for either of them; some glandular disturbance making him premature-impotent would free him from sex soon enough and enable him to cast off the heaviest bondage of pride, for a role of humility and feverish sensibility lot-cast for him on earth by the sneaking fates. "It all starts with the business, then gets to happen bad; it's like a sickness of earth; I blaspheme life; but they cant tell me it's not an evil. Ah, and they did that with me; the old man had me baptized under the steeples of St. Hubert; the wind, the rain; we've only to lose our bodies, to re-find heaven; beautiful blue heaven, nothin there."

* * *

(6)[53]

AND THAT NIGHT HE goes and plays cards anyway. Headed for that switchman's shanty for the game with the railroad men, he and Charley

---

51   The text reads "karpaic" but "karmaic" seems more likely.

52   The text reads "ahunted," a typo for either "haunted" (best guess) or "shunted" (also possible). See p. 78, where the birch are "griefstricken."

53   Kerouac used much of sections 6 & 7 in writing *Visions of Gerard* a year and a half later, in December 1955. See VOG 87–96.

stopped off at the Keith Theater and went backstage and for a moment were standing smoking under the iron fire escape in the gravel alley by the mill spur tracks and the canal, across from where the Post Office now stands, under the moon in the soft Springlike night, joined by some of the performers on the vaudeville bill coming out for breaths of air between acts. There were Rialto & Lamont, "The Talkless Boys"; Lois Bennett, A Ray of Western Sunshine, and The Popular Composer Muriel Pollock, in "SONGS" by Muriel Pollock; dainty, captivating, vivacious Miss Corinne & Dick Himber, Offering, "Coquettish Fancies" with Ben Oaklander at the Piano; Bob Yates and Evelyn Carsen in "Getting Soaked," by Billy Dale and Bob Yates; Clarence Oliver & Georgie Olp in "Wire Collect," Comedy, Written by Wm Anthony McGuire; Billy McDermott, "The Only Survivor of Coxey's Army"; and on the screen, A Photoplay of Speed, Thrills and Laughs, "Monty Banks and a famous star cast in 'Racing Luck,' a fast action comedy production with a Laugh with every foot of the story"; with, at 8 PM, Pathe News, Topics, and Aesop's Fables, and at 8:27 the first act; exit march at 11 PM by the B. F. Keith's orchestra; when everybody went across the street for a soda, in Page's, or in Liggett's, or in Paul the Greek's; the dense dyed neons of brown oldtime citylight night like old cartoons of election night showing the boy newspaper seller with little cloth cap and scarf and knickers holding out a paper to two men, one in derby, one with cane, their coats flapping in the wind, and beyond a great crowd, some reading papers, a placard saying "Vote for ' ' ((3 3 " (blurred)[54] and the wallsides of buildings in the city night and the marquees and the general drizzle of activity in the furthest reaches of the scene where it is incredibly dense, soft, dark, rich as if Spanish night or Indian night or New World City night, the blue of tombs is in the neons, the secret of the Old Fish is on Old Fish Street, the dark spoor of real profound red throbs up from the lights; all Lowell is slightly alien, ugly but soft and kindly beyond the B. F. Keith's backstage door; smoke fragrantly rises from cigarettes of the gathered performers and Eno the ad man and others; crunching slowly up the coal-like gravel of the alley, from Bridge Street, the sudden enormous figure of a man with a strawhat, a cane, a huge pot belly, a bulbous red nose, and a namelessly battered, muggled, eaten up and almost disappeared face; Old Bull Baloon by name.

---

54   These marks were seemingly intentional, representing a blurred name (in keeping with Kerouac's frequently apolitical views).

The Buddhist Years

"Eno, want ya to meet William Baloon of Los Angeles."

"Los Angeles nothing, m'boy," replies Old Bull Baloon turning imperiously and like looking over his shoulder at his introductor, "Capistrano and the isle of Magdalena off the coast of Palomina, what's the name of that gad damn monkey island off the coast thar?"

"Mr. O'Brien, Mr. Duluoz, Mr. Sagely."

"Couple railroad boys told me I'd find you fellas up here," said Baloon paying no attention to anything but the business at hand. "Got ma car waiting across the parkinglot and all set to go. Thot I'd bring me own refreshments with me, in the form of this here little flask of continental bug joi juice, the joie de vivre, ya know"—upending flask for big look at how much left, and offering it first to almost-as-big-as-him young Eno Duluoz, who accepts with a blush.

"Dont take me for a drunkard, boys, but I sure do accept a lotta drinks in this town lately, and thank ya all." Up, slurg.

Then Charley, then Old Bull, demonstrating techniques of opening cap, wiping, and bringing-to-lip developed from Coast to Coast in an incredibly long life so cluttered with a hundred thousand misadventures in a thousand different places the whole story had never been, could never be, told, except you saw it written in the picotee carnation of his nose, the swim of wrinkles in his eyes, the wrinkles there, like eyes of a hardboot Kentuckian on a rail; the crooked mad smile and yellow-teeth of his grin; the big ring on his thick Neroid finger, like fingers of old whores successful and retired, or fingers of Roman prelates given to regurgitation ere their excarnification comes due and all the banquets fall. "It's a little mixture of wine, gin and bourbon, I learned in Panama some years ago with a little man named Low stood about 4 foot 4 inch and was half Chinese for all I know, lived in a wattle tenement on the edge of a river sewer system with dead rats and crapsticks floatin with the tide, and green spiders in his hat when he reached in to find the dice; good man as ever gambled, drank, lost and died." Looking around, spying another. "I know you...I saw you in Cincinnati few years ago, if you will remember, my dear friend, it was the afternoon some hobo from Pratt Street Baltimore I believe and I believe the name was Slats came up to Lady Nicotima at the bar and slapped her rump, congratulatin her for the good showing that afternoon..."

"We met in the backroom, yes. Lord, that was a good old night."

"Ha ha ha,"—Eno Duluoz—"he even remembers what happened in Cincinnati. Say," taking cigar out of mouth, serious, "you must a done a lot of traveling there, Mr. Baloon."

"Call me Bull, E-no…" returning a similar blue-eyed bulgous serious stare but with humor of time and death inside, "rememberin Cincinnati and tryin to forget Cheyenne, you might say. Been everywhere, investigatin situations from this side of the confidence man to the other side a Blackjack, Colorado."

"Ever been to New Bedford much?"

"To be frank with you, I aint been there but once, passin thru one night, O, about 1918, I think it was, drivin in an old Model T with a buncha boys and a soldier that got back from the front as I remember, and we drove him to his house with his warbag and all and his mother and father were waitin in the door for im…with lights, I remember dark streets…a howlin wind…a trolley…"

"Now there's [where] we really go to town and have ourselves a time, Bull…now gad dalginit, cant you manage to be around here in the middle a July when we go down there—there's a whole bunch, maybe ya know some o them…how long you been in town?…where ya stayin?"

The bottle going another round around, "Since yesterday, holed up in the skidrous old inn cracked and weatherbeaten by the wars of the cockroach for nigh onta how many years ya think? no different than any other drivel hovel I been in from here to the other side of Monterey Bay and down to ole San Juan de Letran. Hotel named after your river."

"The *Merrimac*!"

"Bedposts creakin ev'rywhere—"

"Say, Baloon, I think I met you in the West someplace…or Louisiana."— one of the vaudevillians.

"Lou-siana's in the West, the place you met me in…that's right, it's where I come from…around Ruston."[55]

"That's right, I remember the bill…hell we had a gang, we were going ta New Orleans. There was Jackie and Billie, the Thinking and Talking

---

55   Ruston, Louisiana, was the home of William Holmes Hubbard, a.k.a. Big Slim, whom Jack met while in the Navy when both were under psychiatric evaluation. Jack idolized Big Slim as a genuine hobo, and Big Slim appears or is referred to numerous times in Jack's writing. See, e.g., DP 169–82, OTR 24–25, etc.

The Buddhist Years

Birds, Jack Hanley the Eccentric Juggler, O, Smith and Duane, Wilcox and Lacroix, the Meistersingers, Roger Williams the Boy From Dixie…"

"That's right," said Old Bull Baloon biting off the tip of a fresh cigar, "and Joseph B. Stanely and Company in "Waiting," with Jack Egan. I believe you had Stafford and Louise, a world of Fashion, Song and Dance. And was there Ponzini's Monkeys, or did I have a shot too many out of Billy Jo Daddy's white mule moonshine in the fire beyond the trees? Gentlemen," to Eno and Charley, "my car," and they started off.

Oil cups flared mysteriously smoking by a construction ditch in the Centralville Night—the river flowed—Sweet little Gerard Duluoz prayed for me—Little Nin's toys dusted in the ragamuffin world corner—I know— Doctor Sax muttered in his shack in Dracut Woods—Rain splattered—in the night—A woodstove roared, deep and red as the fire lengthened and the bottle dropped.

* * *

(7)

"BETTER BE JOCUND with the fruitful grape, as sadden after none, or bitter fruit," said Old Bull Baloon[56] as he received his hole card and his face card, which was a nine of spades.

"I dont drink as a rule like you do, Bull—by God have you seen that boy guzzle up that whiskey tonight, Charley? Jim? Two bottles now…"

"It's only 5 AM, give im a chance to start…"

"I've had to come from a long way and a lot of snowy country to want that much heat, Eno; it takes to me like water, or vice versa."

"Well, I like to gamble, like a drink once in a while," big Eno glancing at his king of hearts face card and adjusting it over the hole card, which now, surreptitiously, in the middle of his sentence, he raised a corner of, to see the spade smooth black of a ten a spades, winking inside himself to think, "but I never could drink like that and put it away like that—hell, George Dastou and me and Mike Fournier one time drank I dunno how much beer out of a barrel in New Bedford and then had whiskey and a cardgame just like this I guess nine in the morning, whoo, it took ten years off my life— you westerners are drinkin men…those fellas with the circus at Nashua,

---

56   Bull is quoting from verse 54 of *The Rubaiyat* by Omar Khayyam: "Waste not your Hour, nor in the vain pursuit / Of This and That endeavour and dispute; / Better be jocund with the fruitful Grape / Than sadden after none, or bitter, Fruit." (http://classics.mit.edu/Khayyam/rubaiyat.html)

I remember, by God, and some of em rollin and snorin in the hay and the elephant manure, ha ha ha."

"Aint the first time I'd a slept in a stable," Bull said. "And you, Charles, what you got under the queen of hearts," indicating Charley's face card.

"I wouldnt tell you if I knew," said Charley, now looking at the hole card with the same sly up-corner, saying to himself, so the others could almost read it in the imprint of the smoke before the lamp, "ten of diamonds."

Old Conductor Jim Sagely, the other railroad men having bowed out for various reasons from the hotel room by the tracks near the depot where this game was raving like a dream, holding his ace of clubs in one hand, thoughtfully raised the jack of same underneath and pursed his New England farmer lips.

"Sagely," said Bull, slyly, small blue eyes thru reddened eyelid puffs watching, raising bottle for a slug, a simp, "if I had a barrel a beans and I had a store, I'd hire you to count the bad ones and lay the good ones aside, that's how sly your dollar is."

"You western dandies with vests dont dangle enough rope around here to hang a decent Irishman with let alone a hombre of the western plains, you old boomers are all the same, upend a whiskey bottle in front of the caboose stove and let the waybills go, then come complainin you aint got enuf money and those that do 's'got too much, and 's too miserly for your company or your card game."

"You too miserly for my cardgame—? and took 80 dollars from me just this one night? All the jices you got from me I can squeeze out again, you know, I'm liable to, you old Florida East Coast orange you."

"First time I win some real money in a card game in all my life and they's complaining in the sides and up the back…"

"No complainin, Sage, I'm passint king a hearts Eno Pop here with his recent insurance-gatherer just born, bang," throwing Eno a king of clubs face card, and everybody eying them. "And Charles the hammer, bang," a queen of spades, "two kings and two queens showing and where's the marital bed, bang," a jack of spades for the conductor, and bang, for himself, same of hearts.

"The game thickens."

"I bet and raise the ante."

"At this stage, nobody cares."

The Buddhist Years

"A new ace wont do you no good—old Sage could use it."

"Sevens…aint got no use for em, even when I got seven in the hole, my unlucky number, nine's my lucky number by God—"

"Another seven—talkin of the devil…pair a kings high."

"There he is, Bull Baloon with a girl for his jack. Who's gonna win the rainbow pot?"

"Let me look and think." Eno, hi, with a pair of kings, pretends innocent worry. Charley has nothing further to examine beyond his showing queens, but a mentioned forlorn seven.

I lie in my crib, breathless, blind, while my fathers unwind the world to its bloody conclusions, like tragedians in *Macbeth* bloodsoaked, emerging from darkened rooms, from which sounds of wailing emanate, at dawn, by curtains moving in an insane breeze.

"It's a dream, lads, it's a dream," utters Bull upending a lofty big pull on his swiggins, bloodshot returning the cap, spitting over his shoulder out the open window of the room, to where, in muddy March softnight, fragrant flower hints float with premonitions of new earth, new life, new angels, new eagerness in the vein of the flesh of mortal man: Spring.

Sagely has a jack under and a jack on top, and nobody knows, but no advantage his, yet, till that last thrust of fate-cards, from the hands of the dealer, Bull. He leans over to rub his thigh in the night of the world, forgetting his family, lost in the eye-to-eye game of men in America; nights long ago after Dempsey battered Willard;[57] smoke in Butte saloons; Denver backrooms, games; lost heroes of America; Chicago, Seattle; vaudeville; redbrick alleys and forgotten cundroms under isolated signs in the hiway night of Roadster Twenties; long jaws of bo's riding the boxcar from outside North Platte, clear t'Ogallah, mispronounced, sad, spindle legged waiters in the summermoth night, by lights; America, sweaty, poker games, nostalgic with afternoon and man, midnight and weariness, dawn and O'Shea running to catch his train, Baloon examining his useless king hole card, to full deciding to leave the game because even if he gets another king he gets no ace to ace-high Eno.

---

57   Jack Dempsey (1895–1983) won the heavyweight title by defeating heavily favored Jess Willard (1881–1968), the reigning champion, on July 4, 1919, in Toledo, OH, and went on to be the dominant prizefighter of the 1920s.

The others stay; Bull deals, lost in the dream. "Ten dont do you no good, Eno, lessn you got another ten underneath," dealing Eno a ten of clubs. Deals Charley a seven, making a pair of sevens on the top. "You better have a queen underneath," which Charley doesnt have, turning up a ten apologetically. "Another pair of sevens!" dealing Sagely a seven of hearts. "If he has another seven underneath," opines the red-nosed dealer from Butte Montana, "he's got his own deck a cards hidden under his ear inside that curly hair, yass...which would a left me with the ace of jokers," dealing himself, for the hell of it, the final fifth card tho he is out, the ace of spades, death. "Gentlemen," seeing he's inadvertently emptied his whiskey bottle without realizing it in the heat of what he was doing, "is there any beer in the house? No beer?"

"We got some left, yeah, Bull, in the box there."

And Eno, that which made me juicy born, were his greedy raking-ins, raked in the pot, cigar in teeth, big body tensed forward in chair to affairs of the night, as goldpots strew the blue beginnings with incense of aurora and dawn creaks up to crack and boom over the black sad earth now irrevocably I was, enfleshed, sacrificed and given over to, O moanin shame.

"The San Francisco blues," said Old Bull Baloon, "you got me singin with all this loss of money, and travelin money it was to be, at that. Guess instead of Butte Montana, I'll run down to Dracut this fair morn—see my old friend Sax, a man none of yous been privileged to meet in this town, more ill-fated than in all your dreams you'd a bitterly hoped her to be."

* * *

(8)

NIGHT AND DAY in my little crib I was taking the unreal ride now, learning the rope-tricks of Magadha thru my mind's perceiving that, late, I'd wake from a feverish nightmare I thought real, only to be left up on the shelf of darkness to stare and crumple my thumbs and bite my lips, trying to decide which was the dream and which not, realizing both were dreams, from one dream to the next and into another; all characterized by a faint failure in solidity to feel like it was really solidly takeable; realization that the taste of food was more like a wash over my palate, insubstantial as water over the skin, than like a taste to chew in; sound an accidental realization that I was listening, so that all the noises that sometimes formed backdrop for my deep meditations swam back unreal as dreams, discursive, distant, busy;

The Buddhist Years

odors sneaked at me against my impassable smeller a minute, and vanished eternally; sights like black spidery movements that were not there, not even in the lights of passing cars passing over things, but imaginary blossoms in the dark, forgettable at once; sights like the crack in the ceiling being deliberately written in by the White Hand; and feeling, something that suddenly reminded me to cry because it was pain, a dream but a suffering dream, a dangerous and homicidal dream.

"Ah Ti Pousse," they cried, "he wet his pants, ya mouillez ses culottes. Poor little bird, we'll give him some dry rags."

I was able to perceive the street and trees outside, like gray shapes through the window, beyond the hanging beads of the doorways of the house with its heavy monstrous drowse in afternoons of sunshine; or rainy day graygreen deepseat horror among the furnitures, damp; my first unutterably bleak unhappy realizations of the weather, the humidity of rain, the chill of the world, the sordid rotten blear-like crap in my pants. Monstrous as a king, huge as God, I lay there for eternities waiting for everything to come justifying to me, for I had solemn truth; if they could have spoken my language, the others, they would have lived forever, been saved, gone out of the stream, put the world from them. I was so fresh a dream, so near to non-dream which was only recent, so remembering of the essence everywhere filling the different manifested forms, my eyes so moist and pure and undefiled by discriminatory ideas of what I saw, my feelings so blank and perfect like fresh new gloves and white at that, they could have learned how to take off their old clothes and regain the naked pristine emptiness. Flaming in my mind was the first sunrise, going up over a hill, and dew and birdlutes. I knew it was the sunrise of a dream. I had a vision of a great white man like God standing like a giant by the hill, leaning on it to watch his work, the roof of the little house there, the tear in the curtain of reality behind. Another pristine dawn occurred in a wooded valley, another little house, a cabin, with smoke, and sad the banksides filled with bushes into whose leaves I stared from below. There was a woman holding my hand in the first morning of the world, we stood side by side, by a hill.

I had a deeper, stranger realization of something that now, removed, I cant unpiece; something to do with a remembrance of before I was born, of the street, of Lakeview Avenue before I was born; a realization that could

Jack Kerouac

only have been possible to me at the age of at least 2, because I would have had to see the street first.

* * *

(9)

OIL CUPS FLARING in the misty night, the sand, the ditch with jagged concretes of old making little dusty ledges for living strange dusts that are now blowing in the night, the flicker of the flares, the saw horses, the sand piled—somewhere on the mysterious horizon of the suburban night like scenes in Mexico City or Montreal—equally and O most hauntingly like the little salesman with the mustache, the strawhat, saying he is dying, the golden davenport of his house at the top of the street—the wind from the river cold and inhospitable, dim lights in the houses, creak of pines, lost Lowell on a winter night in 1922 and I am not yet born but the oil cups flare and smoke— little rocks on the pile have eyes—everything is alive, the earth breathes, the stars quiver and hugen and drool and recede and dry up and spark—no moon. Black. Shuffling figure of a man in a derby handsapockets going to the latticed house, the Kellostone pine, the great soul of my brother Gerard in sadness hums over the scene like your Diamond Samadhi, O Sakyamuni-Prince—Hear the river hushing over a load of ice—Smell the Smoke of the dump—the little man in the straw hat is going home, newspaper's underarm, he left the trolley at Aiken and Lakeview, bought a new Rudy Valentino box of chocolates for his wife for tomorrow night Friday, "I am dying" he said to me in Eternity in Montreal years later and that afternoon Frank Shephard[58] and I took the two girls, sisters, to the bleak roadhouse outside Mexico City and danced to sad lassitudinal Latin mambos and slow tempos and boleros— the rain came, outside it was a pine, a gray window behind brown pink Mexican drapes of decoration—the hand drummers dreaming—I saw the oil cup flares of the construction job at the middle of Gregoire Street in Lowell in a night before I was born, the moths flying millionfold around, the dense happiness of timeless reality and angels—the incoming soaring whirlwind cloud of thoughts, eyes, the whole shroud, the Blakean wind and the voice in the wind saying "Ti Michel va venir au monde, il va savoir le mystère, il va savoir le mystère!"—*Ti Michel will be born, he will know the mystery, he will*

---

58   Frank Jeffries (1923–'96), whose pseudonym in OTR is Stan Shephard. Kerouac is in part re-counting an experience he had with Frank during their 1949 trip to Mexico City with Neal Cassady (part 4 of OTR but not included in the novel).

The Buddhist Years

know the mystery!—and at the foot of the street the house where the woman had an altar in a room, whole statue, candles, flowers, this dame instead of a TV had in and for her sittingroom of settees and kewpie cushions a bloody sadness in plaster, loss and vim of kicking candle flames hundreds darting to the rescue in air screaming pursuit of lost atoms—The mist of the night, the river beyond, the dull street lamps, the pit of the universe not only like the Massachusetts Street of Rosie Cassidy[59] in another room of the Level Time but (as dark, as fragrant) (later, when I became 16) like the night of the dream of the crowd playing leapfrog around the racetrack with dice, knives and interests—in Denver, in Shmenver, when silently I a goof following a cop who later turned into a woman came padding on my dusty shoe of dreams, amazed—the last gloom, the last barn—horses?—and in the rickety sad immortal NOW-house the swarming vision parting over the heads of little children on the bed and I'm singing a saying—"Where's Earl?"—leaping ahead into my fabulous life's adventures—and that little salesman sipped his beer in Montreal, put it down, adjusted packages, said "Well I'm goin home"—

"You're a real drunk—" (T'est t'un vra soulon)

"Well hey, dont talk like that—We dont say that—"

"Aw—" I was sorry—"In English in the states—it's a joke—we say it like it was nothing."

And he said: "I'm dead anyway—I'm goin to die soon," and off he goes, 98 pounds, dark, blessed, off into the spectral Montreal night like the one we'd gone out to the suburbs of Mexico City in, on some meaningless high drive, Neal and Frank yakking anxiously, pointing, looking for something, Gad knows what happens to us in the end, as I rode in the back seat staring— got out of the car, walked around a field, houses on the other side, the ranked silent adobe roofs under low level stars and the Fellaheen dogs lean and mangy sleeping in mud holes or howling and prowling for slats of debrained cows—a path, starlit, an oil flare flicker of some dugout ditch or sewer hole across the dry brown plateau grass—a kid in white trousers, shirt, holy bright strawhat—4 AM—comes to greet us—we talk in a field—dim brown lights beyond—the sky wild—we dont know what we're doing, saying, "Qué fue amigo esta hora mañana"—the kid has a baseball in his hand, is plopping

---

59   Mary Carney (1921–'93), Kerouac's high-school girlfriend and the subject of his novel *Maggie Cassidy*, written in the spring of 1953, a year before this text.

it—It's like Algiers, like China—the mystery of the outskirts—that last streetlamp—Premonitions without time under the Atlantis Atom Bomb predicted and backseen by self-hypnotists in America, like E.C.[60]

I am not yet born—I have not yet walked the streets of Victoria Texas in the night, run Main St. down to its railroad track and the little cottages with Christmas in the windows, the Watsonville Mexican grocery stores and bars next block—the brown, sad, shrouded Out Our Way and also Kafka factory across the track foaming at the nub of the foot of Main St. which even now you can see, as you turn, illuminated bright beady Xmas in the interiors, traffic, rich—here the gloomy factory and the men in the windows on the spot looking down with sandwiches in their hands at that hobo walking the Missouri Pacific ties in the misty night of oil cup flares, pink lights in windows, far dogs, railroad howls, rumbles of horizons, Texas white cottages dreaming, Christmas in the sad—I tell you, and had feet then and new Thom McAn shoes, dad—Remembah?—How can I forget?

Not yet born, not yet seen, not yet come—to Montreal, Texas, Mexico, Watsonville California, Lowell Mass. or all your poor bedighted[61] and broken jags of land in this same stillness and sweetness of night, this sleepy goodness, dense, knowledge of sleep, timeless, you can live or die, laugh or cry, yawn or yell, sleep or run, walk or lie—The area of the world is breathing for your arrival, your passage, and your departure down the last lamppost—The glow on the sawhorse of Gregoire St. is pink—it shakes—far off, over darkness, blue windows of the river mills—thunder of lost, scarbranded, hidden falls—The myth of the rainy night, hidden in upper capes of darkness—Droop of shadows, Shh—Sweet time in its number: 1922—

Here comes Eno Duluoz the young printer toddling up the street to home—s'been losing at cards all night? Coughs, removes straw hat, wipes brow, hurries on—disappears in gloom—the oil cup flames, smokes, quivers—Now you know the whole river is rushing, hushing, smoking mist forever—that has been the Time Sound—now you'll never hear another sound—Bzzzz of hear's intrinsic hearing, unangry as a *dead* bug—Soon it will be March—Now it's early February—A winter snowbird is sleeping in the crawl pine, the wit little beak is burrowed in the caky feathers of cold wintertime—soon the eyes will be plucked out by hawk sisters, the feathers

---

60   E.C. is Edgar Cayce (1877–1945) (see p. 22 herein).

61   Typo for "benighted"?

The Buddhist Years

tinder for fires, they'll find him under a brakeshoe by the track where the rat runs hiding—the crackle foot still from twittering aghast—(and) at last—bird—

Morning thunders on the horizon, makes a great quiver, sonorous music of gray, the wangdang spreadeagle clink coin of morn about to 'rupt BOOM—Whole worlds waiting with banners waving for the steely infant of Divine propositions with the Angel of Mercy, proposition being foremost "If you live you can die—If you die you can live—the burden of time, all thoughts of suicide, post pubertical problems of love, loss of mates, debt, ignominy and general perfidy of dirt—yours—if you will quake when the giver creams, and come to life—Run on, little ghost—Your doom and dont blame me"—

* * *

(10)

I HAD GIGANTIC FEARS of a big drape ripping, rioting down the stairs in my mid-sleep and all the shriekies of the narrow night crowding in to hold me down, pinned, while sheets dance. Something in the corner was moving, brown, darker than that, myriad, bodiless, it was a lump, it had no soul, it was worse than a ghost and it had no substantial reason to haunt me. The crack down the parting of a drape was the crack through which I could see the reposant elbows of destroyers bent and plotting on my demise, secret, silent, conclaving inside there as tho they didnt want me to hear my own fate being decided. Even in the afternoon religious pictures of Jesus on the cross, for all the torment I understood instantly about it, were somehow part of a general hex to bring me down and lay me at the foot of some cross; the nubs of the nails on the feet of poor Jesus, I studied, with little mind, lamb of god. Laughing bigdrinking adults around my crib looking at my little chins made me see swirl, sad-up, with blue worries in my eyes, and they thot it was a joke. I saw the swarming vision of the parting of the drapes of the shroud in the gloom immensities of the black slick cover on the chair. Day time, night time, I should have had a glass of wine, but was too young; reminds me of a poem on the subject, writ by two little girls of my acquaintance in Calif.

ages 4 and 6[62]

(dictated to me in 1954)

---

62   A reference to Cathy and Jami Cassady (b. 1948 & 1950).

(mindful am I, that when Demosthenes the Greek orator who studied to conquer stuttering with pebbles in his mouth by the essential soul sighing sea of time, was told he was spending more on olive oil than wine, he started to buy up all the wine in town, and threw jokes at the proprietor to boot)

He was a little boy
And his Mother
    took care of him
And Jesus was crying when his mother was gone.
Then a girl came
    with pigtails on
Then she patted the little baby
    Jesus—
Then Mary came home
    and kissed the little Jesus
And told him to go to get
    up and have
A little ride in the buggy—
His mother went away again
And the girl came back
    with the kitty cat
Then his mother came back
    & was drinking some wine
And took the glass & put it away
And told little Jesus
    to have a drink of water
Angels flew around him & covered him
    all up—

(Word for word.) (If I had felicity with my facility I'm telling you I'd be a millionaire.) Also mindful am I, in all this mix of time, grapes, love lost, vicious springtime, slit flesh and general erroneous parturience, I agree with the Socratic Sage, who said, "None of your wives will love you, cherub, and none of ye cuckolds are dry." *Our Lady of the Flowers*, the *Sacred Books*, *Go*, and *The Decline of the West*, and *War and Peace*, and the Holy Bible, and

The Buddhist Years

The Town and the City[63]—nil, till the Urbi Roma Ruby Port Artistic wine is poured, to make my palate crave and rave, pour tortillez les glands d'gout, torture the taste glands, splowf!—another herobook gone down, another face lost, the eraser of heaven's coming down to put an end to this, and with Omar,[64] let me rave in this dream for dream it is, repetitious, alliterative, and sad. Gentlemen!

Old Bull? He'd taken a big belt out of a bottle and laid down to sleep in the cave of civilization, in his clothes, on the skid row bed, and slept as angel-like as me.

* * *

(11)

MY FATHER, with his big thighs, the cigar ashes falling on them, his rough back-of-hand scraping them off, his cough, huge sincere eagerness, gnarled tortured blackened face beside me in some old brownlit smoky coach of the Eternity Railroad and outside thru the unwashed windows we see sad sidings, rails, bits of grass, griefstricken birch on a cut, the wilderness of New England, a few stars, the distant sad lamp of a rear brakeman rolling back up the track with his handful of fusees[65]—my father whose soul I see even today in the speechless neons of cities like San Francisco, Boston, Chi, the big face of him bending over my America, saying to me, "Mike, Mike, my boy—" and shaking his head and pressing his lips together, as if to say, "It'll be hard, it'll be awful hard on you" and as tho he was waiting for me to finish up this life and come join him in heaven finally—The immense uprush of his heartswallowing serious worrying, I see it in the blank void of what's left me since he's gone and's been called the world so far, a great heart drooping like the Sacred Heart with its thorns and blood and inexplicable penitence. "Why do we feel so guilty?" I cry in my sleep, as my Pop used to cry, "It just doesnt do, ca va pas, ca va pas!—on est emorfouillez entour d'la terre, we are mortified into the ground," no truer words could be possible. My father Big Eno, whose bones blear now in the rainy grave in Nashua New

---

63 References to *Our Lady of the Flowers* by Jean Genet, *The Sacred Books and Early Literature of the East* (a 50-volume set originally published by Oxford University Press), *Go* by John Clellon Holmes, *The Decline of the West* by Oswald Spengler, *War and Peace* by Leo Tolstoy, and *The Town and the City*, Kerouac's first (and, at the time he wrote this, only) published novel.

64 "Omar" is likely a reference to Omar Khayyam (1048–1131), the Persian poet whose *Rubaiyat* is perhaps referred to in the phrase "Urbi Roma Ruby" just above.

65 See p. 171 herein for a different version of this same dream.

Hampshire, beside little Gerard's, and God knows where my grave will be, had his own weepy childly beginnings in St. Hubert Canada on a fated day in 1889. I have old records of his baptism. In it I see the mud of a country road, forlorn paisans all dressed up in the wind whip, a bleak font, a black priest, an iron cloud, sticks in the plain, gray brown grass of Abraham's Prairie swept by the Baffin Strait blues mashing on down from the nostril of the moose, the Labradorian Canadian New World howl of it, and all so coarse, vulgar, roughened by the tough needs and potato fields of the lives of the gathered ravenclad shadows celebrating the arrival into the church of another little fold of honey flesh.

High into the bleak shot the iron spike of the churchspire, hopeless to prove, visible for miles; across the river lay the smoking hulk of Montreal, its tangle of shacks and outskirt blues, its Mount, Cross and spiry downtown density of roofs; all seeable through dust clouds circling abandoned upon the colorless earthflat.

Arménégé Duluoz was there, small, grim, strong-knit like a wild boar, stiff as a plank, in baptismal best, boots, suitcoat, tie, watch and chain, hat; a vague unremembered cousin among the hundred cousins. There were statuesque French beauties signing their name in the register, laughing, lifting skirts delicately at the curb, the wind surrounding their Venus rumps with a shroud of shapely wind. The flutter of the bird to the sea, the crack of the weathervane. Eno Alcide Duluoz; his father proud and angry, his mother mournful, his brothers and sisters mad and quarrelsome.

"Allons, it's all over now, let's all go home."

"Well wait a minute, won't you? We just got here. You think I put on my new dress just to jabber in the street two minutes?"

"Ah shut yr mouth, me I'm goin. Grab the horse, he's pullin the other side."

"Wat you got in the neck today, you?"—brother asking brother.

"Eat some…"

"It's like that we talk, the day your little brother's baptized? You should be ashamed…"

"Aaaahhh…"

"Allons, allons, the gang needs a little raisin in the belly; allons chez nous, mes amis, to my house, I've got somethin for you all."

"He drinks like a hole, that moron…"

The Buddhist Years

"Shut up, hold the reins…"

The mournful bickering party, all in black and black ribbons, punished by the winds, moving off down the darkened day-street with the little pink cherub in the mother's [lap] shining like a new flower in an old bog.

* * *

(12)

THESE PEOPLE WERE HARSH FARMERS from north towards the Gaspe, near the village of Duluoz, all of them descendants of an early trapper of Breton mixture and a pure New World American mother whose Old World Fellaheen heart was lodged in the Iroquois nation, the tribe of the Caughnawaga, whose fires were never warm enough, and whose blankets and pots and horses were sorrowful like little March when it drizzles in the morning ground. Crystals of ice mesh on the mud in the stone, the gray blanket moves, vapors rise from the pitiful village of life.

There had been ten or eleven Duluoz brothers, only five survived; that many sisters, two of them dead in childhood; one maniac, several cripples; figures fantastic and impossible to believe. The stamp of the wild Duluozes was the snub nose, the telltale bejawber of the jowls, and batted mouth with the lower lip twisted moist and pathetic, like great crybabies of tormenting life, people made for weeping.

The Legend of Three Houses

ON THE ROAD   June 22—[1954]

I—THE LEGEND OF THREE HOUSES IN THE WEST

WHEN LITTLE ROAD LAMPS shine on the edges of lonely towns in the wide American plains, when this groaning earth turns from the sun, and a car comes and bullets by and is gone forever, and the lone hitchhiker thinks "How indifferent and cruel minded the vanishing of that red tail light, to leave me alone with the wind and the dry grass, the hot road at dusk, the visor of the Big Dipper on my lostness, lostness, lostness," still you can see, in Eastern Colorado, like an airplane burning in the sky, remnant rose sorrows of the long past day burning on the rock of the wall of the Great Divide, showing how the curve of the world in the western desert plateau has not yet obliterated all the sun, and so yet it can be seen on the ghost rock of Berthoud that sad red romance of the dying world, like the flame of mind's magic jewel in the Vast, the Void, the Already Gone, the Already Gone.

Three houses stood on one piece of land in this country. At night on Denver's long low hill overlooking town, near Morrison Road, you saw the lights of the three houses overwaved by cottonwood trees through which the plains wind sang a steady sea-song like the sound of sand flowing endlessly from out of a vast resounding funnel, a sigh grand, sweet, strong, because it came all the way up the hill of the western night, from Kansas on up. Above the three rooftops and the trees you saw the western sparkling stars. From the many-roomed White mansion, built in red brick with white pillars, bright rich lights poured; the light on the porch showed people coming in; the lawn; showed cars on the driveway; two pretentious whitewashed huntmasters with red caps with arms archaically extended like Egyptian offerers. In back, over the corral fence and under the densest biggest tree, was the saltbox plain wood house of Smiley White and his family, also showing many lights but somehow not so bright, momentous, patrician, or as grimly rich, the livingroom always dark where gleeful listeners of radio tales sat fascinated

The Buddhist Years

by the dial glow, in later years by the magic little show of television, the kids on the sofa, the old man in his rocker, the mother interrupted in her kitchen door. Further back, by the dry creek draw and the old barns, stood the one-room tarpaper shack of old Cody Deaver showing brown glow of oil lamp through burlap shades hung from nails; weaving huge shadows of winos toppling around, you saw in there, like giants magnified and thrown on a wall, the frightful secret hood of a looming shoulder, a curse, a crash, a crazy laugh.

Three houses, three classes of people, on one land, in one complex family tragically intermingled, on one continent, in one common and pathetic night.

Above the Rockies, just west, where the hill merged with the foothills and foothills piled to the rock peaks, beyond Golden, Boulder, final jackpine timberlines, there flashed the sad, the beauteous evening star, bright as a new nail in the occidental day-faint plank of dusk, prophetic and like a quivering cross for watchers of the mountain night like Ray Smith who was a child in this legend of the three houses.

* * *

THE SEED, that, had it been burned, would not have sprung aggrandized multiple families to gnash the troublesome air, was planted long before and in strategic places in the North American landscape. The making of the Whites, the Deavers, and of Ray Smith's father Old Bull Baloon was as the planting of pieces of the common potato in torment fecundities of earth; your original potato sprung plants from every eye, like Zeus, then vanished in the weariness; a score [of] potatoes rioting from a dreamlike paternity that because it is no longer here, was never really here, but only a dream bequeathing dreams.

Our fathers, we have understood that they lived, there are records; but only the living and the ignorant consult them; the dead dont care; the dead know that there was no Napoleon, no Barnasha,[66] no John Smith at all; flesh is stamped but nil.

Wade White was the grandfather of all this clan bearing the name. He came from earlier, darker fathers long mush and nameless in graves of the Old South and of Old England before that. Wade White had been seen and known; had sat sons Dan, Smiley and Joe all on his knee at the same

---

66   An Aramaic term meaning "Son of Man," i.e., Jesus.

time; had kissed his daughters goodnight; milked the cow in the very barn out back; posed for lorn snapshots in his eternity shirtsleeves by the fence, wearing old roundpeak black sombrero bought in Butte in the Roaring Eighties; but now that he was utterly gone and passed away, what could be said of "Wade White," of the figure that posed for the camera and can pose no more? "Wade White" then?—just a form in a dream, a conception in human outline that lasted no longer than conceptions ever do last, without selfhood, without substance as evident by now, without any thing; thinglessly nothinged forever, silent under the grass.

Grandmother White took walks to see his stone, marked 1852–1929, and struggled with her trembling anile chin to know this, and knew it.

In the same way began the Deavers; some lost grandpaw in North Dakota, axing wood on a gray Christmas, spawned Cody Deaver and twelve others fore and aft, and they buried his axe with him, and was there, is there an axe? was there, is there an axe-man?

Old Bull Baloon was born Guillaume Million in Quebec, Canada; came west in 1890, a railroad booming whiskey swiggling poker and pool shark with no worries other than the heat and the cold; in 1928 met and married Adeline White, took her home to Riverville, Maine, where she died giving birth to Ray, who, taken in by Sisters of Charity when the alcoholic pater disappeared, was designated as Ray *Smith*, a name not so far different from Million. Old Bull was 'real,' his son was 'real'; but now Old Bull was where nobody knew, was where the rain goes; was one with the lightning flash, returned to the dark at once; like father, like son.

* * *

WADE WHITE had been a little country boy who couldnt sleep at night and would come out on the porch of his family's log cabin in Big Kincaide, North Carolina and look at the moon through cobwebs, listen to the summer pipe of hot night birds, crickets, almost infantlike cries of ditch frogs, the croak of the bull in the Tar River; a thousand night noises under the haunted pines, the heated blurry stars; and on the horizon he would hear war's dull rumor…like horses running, wagons booming, ghost cannons speaking. It was 1863, the sounds were in his own mind but the war was a vast and funereal phantasy. His own father was dying at Kennesaw Mountain; his cousins were buried in The Wilderness. The blood of the bear of the South was soaking in the woods. A lost mammy, eyes cupped, searched the other side of the cottonfield for the

The Buddhist Years

re-arrival of Marse Tim—Marse Tim wasnt about to come running through that fence crying her name. Lost voices of Negras in a clearing, crumbled log sheds, the place where they left the mule…Wade White yearned to leave the woods of the Coastal Plain, follow the bright clouds west, find the dusty road to Tennessee, the battles of men, the ways they had for springing up and out and west, the American Faustian Final Bursting-to-Blow to the furthest last land. This was why he ran away from home—how come a bear chased him one morning in the Great Smokies—caused his arrival in Memphis at war's end—gat him a horse and a saddle jug and showed him riding between St. Louis and St. Joe—reason you saw him, stiff-collared, clerking off the ramps of Westport Kansas—why, like other Americans, he gulped to see the clouds following the Missouri, like white cuttings over the brown flat—what made him ride the Yellowstone range, saddlebum to Montana—gold and silver strikes in Butte, and be-derbied you saw him standing in front of his hardware store—with slitted eyes playing ten thousand poker games in the smoke of old spittoon saloons—events that led to the sight of the prosperous businessman stretching his legs outside a stagecoach at the Medicine River stage, night, beyond the last oil lamp you hear the whisper of the sage, you know there's no end to all that land, that American lone long land—so finally on roaring Larimer Street Denver there's your spindle-legged, archaic, be-derbied and bewhiskered men walking back and forth before swinging doors and there's Wade White helping a lady from a carriage in front of the Windsor Hotel and the goldstrike poets are writing on the bullethole walls. Her name was Annie Kemmerer and they got a big redbrick house out by Morrison Road and Wade became a wheat and alfalfa man; soon you saw him playing cards at the Colorado Wheatgrowers' Association, and in saloons downtown; and you saw him on mornings when the sun poured like gold into his study, bending in grave concern over a big experienced fist at ledgers in the rolltop desk, his handlebar mustache white as snow. From 1895 to 1910 he sires his list of heirs—E. Dan, Joseph, John "Smiley" White and two daughters: Adeline and Sarah.

* * *

THE THREE WHITE BOYS grow up in the summer golden wheatfields, go swimming out back of irrigation lakes, ride horses to the hills. Smiley is the leader, the adventurer; E. Dan the eldest, and Joe who always laughs, follow him. They roam the South Platte River from the railyard viaducts downtown to the open plain again where she flows shining in her pebbly bed. They build diving boards, pan for gold; play baseball on the teams; smoke cornsilk butts in the tall July grass, leg on knee and looking at the clouds. "That one there looks like a big old man layin on his side."—"That one there's a whole river of lambs."—"That one there you cant tell." They scrabble in the junkyards of Santa Fe, roll hoops through the downtown alleys of Saturday pure morning exhilarated nine o'clocks smeared and excited by the smoke of incinerator fires and by the clang and toll of the engine bell as a freight rumbles over the crossing from the mountains that you see there in April still snow-perfect in the void blue. They have rock wars with Mexican kids—they make friends, squat with them like Indians around kid-field fires of October dusk—race bikes around.

But as they grow up, and go to school, you can see the difference coming in their faces. Smiley is lazy and "wont do nothin." E. Dan is an honor student, energetic, futuristic, hurries on little feet. Joe, handsome, smiles and gets his way; in high school he's elected class president. He and Dan go to college (Denver U. and Columbia respectively); Smiley hits the road and works as cook, carpenter, professional boxer, brakeman and blackjack dealer in Nevada and Montana. He comes back home and takes over the work of the farm, moving into the fieldhand shack, sullen and uncommunicative, while Joe and E. Dan White go into politics, law and real estate and live in the redbrick mansion with the family. Only on birthdays they can persuade Smiley to eat dinner in the big dining room. Out in the plains men are playing cards in shacks.

"Smiley needs a wife."

Sometimes the three brothers are together in the bighouse study drinking Scotch around the billiard table Old Wade put up in 1910, and usually they're arguing. Sweet brotherly eyes that used to mist in youngtime joys, pouts and pains they'd shared, now coldly they cast orbs of hate on one another, half concealed.

"Just dont like to understand?—just dont like to see cow men come in their old dirty jeans begging to you two golfplayin college prefessors for a piece a paper for a piece a land that if anybody deserved it, was them anyhow, jess like Indians." This was Smiley's position; he didnt like businessmen, business, laws.

The Buddhist Years

"It's because you dont understand money, Smiles." Joe looking up from his cue with his charming dimpled grin. "You're like a country hick who dont have no conception of what money is, cant even understand a simple sale commission and probably dont know enuf to pour sand out of a boot—if you wasnt my own brother and I didnt know you to smell a buck a mile away, as a White will—"

"As a *who*-White will!—"

And Dan, with his little careful mustache, rimless legal glasses, weary oldworld sophistication, bachelorized detachment: "Go, come now, Smiley, you dont mean to tell me you'd rather break your darn fool neck at railroadin and cookpots and what-had-you than find yourself a nice clean and I may say respectable and *decent*—gentle—way of earnin—hah?—your pittances, pots?"

"You dont know what it does to me to see some old sidewindin fieldhand step inside that office of yours on Champa—always some damn law paper hopin he wont lose his land—" This was Smiley: in his own right a sympathetic, intelligent man, a little underestimated by his own brothers and the world; cross, true.

"—reminds me of the joke about the cow and the kangaroo," says E. Dan White, always telling jokes, always showing triumphant teeth in a small, persistent, needling grin. After five Scotches Smiley stomps out and goes back to his chores, his shanty, his rue.

"At least I'm a man," he says, looking off from his harness towards where you can see West Kansas thunderheads bedazzled and lost in a sky above a dun bleak land so vast, so severally shone upon by heavens accommodating a half a dozen simultaneous storms, it's like a vision of the world from an airplane, the tremendous embrillianted prairies and squares of cultivation in which, suddenly, you notice one illuminated dot in all the gloom where the Lord has oped a hole in the contentious skies and rayed down a worldful of sun on one blessed unbeknowing farmhouse where a good and honest man is abiding. "Must be a good man, or his house wouldnt be shelved to shine like that—"

Smiley needed a wife and found her that winter of 1928 while carpentering on the construction jobs of Phoenix Arizona. She was a real Western gal, daughter of a small rancher; big-drinking all-night-talking, eager, goodnatured, bighearted, with long wild hair, freckles, eyes on fire; some fever in her soul, her high anxious voice, her excitement, tense fretful body. For Smiley, Henrietta Love was the buddy who could drink and stay up all night with him and be his wife and on his side besides.

His rue satisfied, that Spring of 1929 with his own tools he built the seven room saltbox house on the common property of Paw Wade White and no sooner had finished tapping in the last nail on the final shingleboard and married Henrietta in a big ceremony in the main house, at which Old Bull Baloon a gambling pal of his from Butte Montana suddenly gayly appeared, to tender his respects, tipping straw hat over bulbous nose, and to "Give a couple whacks with the hammer so's I can lay claim to the back of yer yard when I lose my last hat," meaning to help him build his house but too late due to adventures delaying him en route; to the surprise of everyone it turning out that he had known Paw Wade White himself in Butte and played cards with him much before buddy Smiley was out of his crib—when, in all this gayety, with visiting Kemmerers, in-laws, a barbeque in the yard, fireworks at which Old Wade solemnly presided looking fit as fiddle, the oldtimer nevertheless sat in his chair after supper and died, grimly and on his own weary account, head bent like a cynic music master listening to his pupils in the other room. Smiley felt a knife in his throat from life; they'd never seen him cry. Old Bull was stopped in his tracks; you saw him in the alfalfa rows hatless, pondering at the midnight ground, whittling tufts of earth with little kicks. "Aw hell fire," sighed Joe White. E. Dan drove to Denver to make arrangements. It was a shock, noted in the papers along with a few funny "legendary" stories. The funeral was a long line.

Not only was it the death of "an old grandtime American" but it was like a prophesy, when, a week after his burial, vastly were the skies to the Southeast darkened by the coming of the Dust—The giant darkness rising from out beyond Kim, from Oklahoma dry and lonely, 1929, signifying the coming of the Giant Depression and the death of something like Wade White in America: the death of the grand, the expansive, and unselfconscious.

* * *

THE WHITES SOLD THEIR ALFALFA LANDS for real estate; the dust cloud passed over unused harrows and brokendown plows. By 1937 you saw neat white cottages built in rows when you looked from the backsteps out beyond the barn, and it was different.

Old Bull Baloon had come to see his friend in time to see his friend's old father die; now, in 1930, he took Adeline, his friend's sister, to wife. Life,

The Buddhist Years

death—it's a swap aint real. It was Bull's second marriage, the first one so long ago in the annals of his huge alcoholical soul it's better not ever to mention it, least of all his age, 55, since no one could tell by his appearance, fortyish enough, and his incalculable demeanor anyway: sandy hair combed to one side, serious blue eyes, bulgant and reddened nose, cocky smile, suspenders, vest, key chain, straw hat, spats and walkingstick, a gay *vivant* with a sneel of satisfaction in every picotee-carnation of his pockish, goodnatured, crude face. Adeline was no chicken herself in 1930, a little old maidish but quick to discern a good man's intentions. And he was a good provider, leastwise a good *winner*; outwardly just a railroad boomer, conductor by trade; this being just a semi-front for a man who could and did come into some town in the U.S.A. and win a week's meals (with drinks) inside an hour in any poolhall or backroom where a game was on—as natural a gambler as ever flashed thru a barroom door. Adeline died of childbirth in the town where Bull had taken her to live, in a five room wooden house in the French Canadian district of Riverville Maine, where some of the Quebecois Millions, sisters of Bull, lived and had provided a gigantic hope chest full of newlywed gifts, dishes, drapes, sad baubles to furnish and appoint the little 1930s love nest, among the scatter of which Bull stood hearing of the death of his goodly wife with a heart of petrified calm.

Because just for a moment the cynic gambler had almost been a man of affection again. Gloom hid behind the sofa he'd just bought her with a week's pay from his new insurance job. No use; in the morning you'd find the coffin, the crape, the undertaker drawing gray gloves at the front doorknockers.

Leaving all his money in an envelope in his sister's hand, Old Bull Baloon in straw hat and coat and carrying suitcase, left town that night on an old freight train, in a spitting rain, and was never seen in Riverville Maine until six years after, after many a locomotive had swum through its valley, when the child, who lived of his mother's death, Raymond, was driven back across the haunted spectral night of that restless, always mistaken, whichway-going, piteous, broken-hopes American road.

And for nothing, always nothing, for no real reason that the eye can see or the hand make use of—solitary, ungraspable, you see the headlights of the lone car crawling down the road underneath huge darkness, you know there are eyes behind a windshield watching, and talk, and that sad twangle country music scratching on a fading station, and hopes. "And time we get there it oughta be near daylight."—"I only hope they'll be there—it's got me worried"—"Well, we've got a long trip ahead—get some sleep."—"Aw hell I'd rather talk, aint no sense in tryna sleep now"—"We've put a lotta miles in this old bugger she's still goin strong, by golly"—"Ten miles ta Cranston"—"Cranton?"—"Cranton, Cranston, I wonder if they got a hamburger, huh? A hot cup a coffee huh?!"—and the car barrels on, dr-r-r-r, the good old American engine, the powerful American headlamps probe on deeper and deeper into the placeless void of night.

* * *

ACROSS THE SUN SHIMMERING FIELDS came a red faced man carrying his coat over his arms, and wanted to know if there was any work needed on the White farm, which in 1930 was still three quarters of its original size. Name of Cody Deaver, from South Dakota. Smiley liked him, had little odd jobs for him, had wife Henrietta give him a good hot meal, invited the man to make himself to home and move into the fieldhand shanty in back of the main White domiciles. Cody accepted, and they played blackjack and drank a jug of moonshine that first night by the light of the oil lamp, Cody sayin' "I caint dig nothin but tracks."

"Then stay."

He was a good serious worker but a wino and sometimes gone a week to sprawl in the backalleys of Larimer and Wazee among litters of broken glass, scabs on his blue lips and froth on his chin like a man beat on and kicked by armies of giants. When Bull Baloon came hoboing thru on a Depression flatcar, after the death of Adeline, there began a binge on Larimer Street with Bull, Smiley and Cody Deaver that lasted thirteen days, beginning each day with a pre-sandwich jigger of moonshine the size of a water glass, ending each dawn in sprawls sometimes the three of them miles apart in the city, or sometimes Bull was out on a rolltop desk where there'd been a game and Cody was in jail and Smiley'd made it out to the farm for a few hours. The whole bill was footed on the winnings of Bull in one night in a Curtis Street backroom.

"Why in hell did you ride a freight outa Maine, if it wasnt to punish yourself for skippin out on yr wife's funeral, cause I know *damn* well you coulda made you ticket in two hours in a dazzling goddam saloon."

And Bull had answered not, but showed bulbous pop of bloodshot eyes that had seen enough suffering.

The Buddhist Years

"Old Cody Deaver from Poorass South Dakota," said Old Bull, "I think he's already gone to meet the birds and here it's six and the other jug aint here. Ace queen high bets, deal out them fate cards"—singing: *"Been in Butte Montana, been in Portland Maine, been in San Francisco and been in ALL the rain*—That's what I heard last week from a little Negra man, oh 'bout five foot tall, hoboin all his life outa Louisiana, outa Mournful Mound Bayou actually. That boy sure could sing and right with the clackedaclack a the wheels, you never heard anything so real beautiful—Well, I admit I ran out on Adeline's funeral but you might just as well a buried me with her I hate funerals so damn much and disbelieve—As for the kid, you say it lived, I say maybe t'would been better if it hadnt lived. Because sure enough all this death and rain and pain, and poor moonshine, aint *my* idea of honey heaven."

"Aint mine either, Bull, but look what you're doing there, ace king high and it must be you."

"Started my life long ago on a hard and poor farm in Canada, since then which time I aint had no faith in the upturned eyes of the Christian saints—A flask, a jug, a barrel, a bottle, a box, with likker in it, I dont know, I guess I'm just a drinkin boomin gamblin bum but I've sure heard the blues sung in my day and got more faith in *them* than all improbable paradises as can be cooked up Sunday mornin in Iowa, Philadelphia, Lutheran Minnesota, Old Medicine Hat Mississippi—"

"Is you sittin there behind ace king high, or is it my Aunt Esmerelda from Slumgullion Pass?"

"It sure aint Saint Benjamin. Let me see you climb over five dollars," and raising the ante from 30 cents, he bets the five with frank blue eyes, in a rare bluff.

* * *

ALTHOUGH CODY DEAVER was a lost and hopeless drunk, so was Henrietta White, who sat around all day in her calico dress belting off gin bottles and trying to visit every woman in the neighborhood at the same time. Something there was in Cody's sad honest blue eyes, that in hers you also saw, that in Smiley's unsad eyes you'd never see, as though he had a million hogs and was counting every hair of em, as though he hated life and the people of it, for which no one'll ever rationally blame him. So that, sometimes when Smiley went on a gambling spree in town, driving his Model T with solemn selfbelief of human ignorance in Time down Alameda Avenue to the cluttered Denver of his boyhood, and Henrietta'd caused tongues to wag up and down the line with her ginny enthusiasms over the backyard fences of the Depression, she had no other recourse but Cody Deaver, who sat head on arms in the kitchen all afternoon mumbling "Yah" to all her long female harangues that had no specific purpose but to make her tongue go "Pa-ta-pa-ta-pa-ta-pa."

Sometimes you saw the poor tired human eyes of Smiley, the rings underneath them in certain light, and he said, "Hell what are we livin for if it aint to jess die?" He signed, closed the barn door, went to bed, dreamed the secret manly dreams that were wont to make his wife stay wondering up, cursing in the night.

"Who is this man that came to the scenes of my girlhood in Arizona, and made me love him with his big arms under that rattlesnake moon, and made me dance to the fiddles of the wranglers with orange bandanas and microphones?—if it aint someone's called John Smiley White, and here's his home, and his Paw's land and but he yawns at eleven o'clock every blessed night… Is it a ghost I see in the bed beside me, or is it a man I can hold on to?

Wino Cody Deaver never yawned at eleven o'clock but had a carnal stupid heavy interest in the world, at which he gazed, like a selfbelieving hero, with far-distant, blurry, beautiful eyes, saying, "We-I-ain-gol-hel-um?"—falling back again, a baby.

Henrietta hated the Whites in the main house with the fury of a black actress in the Italian Masque; E. Dan, Joe and his new wife from New York, the Kemmerers, Sarah, the feeling was mutual and the snubbing far from unofficial. Henrietta'd in her guilelessness managed to squeeze the snake's pouch and all the venom comes out.

Meanwhile in downtown Denver the mist fell on gray drizzly days, you saw the telegraph wires, the miserable honkytonk burlesque of Five and Tens, clunker REOs and Essexes parked at curbs, calico dresses of Thirties Ladies, the inky sadness of the Depression passing by with no millionaires in sight—men in tight suits with double breasted short lapels hurrying by with Early B Movielips pursed in selfimpressive satisfaction, as though the world was real and all the mountains beyond the neon marquees and honk toots of town were anything but solemn vast prophetical heaps piled there by huge gods of geology for no reason but like the unreasoning anxious equally tormented and interested silly sun blatting behind western clouds to the Ute

The Buddhist Years

and long-ago laments of death, pain, disinheritance, for just a lot of bright frightfall blank seeing of it all, so it couldnt have been surprising to anybody to see, on Wednesday March 12th 1931, Cody Deaver and Henrietta White come staggering up Glenarm Street carrying huge battered packages and suitcases tied with rope, their eyes wild with guilt and madness, buying meaningless expensive tickets to San Francisco one thousand four hundred miles to the west so they can run away from a poor ungraspable incapable Smiley. At night there's your Greyhound Bus balling down the road with left front tire hard on the white center line, zoom, the high stars of the desert riding with the window dreamers and flashes of dry grass pelting by, the wash swath headlights on the side of the road—and one occasional lone, western lamp far in the turning land.

"That's awright, Cody, I aint complainin about what Smiley done, only about what Smiley *aint* done!—I'll build you a little home in the West, just like in that song you like so much—we'll go to California jess like everybody else that's got sense—It's the promised land no matter what ANY body says. Damn it, Code, you aint handed me that bottle for a half a damn hour and damn if I aint seen you sneak a few—"

Chuckle. "But you better not talk too loud, if that drinker sees us drivin in the bus—"

"Why *hell*, I'll wrap a long telephone pole aroun his head. Hey bus-drah-ver!" calling from five seats back; "why they call this the Greyhound Bus?—cause it stops at every post?" Then head against head in the long traveling night, "Dont you worry, Code. I'll bullt you a home like you never seen and nobody'll know where we are and nobody'll be botherin us any more—Just rest your head on my shoulder and sleep, honey lamb, Mama'll be takin care of you from NAOW OAN"—with infuriated justified nod of the head, and lonesome, because Cody's already asleep in the long night drone to Salt Lake. So Henrietta broods in the night, and in her womb Cody Deaver Junior's already begun to form and stir with selfbelieving karmaic rue of his own, and everywhere it's unhappiness, though a lot of laughter rings some places.

* * *

THIRD STREET SAN FRANCISCO, you could have guessed it just by looking at them that's where Cody and Henrietta landed on arrival. A $2.50 per week room in the Boston Hotel on Third and Mission. Saturday morning when they checked in, and the street swimming with characters from all corners of 1935 America. Barber shops, pawn shops, secondhand clothes stores, junkmen with wagons, lines of drunks against the battered wall, trolleys clangin by. Sad music from windowsill radios, from ten cent movie, penny arcade. Restaurants with prices soaped on the windows and a stockingcap Chinese short-ordering the chow to seated lines of mournful bread-fisting bo's with coal in their clothes and bumps in their hats. Ruined dark haberdasheries with bottomless insides where you cant see the furthest rack of used boots. Hardware stores with rainy windows selling screws and bolts from the local dump. Okies with families struggling by with cardboard boxes, bagfuls of cabbage, chewing Wrigley's Spearmint Gum all five of them, and "inneressed in laf." Eccentric saints with long hair and burlap coats teaching on the corners of woe man. Salvation Armies clanging the cads with clash, "Lord!" and that shaky nasal trumpeteer of the Lost Land. The paddy wagon passing by, loaded to the doors with headbent bleeding bandaged onelegged drunks, two young cops riding the rear in blue. Bright is the air from the gorgeous rippling Bay, clouds as white as heaven snow roll huge from Oakland and from the Sierras those last humps to the American Final Westcoast. Ships from Manta Ecuador, from Seattle, from Yokohama Japan sit at piers in tangled shroud of boom and tackle. Other ships are leaving, plowing a trail out the Golden Gate to the far Pacific sash of paradise. Whitecapped seamen and whitecapped winos mill on Embarcadero's wide sidewalk. "Whoee!" yells Henrietta out the hotel window. "This is some hell of a gay town. There's more whores on the sidewalk than ya got cows in Arizona. Granddaughters of the Gold Rush, is what they must be, Code. Damn, go on out and get some booze, I got a dry hole in my stomach. If it dont clabber up and rain all over like Smiley used to say we'll go for a long walk tonight up on those hills the other side of Main Street and hobnob with the snobs. Come on over here and look at this damn town—shoo! whoo! I'd shore like to have a snort a what that long tall lanky drink a water's guzzlin down there! Standin in an alley with thirteen Indians and one seventy-year-old gal that musta got her stockins at the you-pickum-yourself ten damn years ago, Lord have a mercy on my soul—"

Cody Deaver Junior was born in the City and County Hospital in San Francisco that year, on a night when like on all nights his pensive sire was panhandling what he could get that could roll him back of barrels, in the last

The Buddhist Years

wino alleys of America, there being nothing but water west of there and no landward saving face and turning back.

Suffering and poverty were the names of Cody's parents.

* * *

JOE WHITE MADE A BIT of money; with the help of E. Dan's acumen in law, a new lumber mill out by Ouray, new mining stock and other sources gathering interest, he was making more each year. In Eleanor Schermerhorn of New York and Greenwich he met a woman who had more money than it would take him another twenty years to amass. She was a cool patrician blonde with bony hips and thin lips and not much interest in men. She was skiing in Switzerland with a tweedy poetess when Joe who was [on] his first European trip in the same summer months of 1931 that were time-wise meshing all the sorrows of the Whites and Deavers with their satellite befumblers, came upon her in her attractive snow suit in a curio shoppe that had a door leading to an inn next door. She was the vision of his Coloradan heart's desire, gleaned from high school skiing parties, from winter barbeques at Denver U. where he'd been such a popular political successful type with the gals. Oddly, Eleanor liked him for something strangely asexual in his guileless childlike and thoroughly predictable "American" behavior, such as it had been the fashion among smart tourists in the Twenties to deplore, but in contrarious Eleanor, independent of mind and possessed of an intellect not completely thieved of its original class in common snob schools, it was a gimmick felt less deplorable than quaint, archaic, as if she'd found a real live doll, a paper charmer in and out of a book. And he looked like old Schermerhorn her father, who'd built boats and invented turrets—he looked hauntingly like him. And he was sweet, because he liked her. They went through the little door for a drink. At midnight they waltzed in her moonlit window, drunk, like in Irene Dunne-Cary Grant comedies, the bubbling lovers.

Already getting stout at thirty you saw Joe White in striped pants and tailored appropriate cutaway getting married in St. Bartholomew's, gently sustaining Eleanor's lily-light hand in one upheld be-ringed paw that'd had its roots in the bones of the earth of thunderous Carolina, piney woods, old platforms, cheekbones, loss; skies that say "Yah!" above the gnawing human scene.

No mention of that at Gotham cocktail parties or gay champagne breakfasts at the Denver Country Club, no need to mention it.

From this union of naïve ambition and dry intelligence, came three children the heirs of the White estate whatever it was, had been and would be worth: Chester, Julian, and Laura White.

These, commingled with Cody Deaver and Ray the orphaned son of old Baloon, gathered together in inheritance the spill from the bin of mistakes heaped by predecessors with lips as serious and as primly-selved as theirs.

* * *

DURING THE FIRST FEW YEARS of their marriage Joe and Eleanor were like lovers, turning out the three children in succession; after that the cold wave set in, Autumn gave way to winter but that winter was a phantom winner. Something went wrong with Joe himself, ulcers from business anxiety, from alcoholism, from decline of his sexual apparatus into impotence, from general lack-gravity of zeal as if you saw a silly airy space of dont-know-what-to-do between his eyes all the time. He mumbled and fumbled, kicking his shiny shoe points up and down, legs crossed, in his office swivel chair, in the gray void of days. Doodling and yawning, the tragic waste of doublechin folding over the white collar: waiting for 4 o'clock cocktails at the grille room of the Brown Hotel; where women attracted by his smile and boyish eyes, seeing the expensive leather of his wallet, would wave martinis with him till cockeyed midnight, ending up in blur of memory and haggard hangover. "We went to the Windsor for beers? I dont remember any of that—Gosh, I feel awful—I'll jess die before I get to my office—Uff, year after year after year it's getting worse every time—My skin here on my bridge of my nose used to be smooth, like shoe polish—Now it's come all dull, dry, old —" [* DHARMA POME][67] He had no idea why he was born, or what made him want to prove that he would never die by the way he drank and rushed around with everyone. At Cheyenne Wild West Days you saw him in cowboy boots and ten-gallon hat yelling "Yahoo!" with gay parties of jeaned businessmen in size 45's and orange scarves, the cowlady wives wearing buckskin skirts with holsters and holding Daquiris with that official serious unshame of masquerades, the swinging doors of the saloon bulging out from all that wealth and ampleness like the folds of a fat wallet.

Regretful faces that look in mirrors wondering why there is birth, decay, suffering and death and why it should happen to them and so soon and in

---

67　The "DHARMA POME" that Jack indicated to insert here hasn't been identified or located.

The Buddhist Years

such a strange, gibbering, intolerable way. Rarebit, sterling silver, White Horse scotch, only add irony to the pain.

Joe's West, Joe's life, Joe's futility.

Eleanor rarely left the big redbrick house; she hated Denver. As the children grew she spent more and more time in her apartment off Fifth Avenue near Washington Square in New York. It was lonely beauty, lavishly furnished with heirlooms and canopied beds that had shook from the snores of Schermerhorns who'd crossed the Brooklyn Bridge on sea-bright 1880 days grave and motionless in brilliant phaetons, Julian the eldest son had a room of his own with fireplace, canopy over bed, the 11th Edition of the *Encyclopedia Brittanica* and a rug his maternal grandfather'd bought in a Ctesiphonian market about the time his paternal grandfather Wade White was aiming at the spittoons of Coulson frontier days. The children enjoyed that rare combination of Western carefree summers with Eastern blasé winters; they grew in an accomplished tho melancholy atmosphere that combined the advantages of two kinds of money and two kinds of education. Money of their father's in Denver meant wild rides in their own new cars, gay weekend parties at Estes and rodeo festivals; money of their mother's in New York meant rainy Saturday afternoons in the Metropolitan Opera, smart shops on 57th Street; education in Denver meant reverence of alfalfa bales, horseback riding, the study of mountains head on hand; education in New York meant the new plays, programs in *Cue*, the *Times*, Andover Academy, tennis parties in Rockland County.

She had much more malicious intelligence than poor sad tippling Joe, so the three children incontestably banged onto her side.

And Joe was lonely, and he was lost.

* * *

JULIAN WAS A BRILLIANT CHILD. At eleven while thumbing through a book of wildlife pictures, "Mother, a great unequivocal dog is all a wolf is, arent it?"

"Sure are."

Being blond and green eyed like she, he was her favorite; his brother Chester took after the old man with dark hair and a less airy manner and no Julian's mysterious forsaken look. Laura was a beautiful girl, tall, shapely, gray eyed, as detached, cold and haughty as an indulgent princess. The three of them all dressed up in the Fall for the train trip to New York (on the Rock

Island Rocket across the wheat), they looked elegant and all a mother could wish for. You saw Julian in a tweed suit, ironic looking already, clutching *Time*, *Life* and the wicker lunch basket under one arm and being led by Potchki the black spaniel on the leash, shouting gayly as he led the others through the car to their reserved seats: "*When you put cattle in cars they copulate.*"

"Julian!"

"No one knows what copulate means, Mother."

"*I* do."

And all four grin—Chester has a malign minister-of-state smile, something secret, gleefully snaky in his manner, snickery around the lips, like his sister. Often you see Laura and Chester in one corner, whispering and going s-s-f-t, having certain sophisticated secrets known only to them and avoided all too wearily by frowning Julian, whose attention is smothered in the subject of life and death. A bleak glaring light prophetic of his empty future, like the light reflected off sweltering new cars at high noon in American parking lots, hangs above his head like a shapeless halo. His blond hair is sad. Chester strides behind him carrying the suitcase in long loping shadowy steps, like an Arab, snickering. Laura is well dressed, in trim teenage suit, carrying dark glasses and a Mexican purse. They all have healthy tans from the long summer at the Denver farm. Mrs. Eleanor Schermerhorn White, often mentioned in Denver society pages as a guest at some important social function, at which she might appear for just a few minutes ("I'm on my way shopping"), also often mentioned in social notes in papers back East, and who hadnt cared much, takes up the rear of the aisle procession through the back-to-school streamliner with an expression giving away nothing, save a faint twist at the corner of the mouth, where she's appreciating the fact that her children have inherited her own tremendous sneering understanding of life and arent going to be stepped upon nor outclassed nor outshone during their tenure in what she thinks is time on earth.

They have plenty of money, the old man's disposed of, and the gladsome old hope of Autumn gold streams on their slippery young heads.

* * *

MEANWHILE SMILEY got married again, Henrietta having disappeared completely like a bottle smashed to a thousand pieces in the howling night.

Louise Marshall was a good old soul from Oklahoma who'd been a longtime friend of Adeline White before she died in Maine and had lived

The Buddhist Years

from time to time in a trailer under the cottonwood in the backyard of the big main house with her sister Jennie Marshall. They'd been waitresses together in lunchcarts up and down the West and migrated everywhere hauling the trailer with a 32 Chevy half-ton pickup, happy. You saw them in Jiggs Buffet drinking beer and eating big chickenfried steaks on Saturday afternoon.

Adeline was 40 when Smiley, alone in his selfbuilt sadhouse, became enamored of a need and married her. Louise's sister Jennie, a wild woman in jeans who also delighted in manly jobs such as hauling coal in the pickup in the mountain winter, stayed on in the trailer and in later years when the children of Smiley and Louise became numerous she moved into the house and became the helpful Aunt Jennie. Louise was stout, oldfashion'd, compassionate; she took good care of Smiley and was a good mother. In later years when he became conductor on the railroad and had gathered a lot of serious seniority and quieted down from his bigdrinking largegambling ways, he began to appreciate the fact he'd married a right woman.

Cody Deaver he never blamed for Henrietta's madness and never thought to see again.

Smiley's first child was born in the west room of the saltbox house on a July evening in 1933, facing the huge milky-rilled moonblue wall of rock mountains we call the Great Divide because there is where rain and rivers are decided for better or for worse, in our Vision America. Karma-like a raindrop falls, tends to the western slope, say, instead of the eastern, much as a spirit decides here or there upon its ridge of sentience; and, so, the infant was born Mongoloid, with vaguely pointed head, Oriental eyelids, pug nose, dark mole of destiny square on the forehead like the chief of the 32 India mystic marks of excellence. Anthony White, his given name; but his mother wasnt about to send him off to institutions where his hideousness could be cut and cauterized from her thoughts; instead she kept him and longed to love him and her piteous decision bore fruit some years later when he began to mature and show signs of an excessive, almost saintly kindness, to everyone, wherein monster-like he frightened even some grownups with his froglike voice and gawp of interest and abnormally large hands tho he was absolutely harmless. At the age of eight he found some boys frying a snake in a tin can, and removed the snake and placed it tenderly on the grass as it turned and bit him. No boy in the district had the nerve to oppose him, but he exhorted none of them, saying only "The snake hurts too."—Because of his reddish hair and freckles he sometimes answered to the name "Red" but a curious habit grew around the neighborhood to refer to him as the Imbecile—since most people cant pronounce "Mongoloid" or dont know what it means. At Christmas time the "Imbecile" was first to place his gifts beneath the tree, bought from savings sawing logs for a local coal wood and ice dealer, tho he was only 10.

Freddy was the second boy, born in 1934, a happygolucky skinny hero of all the kids around those fields because of his tremendous joy and driving wild laugh you could hear caroling from every haystack and swimpond around Morrison Road on drowsy summer afternoons when you see the fields with all their yellow weight of buttercups and Ah Sunflowers sloping down towards distant Denver redtop vistas like a multidetailed vast and wonderfully happy Rubens landscape. "Bring me my boots and shoes, I'm goin train ma filly." Freddy White who was so gay he didnt care whether he lived or died and at 18 ran his hotrod head-on into the only tree you could see on the horizon outside Cheyenne Wells, Colorado, at between beercan midnight and yahoo dawn, and that was that, for five other boys as well like him. Svaha.[68]

Lucille was not tragic, was the apple of Smiley's disillusioned and tired eye, was the last and only comforting progeny for him, progeny being what it's worth in this world of suffering, where it should be apparent to desirers of self-propagation through children that suffering multiplies suffering, and who can separate the multiply-er from the multiply-ee after generations of intermeshed groaning in all this harassed bloody dust with its underlying maggots waiting for the gnats of vexation to drive us reposeless down there— for God's Sake why dont they stop?

Tony, Freddy and Lucille; and on evenings when Ole Smiley White chanced to be home from a summer extraboard run, waiting for the next phonecall from the crew clerk "Smile-eee? It's deadhead on 85 to Saltpeter Junction for a dog-eared drag east, get that m'boy?" and so was taking the opportunity to enjoy his favorite radio mystery and doing so with the kids in the parlor, sweet little Lucille cuddled on him, Imbecile Tony and happy Freddy rocking furiously in the dark to see the voice-actors in their mind's eye, and Maw White the good old big Mamacita in apron drying dishes and her gray wispy hair the sight of which sent pangs of sorrow and love thru

---

68   "So be it" in Tibetan.

The Buddhist Years

poor moaning Tony when he looked at her, the smells of a recently fried and eaten porkchop supper still filling the happy parlor with the lights out—the glow of family order in all their souls—on such evenings, and later on when Ray Smith was brought from Maine by Old Bull, at Louise's and Smiley's insistence, to live in their home a normal out-of-orphanage life with children who were after all his blood cousins on his mother's side, making it four kids in all and Aunt Jennie too radioing in the parlor with aging Smiley—and after Cody Deaver had reappeared, completely disintegrated and unmysterious with all his teeth and 90% of his memory gone, accompanied by little Cody Deaver Junior who'd spent the first decade of his life wandering the backalleys and pierheads of San Francisco and all the freight yards between there and Ogden and El Paso to the south wearing a weird collapsed top hat old Cody said he'd found outside the Palace Hotel after a fire, Smiley with mysterious and sad compassion offering the poor vagrant the use and whatever comforts of the old field shack, into which father and son mutely moved, lighting candles at night—There, on summer nights when Eleanor was back in Denver with the three sophisticated offspring, and E. Dan White hurried to his businesses on phone and gas pedal, and Joe White the supposed Papa contented himself mixing drinks in the kitchen or sneaking out at midnight to meet the gang downtown, you saw the lights of the legend of the three houses spilling their variegated glows on the land of Old Wade White as that selfsame plains wind blew hugely sowing through the cottonwood trees, vast shhh's of seasong mourning portent sighing for the angels within, the human forms, the deep, wild shapes in the snowbright neon kitchen window of the rich, in the rose parlor window of the railroad man and his raggedy joy kids, in the flickering shantified glooms of the bum and the boy—three houses; three families; in one common, compounded, unhappy mystery.

II

BACK EAST, the son of Guillaume (Old Bull Baloon) Million, Raymond Smith. Orphaned and emancipated by his dying and disappearing parents as completely as ever a mammal could wish in this hymeneal world, but unfortunately being cast from the frying pan of family involvement into the fire of the orphanage, found it a melancholy imprisonment.

There was a hole in the wood fence of the orphanage playground on Bridge Street, in Riverville, Maine, through which the boys took turns looking at closeups of the world.

One afternoon Ray was brooding at his Catechism desk as the nun educed answers from the pupils, in French (it was a French Canadian orphanage) when suddenly his mind roamed into a vision of the dreamlikeness of existence and he saw everything as visionary flowers in the air—the unknowing nun with her stern stupefied anguish behind glasses, the things written on the blackboard, he saw it all as dumb shapes imprinted on the air, ethereal as ghosts, insanely innocent. Suddenly the Mother Superior came in, her black garments waving as she hurried, and six-year-old Raymond stopped in his mind the fears and involvements he'd had of her ever since he could remember (her stern sense of Work had transformed her original loving image of the Virgin Mary into a shadowed necessitous image of the martinet) realizing she too was but a visionary flower in the air, a morbid, appalling, crazy apparition in a dream, twisted, streaming thru open space. A choked giggle broke from his throat.

"*Raymond t'est malade? Vas à toilette!*" The Sisters stared at him anxiously, thinking he'd just repressed vomit. Glee-dingling in freedom, Raymond ran to the toilets where he kneeled for twenty minutes at a bowl by the dank drips of the concrete general urinal, motionless, pretending sickness, staring at a square view of the white clouds sailing across the afternoon sky in the one window, fully realizing that he was at the end of the world. "Who am I?" "Where is this?" Like waking up from sleep, everything was imprinted on liquid. An enormous woe of antiquity lurked in the stone of the basement, in the signs of human use on them. The clouds, shining in the pure empty space of blue, seemed older even than the stone of earth in basements of man, but ageless, crinkled by gold and old heat into shapes that kept insubstantially changing in heights of cool vapor. Something immortal was in the perfect emptiness of the blue firmament, so that he had the eerie sensation that his true self was this emptiness and everything else was a big mistaken junk-rack of imaginary things all around, including his body which was suddenly like a spectral giant.

"Come get the caramel!" whispered Dinky in his ear at night, waking Raymond to realize how much he liked caramels and in astonishment look around at the frantic afterlights activity that always went on when the caramels

The Buddhist Years

were ready to be sneaked in. His mouth watered and he ran barefooted down the dormitory after Dinky.

Later that night, with an aching heart, he watched the star that burned in the upper right hand windowpane. "Mon étoile" he always called it, in French. He couldnt understand all the dark sky, he had to keep looking at the place where the star was. "Just because it's like a star?" Why didnt he look beside it equally, just as, often, he would look at Sister Marie's face and then at the blackboard beside it and it was all the same as far as his eyes were concerned. But always they kept calling his attention back, to the *face*, scolding him for dreaming in emptiness. He felt like a dullard.

He never gave much thought to his father or mother, never having seen them, and he hated to be noticed by any adults or nuns who were around. He was not lonely; worse, he wanted to be alone, there was no chance; he gnashed his teeth in anger because they couldnt leave him alone. His fantastic reverie was of sneaking out at night, over the fence, down the fields to the river, where he broke the lock on the rowboat and floated with a magic little river 12 feet wide, under vines, the shores widening to vistas of a great sea ahead which would set him free to roam to China. But he cried in his dream remembering the poor kindness of Soeur Marie, her continual worrying, "Raymond vas lavez tes mains?" and all the time masts of ships ahead, seaside post roads like in England in the book *Kidnapped*, some strange Oriental city where he would come under the care and tutelage of an old Chinese Mandarin and come back to the orphanage 20 years later a mature, cultured, wealthy man of great physical strength to the amazement of Soeur Marie (pure heart!) who'd cried for nothing. So he lived in a blue house, in China, behind shutters, upstairs, over a narrow street, remembering his little river that took him from the orphanage far away.

At the age of nine he was small for his age, brown-eyed, dark, quiet. They came for him one Sunday afternoon.

"It appears your father has shown up," he was told coldly in French.

Old Bull Baloon stood there, hat in hand, combed, rednosed, sheepish to see the boy the blood of himself had perpetrated on the Void and just a little thing innocently made to walk around in all this enormousness and evil. A world nobody asked for in the first place.

Bull's eyes smarted for the first time since all the blue moons. Just the sight of the pitiful black stockings, the little pants. His big cirrhottic alcoholic hands opened. "A couple months at your aunt's house, son, then we go West, m'boy."

* * *

BULL HAS SEEN TO IT that Ray can get out, he's brought some judge friend that you see in the background in shirtsleeves with a notary seal in one hand and a pen in the other and it's Sunday afternoon and both of em smell like liquor—The nuns are disgusted, the Mother Superior is glaring at the judge (who is an old poker friend of Bull's in the outside free world that now Ray sees flaming in his imagination of white shirts, sleeve bands, sweat, cigarsmoke, maniacal activity)—"Madame," the Judge is saying, "this paper is copacetic, I had it notarized a week ago and it's got a copy in city hall, you cant tell *me*—" he's a little high and flounders and almost trips, meanwhile a cigar fumes in his face and he has red on his nose just like Bull. Meanwhile Bull has Ray in the corner and is asking him "Raymond—I speak a little French—I'll tell you the whole story of our family—this afternoon—and the whole story way back, the family you're going to, in Colorado—you'll love it, boy."

"*Oui, Monsieur*"—

"Appele mué Pa—call me Pa," says Bull and he almost cries right on the spot—Little Ray's clothes are brought in a little bundle, laid on the bench— The freedom is so enormous he doesn't know what to say, think, he can only watch—He is fascinated by the way Bull's cigar ashes keep dropping on his huge thighs and how he keeps brushing them off with a rough scrape of his horny-back-of-hand (frozen hard-skinned on many a 12 hour local in below zero yards of the railroad)—It's Sunday, it was the day of the best meal of the week, suddenly Ray smells it being cooked in the boily beefy kitchens below, his mouth waters, for the first time he's a little afraid—Old Bull and the Judge have an old Pontiac parked outside the orphanage, there's a bottle of whiskey and a bottle of wine in the back seat, in paper bags—it's their kind of Sunday afternoon, they're going someplace—It's like a dream, the Judge's papers are unbeatable, the orphanage has to let Ray go at once, just as the old man wants—The Judge is making an angry phonecall in the hall phone— In the dream of golden afternoon Ray is suddenly liberated by two strange funny angels descending from a heaven he never guessed.

* * *

The Buddhist Years

AS THE TWO MEN AND THE BOY go across the orphanage yard, past the grotto and the cross, the kids lean from the window and watch and comment—"Eh, Ray s'en vas—la on vi vwera pu?"—"Be non, vieux fou—c'est son papa ca du a mar le charchez—"[69] Old Bull meekly humbly takes the hand of the little boy as they walk, and so you see them, their shadows on the gravel, walking along, as the kids watch and suddenly at the foot of the cross (still holding his Pa's hand) Ray wheels to kneel very quickly and jumps up again almost not disturbing the flow of Old Bull's step and you see the two big men fumble in their thoughts, the little steps of the boy going on gravely and steadily into a world he does not understand and wants to love—and the children watch their shadows on the gravel disappear—out the gate, to Bridge Street, traffic, redbrick buildings, the river, the city of things—

* * *

"SON," SAYS OLD BULL as they step into the car, holding flapped doors open in the bleak of the Sunday afternoon street where lost little girls suddenly Ray sees with new eyes for the first time are in their favorite best new white shoes and pink coats and purple bonnets, stand undecided, throwing shadows on the pavement—whether to go to the Rialto or the State, see Rex Mix instead of Taipan—Tom Neal or Mawlk O'Rooney the boy with the derby hat, Mickey Rooney rushing around in gray comedies with little fat negro boys in hole hats in incorruptible backfences Ray'd so long dreamed to be free to roam in—"Son," says Bull, "I'm gonna take you to your Aunt's house and leave ya there for a month or two—with yer cousins—Uncle Freddy, that's my wife's husband, I mean my sister's—Then I'll go to Ole Mon-RE-ALL, and earn me some money for our trip west in this Pontiac—I've been called back on the board of the Canadian National Railroad and I'm goin braking till I get a stake" (that I gamble on Ste. Catherine Street, he added inside his own mind, no sense in telling the boy all the details, and he was gonna be well taken care of, as far as I can see), stoic old Tar' Bull says to himself as he climbs laboriously into the driver's seat of his 1933 Pontiac.

The Judge meanwhile having waved papers and notarized legitimacies, pop eyed for his next drink, they drew off, down the Bridge Street traffic, in the gray horror of tenements of wood on cobblestoned trolley streets, banging over the tracks, the old clunker Pontiac picking up speed with a

---

69   "Eh, Ray's goin, now we won't see him anymore?"—"Well, no, you nut, that's his papa come to get him"

sure, loud growl—Bull's got his hand firmly on the knob of the gearshift with a majorious magnificent elegance of kings, sending his old pot-pot putputting down the road of the Thirties—

"About time for that snort," reminds the Judge, as they come to the first street light, at an intersection of the mills and the railroad track. Entering Riverville Maine now—pine trees behind the mill canal, cold look in the hills outside of town, the long open plains of flat emptiness (like Klamath Falls, only on the other ocean)—brisk—

"My boy," says Bull, now to Judge, "it's a well known fact, every one of your inactive and unemployed son of a bitches has had it that way since Eve married Arden, Dad—"

Judge's name was Daddy LeBlanc, he had a "blonde" he said on Main Street Lewiston, Maine, that was this and was that and was actually a retired old dame of the stageposts seen many a moon in the Twenties by the fence, with mascara, now with pendant longpearls and perfumed front sat as majestical with one hand on pup head as Bull Bleakbone with hand on shift knob—"That drink," Judge says, "besides I gotta go home," he adds quickly, "wife's waitin"—Bull pulls into the millyards and parks under enormous afternoon smokestacks of eternity poking their redbrick fingers thinly into a vast and perfect Blue Sunday Sky with muff mipplemops of white cloud pushin on by, to make a little kid like Ray lose himself in reverie, in freedom.

"Son," says Bull, and up goggles the gurgle eyes to his bottle-O—of beet juice granddaddified Ole Smerlt, straight from the Veteran Vat—wop, and Judge imitates (it's whiskey) and it's plain they are going to have another one, being parked in a good spot—as Ray, even Ray can already judge of the Judge and Paw Pop Bulloono (in heaven now) they cant be caught drinking out of bottles when parked on the street, they've got too much to put away. He watches now as they *caramel* their mixins, swallowin with big ugly lips thirsty to gulp the throat down, he could scarcely understand what they were putting down their throats—"S c l u u p," and down went the drink, and their eyes be-popped themselves and they licked tongue on toplip and said "H - a - h !" It tasted good but smelled sour in the car. Everything was interesting.

The judge—Daddy Le Blanc, dropped off at corner of (?) and Van Horn street and down they went, father and son, driving to their own destination. Bull had just stolen Ray from the orphanage.

They were off.

The Buddhist Years

* * *

BULL PARKED NEAR A PARK, said wait for me a minute, and went in and drank ten beers at the counter, exchanging funny remarks with bartenders, bar hangers and general beer watchers of Riverville Maine in assorted conversawtory lost among the sawdust and the cats in the kitchen in back—Kicked his foot and came out of the glooms of the saloon and got back in the car with Ray. They sat a moment with both front doors swung open to let the air blow in—hot afternoon.

"Now, me boy," says Bull yanking up on the gadget, "we're going to—here's what I—now I know we should be in the park a coupla minutes and I be showing ya the pool and the swans and all that but we got to move along in our story. The Aunts'll take care of ya—and I'll be back this time." Ray hadnt dared talk about that. Bull saw his good little heart, and drove on.

Riverville Maine—The locomotive comes swimming thru the newsy village—In a deep cut it rolls swashing, the lonely brakeman, work almost all done, stands, homecoming with lamp on the tenth car back, over bridges, under signal lights, gaunt, bandy-legged—The town is full of living lights, talk of families in eventful kitchens—The crazy farmer's riding his white horse—The construction ditch has oil cup flares around, they flicker in the misty night—A Ford parks at the little bungalow on Cross Down Street—Husband's in the garage making chairs, little girls that hope for piano lessons and half slips made of silk are being put to bed in sweet upstairs rooms—The moon rises resplendent as a rose over the pines—The river over rocks comes tumbling over—Sand shines—Lights glitter at the movie house—The 5 & 10 is closing—High on the bluff overlooking town the two dozen houses make a skein of jewelry in tree, road, cut, walk—The mill's windows are blue down by the thrash near the falls, the locks—Over the old wood bridge of the factory a truck from Portland makes a rumbling like war, there are blue dyes in the tarns and bridge biles at girder's bottom where bums over barrels and wino bottles now their hotdogs munch—

"How long you been in this town, Red?"

"You mean Riverville? or Killinuck? 'bout two days—I'm 'bout ready to roll—I wanta get to Bangor and get some fishin in—"

"I jist come down from Gardiner and up that way—worked a bit on the Kennebec—"

"Aint no sense workin just spend yer money again—"

* * *

BULL LOFTS A BIG STIFF GIN and ginger ale in the parlor and drinks it all up and starts getting drunk and suddenly he's alone in the front room and wants more—Ray's in the kitchen meeting the kids, the old man, Fred Couture, is gone into the kitchen. Bull curses, "I'm running out of money— I've got to stop spending it. Gotta—No drinkin till I get there—*Un ti coup* never hurt the nozzle, tho,"[70] he adds as he sees Uncle Fred returning to the front room with a fresh quart of his best hidden homemade beer—"*Comme les vieux Canayains!*"[71] calls the uncle, spilling the suds in glasses—Afternoon sadsun falls in by the lace curtains of Mme. Couture—Old Bull, dismally waiting for his pap slug of hangover-killing beer, hears a lonely baby crying in the tenement across the canal—The men sit together.

* * *

THE COUTURES live in a tenement on the mill canal—From the back porch where Mme. Couture hangs out her wash and you see it flap like eternity sheets in the long afternoons, you could dive four flights down into the canal—This Victor did every summer, a tremendous dive that as he grew older he less and less felt the need to boast—But now little Clement, 10, was doing it; you'd see his little brown body tanned from swimming among the rocks of the river under the Bridge Street bridge where oils and skeels of factories bothered none of the local boys, and in the nude, falling from his mother's porch in an arc-y crazykid dive that had the mothers of Beaver Street gasp with anger—"Ti mau di[72]—Couture, he'll kill himself yet"— (only when the mother was out).

In the kitchen of the Couture house, shiny neat linoleum, sits a magnificent oldfashioned cast iron stove with rose paintings on some of the panels and beautiful silver scrollworks, the iron polished black and shiny like a new pair of shoes and kept that way for generations—written, in the chief part of the front, in imperishable hammered letters, "Armemger-Leonide Couture, Kirouac, Province de Quebec, 1845 AD" the name of the paternal great-grandfather who bought the stove—On this stove Mme. Couture cooks delicacies, you smell them out in the noisy hall where raggedy children count licorices and slap at walls and banisters and scream, the solid odor of *cortons*

---

70   "*Un ti coup*" = "A quick shot."

71   "*comme les vieux…*" = "like the old people …"

72   "Ti mau di" literally this means "lil damned," but it really means "Little brat," or "Little shit."

The Buddhist Years

porkscraps, the Sunday morning nostalgia of *crepes* with sausages, French Canadian pork sausages soft as butter—strong coffee—on New Year's Eve when sometimes the snow is piling upon the ice of the canal, the succulent odor of hot pork pies *les tourqueres!*—on Saturday evenings when shadows of the noisy court bring in vague brown windowlights and even a little starglow into the now-abandoned bottom steps where the little ones had wrangled all day, the molassy smell of New England baked beans and saltpork and brown bread and fresh white bread baking in the same vast oven—M. Couture himself is an intelligent, well-read Franco American, editor of a small French weekly in Riverville, a good man, eager, indefatigable, kind. He also has two daughters, still babies—You see him walking along his favorite shortcut thru the millyards, hatless, in thought, hands professor-wise clasped behind him, pondering the editorial for the week—"Nos Docteurs Franco Americains S'Ont Distingués dans L'Etat" (Our Franco-American Doctors Have Distinguished Themselves in the State) (of Maine) and at dawn waking with a start with what he thinks is a brilliant lead for a new editorial he finds he was only thinking "La grancher vas timbez"—The Barn Will Fall—"le vent vas mangez l restant"—The wind'll eat the rest—A good home for Ray, at night the evening star sat overhead and dropped its reflection on the canal and Ray leaned his face against the porch rail and kneeled to watch the world.

"A letter from your father!" they tell him a month later—It's in English—

"Dear Kid,

Well I made a hundred dollars on the railroad and tripled it twice on a stroke of good luck that means our trip west will be OKay. So Kid, hang in and wait. Do the errands asked on you and be a good and boy be patient.

Yr 'Paw'

Ha ha Papa"

Afternoons Ray spends wandering around with Vic and Clement, among dumps, locomotive graveyards, river rockholes, fields of Maine town—His soul bursts with the freedom and gladness promised him in that vision of the narrow river leading to the sea. "Ray cossez tu pense? T'est toujours apra pensez."—"Ta pas eu une chance a pensez dans l orphinage? T'a manquez toute cosse sh te montra—Gard encore—"[73]

---

73   "Ray watcha thinking? You're always thinking."—"Didn't you have a chance to think in the orphanage? You missed everything that I was showing you—Look again—"

Suppertime comes and Ray and his smear faced cousins rush home for hamburg and bread and butter and boiled potatoes and milk, great glass after glass of milk till, after supper and time for the radio, their bellies stick out and they compare—

At night Ray sleeps between them on the big double bed, they snore, he repents the day he ever hated anything—

Morning is a bird luting on a canalside fence with a cry so pure his heart sinks with sadness, to see the rosy east and smell the pure mist—How perfect, Tao, is the afternoon blue of the sky when he watches it sprawled on his back on the porch, seeing it through the flapping sheets, hearing the guitars of the long sideburned heroes of French Canadian doorways below "Oh come back to ma side lit-tle dar-lin, we will see that you bid me adieu, jess remember the Red River Valley…"[74] sad, and at night he'd see them roaring off on their motorcycles—The mechanics sprawled on Beaver Street under hot noon cars, the drowse and click of Fellaheen tenements, the laze of the slow waters—tires and oil rainbows in them—

In the front room, shiny floor, shiny oil stove to add to heat in winter, clean windows, lace, the scene outwindow showing the fronts of Beaver Street and other laced parlors hiding itchy stuffed sofas and gloomy oil stoves and sometimes gloomy pianos with sheet music—in home sits Mme. Couture and her daughters, working with cloth—long stories to tell all afternoon, and the French weekly comics showing forlorn little French characters trapped in chapter after chapter of some story—the daintiness and joy with which little Annette removed the ribbons from the box on the sewing shelf, when the mother asked for them—Ray, on the couch, digging everything— "Ti Raymond, tu waite un homme perceptif mais j pense pas tu va savoir comment ti prendre, tu rèves trop—Ton pére s t un soulon, c'a tu sais, c'a je sui certaine tu sara jama tué même"[75]—And she knits swiftly, the needle as well as her glasses and even glass rims shine (the silver), her mouth is prim,

---

74   The actual refrain of the folk song "Red River Valley" is "So come sit by my side if you love me / Do not hasten to bid me adieu / Just remember the Red River Valley / And the cowboy that's loved you so true."

75   "Lil Raymond, you'll be a perceptive man but I don't think you'll know how to handle things, you dream too much—Your father's a wino [drunkard], that you know, that I'm certain you'll never be yourself"
[Translator's note: The added beauty of the French here is that the "tué" means "toi" (you) but is spelled like the verb "killed," so it has foreshadowing connotations that the drink will kill him.]

The Buddhist Years

tricksy, pursed, sure self certain, like mouths he's to see later of Wyoming farmwives in the travels of the spectral world before him—

The pinned *couturier* dolls cut out of the fashion cloths page, the mannikin ribs, the piles of material.

The night that Bull comes back is a beau lit fullmoon night in September—He has new clothes, the car is simonized and shining, he looks happy and isnt drinking so much—He tells the story to the howling family in the kitchen—"Fred, I earned $150 in those six weeks and boy I'm tellin you every time I yanked a brake over my whole body and ribs just killed me—j eta malade, j ava les jambes enfflé encore"

"Ben tu boé trop, Bill"—

"Ah ben, ca c'est compri, mais j Boué pa, j peu pas vivre[76]—I tell you I worked like a sonofaguy then I went down to Ste. Catherine Street and got into a game I tell you—Those Canucks, when they start playing cards— Ben, tu t en rappele comme c'eta—Mon frere Jack pi tué pi l bonhomme Couture pi ton oncle s foi la a St. Pacôme[77]—Yah—" Everybody laffs in the kitchen—When Bull walkt in he'd slipped his brother in law a big bill to cover Ray's expenses—"I lost every cent of it, Fred, and had to go back to work—The game was in back of a garage on Papineau Street, a barn, something like that—I had to bum a ride off a hunter back to my division trainmaster—I made another 50 and came right back to that damn barn and we played, and there were some old Bretons there and you'll never believe it but we each had a glass of Caribou blood before we started—(sh te dit)[78]— and I won $900 and it took two days and two nights and as I kept winning the money I kept sending out for likker and sandwiches and when the game was over I was feeling pretty good, but pretty tired—Got the ole clunker outa hock and here I am—spic 'n' span and ready to go to the Coast—"

Bull, Ray, Uncle Fred and the two boys went out and saw a movie that night—The movie was some dismal silver drama about big faces kissing close and sobbing all over and Ray sat in the deep plush seats of the Grand (newest theater in Riverville) admiring the great purple shades of the ceiling with

---

76   "I was sick, my legs were still swollen"
          "Well you drink too much, Bill"—
          "Ah well, that's understood, but if I don't drink, I can't live"

77   "Well, you remember how it was—my brother Jack and you and that Couture guy and your uncle that time in St. Pacôme"

78   "(sh te dit)" = "(I'm telling you)"

its fixed stars glittering and the places back of vases where a golden light diffuses—he sees ghosts of Lon Chaney stalking on the unseen stage behind the screen—the picture drags, it has jokes in it Ray doesnt understand but that make Bull and Uncle Fred yukkle and comment to each other and chuckle richly—The great plush carpets in the aisle when you go to the toilet—The marble nude girls in the fountains—After the show, in the glittering lights of downtown River Square, they go to a Waldorf Cafeteria with the big red apple sign and Ray wide-eyed orders apple pie with vanilla ice cream, which he eats very slowly watching the ice cream melt in the apple mush—The tiles on the floor, the brown wood panels and coat hooks on the wall, the gleaming counter with chipped ice and cantaloupes shining, the hole where the food was shoved from a fragrant steaming kitchen, even the Negro man mopping the floor, all of it awed Ray for whom all this was the incredible gold and rich darkness of his newfound father's world—In his imagination pictures blazed, showing railroads, betting rooms, lunchcarts in vast intrinsic nights where his father moved, toddling, straw hat, joking with everybody— He wanted to hold his hand but they had never done that since walking out of the orphanage—Uncle Fred's pipe, Bull's cigar, as they drive back home in the Autumn night chill—sparkling moon high in the sky—

"It's gonna be a good trip," says Bull. "Oughta make it in seven weeks at the least. Ray, I'm gonna tell you all about the family tonight—we'll sit on the porch—"

At midnight, the Coutures all asleep, father and son sit on the porch high above the canal that shows the shimmering maya-image of the moon with a long mysterious sash—Bull has a bottle of whiskey on the floor, legs up on rail, and tells Ray the story which in substance is the substance of Ray's life.

"We're goin from here to New York City where we're meeting Smiley White, that's your uncle in the West, he was your mother's brother— Smiley's a railroad man like me—He had an old buddy one time called Cody Deaver, man from South Dakota, a hobo—ran away with Smiley's wife—she was a hobo too—but they had a son, the two hoboes did, lil Cody Deaver that you're gonna meet in New York because Uncle Smiley has driven the old bum and the boy straight clear from Denver to help them get started at a new job Cody's s'posed to be havin there—I dont know what's goin to happen—but you can see, Smiley is a good man, he bears no grudges— Smiley has a Model T and they're s'posed to be in by the 10th, of October,

The Buddhist Years

so we'll leave the 8th—Now I got things to do down South and in Texas and in Mexico so this is our route from here—See, Ray, I had two wives before your mother—my first wife was a Negress woman—she was a pretty dancer on the border—We stayed together about a week—but she came from Big Kincaide North Carolina which is also the location of Old Wade White, Smiley's father, where he was born—so I asked Wade, O many years ago, in Butte, if he'd known any Negroes in Kincaide by the name of Jackson, and yes he did—her name was Jackson—Her brother killed a man down there and was sent to a chain gang somewhere and broke out and's never been heard from—His sons, two of em, are down there—When she came to my room many years after that week of marriage I'm tellin ya about, the Jackson girl, she asked me a favor—that whenever I passed thru the South to stop by at Kincaide and find the two boys, the penitentiary man's sons, and give them this $250 she gave me—'Course I didnt want it, but she cried and everything and said she'd not done her duty and talked about religion (she wasnt pretty any more)—So I said Okay but I gambled all—'Course I've got it now and I really got to go down there, find those boys and give em their money—which is what we'll do—after New York—Now my second wife was a Mexican, married her in Mexico City in the days when I was smokin opium with her brother Dave and an old Chinaman from Dolores Street called Yao Shieh—" They both laughed, because of its connotating sound in French— "But that's his name"—[79]

And the moon was bright on the waters—

"She was a beauty, an Indian beauty, Angela was her name, means Angel—she was an opium smoker too—Now I got to go down to Mexico and find her brother Dave who's either in Juarez at the border of El Paso, or in the city down in Mexico Valley—man I know in San Francisco, old gambling friend of mine, dying and sick, made me promise to bring him certain goods over the border and I owe him almost a thousand dollars gambling debts which he's consistently said I dont have to pay back if I bring him this opium—so this I gotta do and get that debt out my mind—Now you keep yer mouth shut about all these things, Raymond."

"Okay Pa."

---

79   Said out loud, "Yao Shieh" sounds like "He took a shit" in old-time French Canuck (yaa-shee-ay, perhaps spelled "y'a chié").

"From there we drive up to Frisco, pay off ole Moaky—take a quick look up 'n' down Third Street for Henrietta Deaver—"

"Who's that?"

"She's that wife that ran away from Smiley with Cody—she's little Cody's mother, boy—You'll meet em all—Then finally we head across the desert to Denver—There you'll be in a comfortable home with Uncle Smiley, Auntie Louise, and yer cousins Freddy and the imbecile kid Tony—dont be afraid of him, he's a good boy—And you'll have some rich cousins across the field, the Joe Whites—lessee, I cant remember their names—a buncha brats anyway—the old lady's no good—the old man's a good boy, Joe, you'll know him, damn good old boy—and there's Dan White, he's a card—You'll have snowcapt mountains, boy, and plenty a place to play in—"

"Why cant I stay with you?"

"Got too many things to do, Ray, too many places—no place for you where I go, where I stay—cheap hotels, drinking sprees—it wouldnt do—I'll be visiting you there, dont worry—And one more thing, Ray," without looking taking the bottle from the floor and uncapping it dreamily, eye-on-moon, and swallowing a shot, "I got a brother Jack Million, *Jacques* est son nom, oldern me, aint ben heard of for years, not since, O, 1915, but he's in Mexico too and Dave saw him—that's my Mexican brother in law—and Ole Jack had white hair and called himself Zacatecan Jack—said he lived in a dobe hut in Zacatecas—we drive right thru there on our way down from El Paso, so I wanta see him too if I can—I hear strange things about him, one about how he walked from Mt. Shasta in Northern California clear down the West Coast to Mazatlan—and something about he walked to Canada—I dont know what it is—but something about WALKING—and something about SAINTS—we'll see—"

"Wow—we got a long trip, uh Pa?"

"There you go—So relax and rest, because when we leave here the 9th, you wont be getting much sleep any more, till we do get to Denver—Thing *I'm* worried about is that damned Old Cody, he'll never be able to stay in New York, we'll be stuck with *him*—it's the worse mistake Smiley ever made, tryin ta help such a helpless drunk—but like we say, shuffle the cards and cut the deck. I'm takin one more snort, son—I'm goin to bed on that couch and dream sweet dreams of another life I had somewhere where nothin happened and I didnt even know I was there and all my likker was poured thru me like milk of manna, goin through the universe, the color of that moon—"

* * *

THE BIG MORNING COMES, it's a gray windless, dumpsmoking day, a little drizzly misty at times, you can see clear across the river to where there is a smell of wood and damp and fog and burning rubber—Bull and Ray pack their things and wrap them up and tie them on the roof [of] the '33 Pontiac— It has its sneely snout pointed west, waiting—Waters in the canal flow slowly over an old rusty wreck of a car chassis Ray is watching, thinking now, "And this my father's Pontiac'll see the same fate?—be forgotten rust and iron in some Time Canal as the souls bespake even more forgotten thoughts about it, infinitely more invisible if such a thing can be."

"Ah," says Bull out loud as he yanks at ropes, "Ray, when you start hearin the senoritas of Mexico singing at their guitars at sundown your heart'll open upt like ya never thot it would—you'll get a vision of evening make yer blood so warm, sonny—I'll show ya, I'll take ya—Out beyond this American New England mist's your Holy Mexico—prayer, cathedrals, pulque sprouting binges outa the groun earth, milk of the cactus, sour saloons, ole fellas with wide brimmed black Revolution hats—burros—you aint seen it yet—there's a lil ole blood cousin waitin for you there—La Negra I think they call 'im – because dark, or because sumptin—We'll roam and roll till we come to some rosy golden end, son—The sun goin down over Golden, that's where you're goin, Morrison Road, Denver—yes yass sir."

Uncle Fred is down in the street in his suspenders—he and Bull have a parting handshake, it's 6 AM nobody else up; and so Bull gets behind his Thirties wheel and sings, "If this thing holds together from between here to the ribs of North America and over to the back and back to the belly, I'm a better driver than Will Rogers and Wiley Post[80]—but let's hope—So long, Fred—Thanks—May luck come for you on yr left hand, laughs on the right side, hock, hor, there's the best speech I ever made—Yass" chewing on his cigar and smashing up to start it.

"Give my regards to the family when you get thru Montreal."

---

80   Wiley Post (b. 1898) was a famed aviator, the first to fly solo around the world. He and humorist Will Rogers (b. 1879) were killed on August 15, 1935, when Post's seaplane crashed on takeoff near Point Barrow on the Arctic Coast of what was then the Territory of Alaska.

"I wont be back to Montreal for a long time but I will be back, because, Fred, gol damn it, I never saw such traveling as I been doing for 40 years now and it all seems like a futile, futile circle—which it is—but thank God anyfrigginhow"—shaking his head, red faced, the hat waving.

The old French Canadian editor watches the car go roaming down the street in the bleak morning gray, thinking, "There goes a brave old bastit and a brave but ignorant boy and if that's not *la vie*, what is?

* * *

TO HIS WORK BENDING, BULL, jaw out, pushes the old car down the road.

"Some people have nice homes with thick trees out front, kiddo, but we got this old car and the hat on my head and your new shoes—and it's life, you come, you go back and forth, you go—Dont ever cry about life, Raymond— And anyway this old man loves ya"—

* * *

IT'S SAD NEW ENGLAND TREES over the raw cuts of orange earth, the birch—the crow in the middle of the mealy woods, the road—They move down the state of Maine and into New Hampshire, stop at a diner— Bull has hamburgers with ketchup and onions—"I dont know who invented this ketchup but I like a lot of it on my hamburgers"—With glee Ray sees the smears of food on the sides of his father's mouth—Bull slurps up coffee from a cracked mug, lights a cigarette to conclude the meal, wheels on the stool seat and looks in the old melodious waters of the jukebox to see what's to play—Plays *La Cucaracha*—Dances a little, sings, "La corkaracha, la corkaracha, la le ca lo mun ya"[81]—Boy, if you know what that really means at your age I dont think it would make much difference—Hey, go ahead, eat, eat another one—Come on, now, you gotta put on weight, we're going 7000 miles before you get to Aunt Louise's Columbine stews out there in Denver Smullion Pass,[82] damn I've only got one Dexter left"—eyeing his cigar box, tilting back his coat lapel.

"Goin far?" calls the counterman.

"Aroun and aroun—"

"That's far enuf," says the counterman holding up his hand, stop.

---

81 Once again Bull is botching the lyrics, which actually are "La cucaracha, la cucaracha / Ya no puede caminar / Porque no tiene, porque le falta / Marijuana que fumar."

82 Bull is mispronouncing "Slumgullion."

The Buddhist Years

"You look like a friend a mine 's a cook in Wyoming, Ole Dusty Morehead, swing a knife if he got mad, long one—can you tell me why cooks always end up in the can?"

"Too many long wives, knives, lives—mebbe."

"Mebbe."

"Looks like it'll rain—"

"I got my little Pontiac roof all patched, let it rain—"

"I had a Pontiac last year, had to sell it tho—"

Two truckdrivers come in.

"Mack truck?" says Bull. "More heat blast up at ya outa them floorboards then'll feed the furnaces of a Montana smelt—"

"That's life, Mac."

"Aint I seen you some place in Boston?"

"How'd you know I was from Boston? By gorsht s' just where I *am*—You a Maine man?"

"Maine man, extra man, major and minor man—"

"You look awfully familiar yourself—Not where'd I see that face before?—"

Old Bull Baloon was the spittin image of W. C. Fields, small wonder— He passed them a snort from a backpocket flask—

"Fed, Kid? Got yer belly warmed up?"

"Yea Pa."

"Then lessgo—no eats till we get south of the Connecticut line and that'll be supper and it'll be dark by then—Enjoyin yer trip, Kiddy?"

And Ray wants to tell him, he never dreamed to deserve such a trip and such an adventure with such a loquacious and interesting and friendly goodlooking man as that, and turns out it's his father to boot—Like Bodhisattva saints when their Nirvana appears and from all Ten Quarters of the universe come the merciful radiant Tathagatas to lay a wheel of hands on the hot and sentient disciple brow, he couldnt believe the bliss and the reward for suffering.

At noon the boy was asleep against his father's side. The old fellow touched him and tapped him and awkwardly turned to cough, and his eyes watered from cigarsmoke but he thought "Guillaume Million, depuis q té t un ti gas au Canada t'a oubliez le coeur simple—Farme donc ta grosse guèle pi prend l'example des ti 's ange come ça, ton fils mystere."[83]

[COLLOQUIAL DREAMLANGUAGE][84]

The Pontiac doesn't go fast, you push it along at about 30 mph or it'll run down in a thousand miles and Bull's got many to make—The road has a white line in the middle, he'll see it from here to Timbuktu California and get dreams of it when he closes his eyes—Here in New England it's stone walls and farms with apple orchards, there in the New Mexicos and sad horizons of the final promised America it'll be lost windmills of shacks in a dry vast—This makes fear in Bull's fearless heart as he sees the little curled up shoes of Ray on the seat, the little hands joined together at the crotch in sleep—"I sure wish I hadnt met Adeline and made him—I love to see my own blood beside me but Lord, why dya do it?—Why dya do it to me too in that rain in Quebec in 1879?"—Old Bull Baloon reached into the glove compartment and put on a snort—drove on—"Gas's running low—"—Cars swashed by in the opposite direction, it was like a dream as he lost himself in reveries of drivin and Ray who was half asleep dreamt he was in a chariot being driven thru the Roman crowds and out to some blue sea where a small figure was seen falling from the skies—images of old mosques made of rotting wood, watersides, spectral airplanes around—1935—Autumn—the red leaves twinkling from trees, mushing in culverts, piling in crinkly heaps for foot slushing and voters of November—At 4 PM Bull had got a new tankful of gas and driven through Portsmouth New Hampshire and was now entering the city of Lowell Massachusetts, according to his plan to swing west from there on the Worcester Road.

"Wonder if old Eno Duluoz is in town today?"—have I got time to stop and say hello?"

He didnt. He drove in by the end of the trolley tracks at Wx Ctr.,[85] and came into town cla putt ling over the cobbles of Lakeview Ave. into the community of Centralville—A baseball game was going on in a field on the river. Bull stopped the car at the curb and watched. He got out and got up

---

83   "Guillaume Million, ever since you were a little boy in Canada you forgot the simple heart—Shut your big fat mouth and follow the example of little angels like that, your mystery son."

84   This notation, in the handwritten ms., is interesting and fitting given what's about to come, as the story becomes decidedly dreamlike for the remainder of Bull and Ray's journey, as they pass through Lowell and beyond.

85   Kerouac abbreviated here, but cryptically: there isn't, nor was there, a Wessex Center in Lowell.

The Buddhist Years

closer. The count was 3 and 2 and the pitcher was bounden to throw the ball over the plate. He was a tall, thin pitcher with a hawklike face Bull had seen somewhere. The batter was squat, hunky, vicious looking with a swivel of jaw comin out of his compact hat-head-and-neck, the uniform bursting to accommodate a bulge-huge-O of shoulders. But the hit and run was on and the big brute wanted to slug at the ball. He stepped out of the batter's box, struck his shoes with his bat to get the mud out of his spikes, presumably, but was looking at the third base box when the manager, Ole Rubber Doyle, dark, dissatisfied, hewer and roller of bats in the wintertime in a hobby garage, was sending out the orders. He repeated it, the count was 3 and 2 and with a man [on] second and a man on first it was imperative to get them off and running at the pitch, one out. But Rolf de Boutcho the French Canadian terror of West Street of Archambault Street wasnt about to have his fun spoiled just by old foolish strategies of baseball. He sneered, you could see a corner of his face move, a piece of his mustache twitch. He grew huge to stare ogling at girls on the corners of Moody Street Saturday Night—1935—Ole Essexes parked, romeos with straw hats at the Silver Star Café—The pitcher was winding up. Bull was winding up in watching—by now he'd gotten behind the screen among a cluster of men and was commenting as he watched, "It's the bleeding bugger of North Central High, Samoshant, Saoyshant,[86] Tao Vermont—or Wisconsin—boys, let's play ball. It's a long time since old mustachio bent down with stripes on his stockings to pick up a soft grounder in the hard days of balloon Sunday afternoon, and the Strawberry Blonde wasnt nothin but a splash of soda in the street—Home Run Baker from Ole Sweet Home Pennsylvania"[87]—

Nobody was listening. Ray'd woke up and got outa the car and come to see the news. "Where are we?" Nobody thought to answer. All noses intent on the game, like the noses of Popeye Ringsiders sticking over the ring like potatoes on a canvas and the fighters upright and insane with balloons and #iiS! & S P P L A T—Rubber Doyle called time and came down to instruct the batter, halfway down the third base line, "He's dragging his

---

86 The word the Bull seemingly is searching for here is "Saoshyant," a Zoroastrian future savior of the world who brings about the final destruction of evil and redeems humankind.

87 "Home Run" Baker (1886–1963) was a professional baseball player with the Philadelphia Athletics and New York Yankees, leading the league in home runs from 1911–'14 and considered the original home run king although he never hit more than a dozen in a season. He was actually born in Trappe, MD.

foot again," calls out an ole hoghead[88] of the Boston and Maine, who's with Charley Tarley the tile setter and his three brothers Billy, Jim and Jack—and another baseball player out of uniform, old Wes Bestrum the catcher for the Bedford Blues—

"He doesnt want that bastat ta hit to third or short on a double play, pull, he dont want him to pull it but rightfield it—just *plack*." Old Bull demonstrating to these fellas what he means, holding out both hands and as he gestures, lifting vulgar leg, you see his coat flap and the flash of a flask in his backpocket—"*Plack*," says Bull, "*right—inta—right—field* —" (doing a little jig of certainty and senility and unbelievable)—

"That ole guy's got a nip" is the comment—

Bivouac at bat leans in to Rubber's voice lips, in the yelling and booing of the crowd—a suppertime classic, and across the high road you can smell a thousand suppers—over the turnip green fence—of Old Thoreau American towns thereof—

"Now," says Bull, "if he refuses to take that hit and run, the manager's— wait—"

"Place it in the hole by second and first, dont you see how wide they're playin ya?" Rubber saying in Boutcho's ear—

Boutcho "Yeah, yeah," impatient, nodding—Goes to the plate, steps in, straight stance, feet firmly planted, legs a little wide, but swinging the bat with sure hands and wrists and muscular arms and the bat looks loose and shiny but you know it isnt loose, you wonder if his hands are sweaty and slipping at the bat handle, but they're not, the clean clam bat is waved in waiting.

Ray watches his first ballgame; the bat holds his attention, "Yé t apra son bat."[89]

The pitcher winds up, long, loose legs, wide at the mound, pulls in to waist, watches second and first over the same shoulder once, and pulls in his pitch to the plate with a long arc-y overhand arm, the ball comin in high and hard at the plate and straight, a smokeball, because he couldnt control his curve. It had to be over or the bases would be loaded and the manager'd yank him maybe. S y r i a n the batsman, with a little movement of his front shoe into the dust ahead, brought the bat around with his shoulders and

---

88   "hoghead" is railroad slang for a locomotive engineer.

89   "Yé t apra son bat." = "He's after his bat."

The Buddhist Years

with his wrist without using the intervening arms you'd think but as quick levers snapping S P R A M ! !, he's got the meat part of the bat flush on the seamless noggin of the baseball—and a line drive emanates from the plate, leaving a super thick clout-sound, an almost silent sound, as tho the contact had deadened the ball so you see the ball being drilled into the outfield as if by main push together with the clack of the wood—it was pulled, head straight over short, into the outfield where the outfielder grabbed his hat in a flash and looked up and jumped reaching high for a line drive that was hit out of a more eternity infield than the one he'd bargained for, the ball is hit for a farther shortstop than the dark one there—Sprawl, the ball falls into the distant lover bushes by the cut of the bank, and runs down white sand to the lip of the Merrimack River where it (oily with heavenly rainbows and cruds of turd) (rods of turf turd) smokes slowly to kiss the ball which has rolled to the edge of the sand and leaned on a water lily scummed by Time and Industry.

"There's your hit and run," says Bull to the congregated coaches, third basemen, visiting firemen, rail brakemen, weavers, skinners, skivers and dyers of the local assemblage.

"Boy," says Ray—

"Let's go see old Eno—that game made me feel good—"

They drive to the red heart of town. "You'll see San Francisco too," says Bull. "But like San Francisco, like here, it's better to get a good hold a the ball and make sure, than take only a piece of it and make sure—make sure longer—There's no such thing as un-false charity—dont get yourself all confused between what you want and what the other wanters want—you want enough to know you want everything and what you want is a sign of what you are"—Aint no harm in imitatin heaven, or space."[90]

Down among the redbrick alley of the Lowell mills Bull drove his old potato "lookin for Eno" as Ray, all-eyes, saw the river beneath the bridge crashing, washing slowly over its rocks, foam snow sometimes foam rubberbrown from factory stinkpipes and steam jets sticking out of the mills along the tide—Deep in the heart of buildings they drove from the shining sun of the bridge into the shadow of warehouses and factories with ivy—old traces of ivy—Left, and over a little cut of tracks, ramp and house tracks for

---

90   Notebook "R(1)" (Berg 24.1) ends here with the following notation. "To R(2) / It's all style no story."

the railroad switchyard, a little bridge, with a thermometer registering upon it and one as-if-in-the-water to show the height and varied measures—a narrow Frenchtown 1763 street—a toot, an old watchman, right by dark and dank doors of ink—to Eno Duluoz's printing plant. Bull parks and riffs out, crawling over the seat, so Ray can see how really old his father is, how struggling in the void, and his heart pains.

"Wait a minute—I'll go see if Eno's in."

"Let me come."

"*Come* on."

There goes Old Bull toddling into the printing plant which has a vast oily floor all caked with dust and ink and showing slivers, an outside nameless stove hangs stable—ahead Ray sees the machinery of the printing plant inside a narrow door in cardboard partitions—There are low wheel roll trucks with piles of paper a half a man high—The late sun streams thru the glass all-around windows of the print plant, outside is the canal with a glaze of evening pink on it splotching by but not moving—The great presses are still, only one boy is seen at the far end of the room bending absorbedly over the type racks.

"Where's Ole Eno Duluoz," calls out Bull. "Z' that yar father?"

The kid looks up, lost—he looks around, calls "Omer"—and you hear a voice in the far corner toilet, "Okay—"

"My fa's gone to the racetrack," says little Hunky Duluoz, 12 years old.[91]

"What ya doin there, boy?"

"Making a paper"—The kid holds up a sheet on which is printed in a big headline:

REPULSION ROMPS
IN MOHICAN SPRINT[92]

and underneath a half column headline

Takes Western Stakes
Opener in 1:11:45

---

91   Eno is, of course, Kerouac's father Leo, who owned a printing shop until he lost it after the Great Flood of 1936 (as detailed in Book 5 of DS) in part because of his excessive gambling on horse racing. And Hunky Duluoz is Jack's twelve-year-old self.

92   In DS, Repulsion was Jack Duluoz's "greatest horse" in his simulated horse racing game in which he used marbles (and, in Repulsion's case, a "solid ballbearing a half inch thick") (90).

The Buddhist Years

and underneath, lines ruled in, and the beginning of a typewritten story filling it in. This is Eno's boy, inventing his own racetracks—The foreman is belting the bottle in the head—

"We came to see if he was in—See that back door to the Keith Theater across the canal?" Bull points—"well that's where we played many a big game, and in here too—I'm sorry he's not here, Lord knows when I'll be able to see him again. Can you tell him that for Old Bull Baloon? This is my boy Ray, we're goin west together—So long, kiddie. Hey. Take this cigar. Your Pa likes Dexters. Give it to him for a gag. Tell him to try to guess who was here—It's a big world, Ray—It's good to shew friends a little hello along the road—a little goodbye—We were here one night with nothing but railroad lamps because something got wrong with the fuse and we had Charley Sagely the Old Conductor with us—game ended in the Merrimac Hotel uptown, over those stars, stardust and city lights—But less roll, no sense in hangin in a place."

They drive off, Ray's all interested in the world.

Hunky (Henri-Michel) Duluoz watches their car bounce over the canal bridge, sees their heads bent slightly forward to the goal. "L ti ga et avec son pere," he thought, "pi s en alle ensemble—loin.—pa-reil comme Lad Gavin l'outfielder des Chicago Nashes[93] quand ya parti l matin de brumes a Arkansaw a travers les montagnes a Cumberland trouvez l dernier Faire, Lad, qu eta cachez de la loi dans une vielle log cabin—le jockey qui ava la strappe dains main, par la fence—s en von—c'est toute un reve"[94]—(a very strange boy) (whom Ray would meet again in his haunted travels in this haunted life)—

* * *

NOW DARKNESS. Lights on the highway. Bull is pushing the car down the line. Bleary forests all around. Lost farm lights in the woods. The evening star is a hole of old clouds forlorn above the railroad crossing. The granite

---

93 The Chicago Nashes were one of the teams in young Jack Kerouac's fantasy baseball league. Other teams of this era included the St. Louis Cadillacs, Washington Chryslers, New York Chevvies, Pittsburgh Plymouths, Philadelphia Pontiacs, and Boston Fords.

94 "The little boy and with his father," he thought, "and they set off together—far—just like Lad Gavin the outfielder for the Chicago Nashes when he left that foggy morning in Arkansaw through the mountains in Cumberland to find the last brother, Lad, who was hiding from the law in an old log cabin—the jockey that had the strap in his hands, by the fence—they're leaving—that's quite a dream"

quarry. Wolfhowl of dogs by logs. The fox is loose. Sariputra[95] rides the night on a magic flying garment, beings of another vibration swim thru them like transparent veils—

"It's been a long day, hasn't it, kid—Sleep, lean your head on my arm or make a bundle pillow with my raincoat there, and sleep—sleep and sweet dreams—the trip is long, the goal is short and squat and so much so you'll probably never find it."

Outside Ray feels the rushing cold of Autumn night and the holy prescience of winter in the land again, of bare trees denuding to freeze for the squirrel again—Over the pines on a sudden ravine he sees the bleak windless rain hanging like a wet shroud over the heart of the mystery of the entangled forest floor—

"I'm a long way from my bed by the window in the orphanage," he divined with a shudder.

In the reflected roadlamp light, jiggling and tragically quivering, he saw Old Bull's face grimly bent to the night of sorrows.

* * *

BY MIDNIGHT, out beyond Hartford, it's raining hard, the sleets of shrain are sharding in a wide flout across the lonesome headlamps. Ray wakes up with terror in the storm of time to see it—The roof of the old Pontiac leaks a little in the front, drops fall on Ray's lap—"Sit closer to me—or against the door, *one*—get that raincoat and lay it under here"—Weary, bemused, Ray kneels looking backwards as the car washes on—a few distant lost cars, much darkness of rainy woods, the gone road winding back and snaking away—

"What's future, Paw"—"This's a word you heard?"—"Yeah"—"It's sposed to represent not now, not what came before, but you figure *now* as the *future* of what came *before*—they's the way I always think it—Boy, you been asleep—We passed a castle a while back, I wish I coulda shown it to ya—It was off the road, behind a stone wall, way up on a hill, with two, three lights in the rain and it was somehow you could see the stone towers against the gray[96]—Castles always surprise me—Been in one in Denver once—big yard—long ago—Put up by eccentric old miners and desert rats that hit gold—Seen one in California once—and a great big one in Mexico City that

---

95   Sariputra was one of the Buddha's chief disciples, foremost in wisdom, known as "General of the Dharma."

96   Bull's description is suggestive of the castle in DS. See also pp. 157–58 herein.

The Buddhist Years

was for Maximillian Cortez Junior the headwiper of the Europe Axe—Castle they tell me on a white high snowy mountain somewheres in Montana—" —"Is there ghosts in castles?"—"You damn tootin right there's ghosts in castles—I wish we had a radio in this bedoodle, we could be listening to *The Witch's Tale*[97] about this time, isnt this Friday night?—O well, purty soon we'll be through Meriden—Lonely lil town, I stopped there one night in 1919, in a rooming house, slept, woke up and didnt know who I was[98]—same as ever—How would you like to be eatin a big steak right now?"

"I'm sure *hungry!*"

"Wait till we get to New York, we'll be there by mornin, take a lil nap someplace and then we'll go down to some old chophouse by the waterfront or seafood and put on a feed—"

In the back of the car Bull's extra pair of shoes in a paper bag, a topcoat motheaten, an old newspaper, a can of spare gasoline, nameless junks and sediments of time on the ponged spring seat with oily old upholsteries jiggle and jump with the ride of the car like little live things partaking of the adventure with them—

* * *

IN THE MIDDLE OF THE NIGHT Ray is awakened by the sudden stopping of the car—

"What is it?"

Bull is sitting at the wheel dumbfounded, hat back, thinking, stroking his jaw—"Seem to me like I just saw an old man with white hair walking along the side of the road—but I looked back, and stopped—stridin along, real purposeful, long…streaming…white…hair…" Ray had chills in his bones…"The ghost of the Shasta Mountain Top, promised I'd be seein that—Zacatecan Jack that wrought miracles and was seen no more—But it's jess half my imagination, half the night—I'm tired, my whiskey's gone, no place to buy it, long hours till morning and even now I can see afternoon swinging doors of New Orleans…the dreariness of it…The bigness of it"— Late. Fall crickets cracked rhythmically in the high weeds by the woods road—"A shortcut road I'm takin, Ray—while you sleep in yr fleecy universe

---

97 *The Witch's Tale* was a syndicated horror-fantasy radio program which aired from 1931–'38.

98 This is a story Kerouac tells many times of his own, similar experience in a ramshackle hotel in Des Moines, IA. See, e.g., WW 363–66, S-P 137, OTR 14: "I woke up as the sun was reddening; and that was the one distinct time in my life, the strangest moment of all, when I didn't know who I was—I was far away from home, haunted and tired with travel, in a cheap hotel room I'd never seen."

I guess populated by angels I go aroun plannin ways to save 17 cents on gas and have visions of old walkin saints hauntin the America road side—Born in Canada, raised in Saloon, raised in…Hear that train whistle? One two three four, whistlin for orders at the yard limits, I can just see ole Hoghead Loudmouth Hofftaw chawin his cigar t'bits, cursing the sticky rail—For the rails are sticky when you touch em at night, Ray—that's how cold and clammy your steely death—and out at sea in the night do you know what you see in the water?"

"What?"

"A billion live lights of little livin fish, come off and on like signals and never show again, by which you know, if I commit suicide in that tide, I'll never be reborn—"

Ray in his duffed halfsleep could not understand how the world raved at this hour.

* * *

AT ABOUT 2 AM OLD BULL stopped at a railroad crossing where a long freight was slowly moving by—"Slow for the headin in!" he shouted, to show Ray, got out of the car and leaned on the door and pointed and shouted over the rumble of the wheels. "Headin in at that siding right here, either big train orders, or because of schedule—slow, slow—head man's lookin back to see that mainline red turn yellow, then when rear man jumps offa that crummy[99] step to throw the switch and lock it, *green*—s'when they wait—Yep, hear it? Here comes the scheduled old hotshot passenger line around the dream world—Sleep, sleepers!"

A wave of lights, a growing rumble, the vicious chack-a-chuck of a powerful steam engine racing up—"Race you motherin ghost!"—Upcoming in a wild flare of coal fire, Zvroom, the engine with ole C. S. Griffiths sneering at the rail with famed glove bought for 85¢ a pair at Sears Roebuck on oily old throttle ignored by hostlers in gum wadded roundhouses of bleak coalsmoke sigh night, balls on by pulling a string of named sleepers and stay-up coaches with lights, opulence framming by in the dismal thicket by the lead—"Swoosh!" yells Bull. "Go on, Go on!—Old train, you're six minutes late, or 60, you're going to buy what ya think is happiness at the terminal of the city but I have the night at the bottom of my shoe to step on—and I bet I'll last longer than your kind—"

---

99   "Crummy" is railroad slang for "caboose."

The Buddhist Years

III

NOW OUT IN THE WEST the others had prepared their own journey. Arrangements had been made by Smiley White with an old Chinese friend of his from Butte Montana who was now a rice merchant in Chinatown New York, name of Yao Shieh. Mr. Yao was the same man Bull had known in Mexico City and Culiacán. Both Bull and Smiley, during World War I, had worked in the copper mines of Butte and worked nights as house blackjack dealers in two adjoining saloons in Butte, where Mr. Yao was wont to show up from his chili restaurant on the corner by the tracks. Yao had a warehouse loft leased on Pott Street just outside Chinatown on the outskirts of the Bowery.[100] The idea, exchanged and arranged by letter, was for Smiley to drive up with Cody Deaver and his kid and meet (at 18 Pott Street) with Old Bull and *his* kid drivin down from Maine. Arrangements were going to be made, during a big poker game, to get Old Cody a place to live, like a coldwater flat that would rent for about $2 a week and which they were going to pay in advance for a couple months to give him a chance to start in at his tinsmith trade which he'd learned in South Dakota from a friend of his father's, an old German with walrus mustache Hans Otto Bach. So they all drove there and met. Smiley took three weeks off the railroad and took the last of his big trips reminiscent of his young days when he was the bum of the family and Joe and E. Dan were in college and he'd drive up to Butte or over to San Francisco or down [to] Lubbock Texas where he'd carpentered or over to towns north of Cheyenne where he'd been a lunchcart cook—

So he left Louise and the kids Tony, Ray and Lucille on the hot fire of warm homelife in comin October, and drove the clankrous old Model T clear from Alameda Avenue outskirts Denver, to the hems and lips of Lady Sea at the rock rat of New York Manhattan—one thousand eight hundred miles and three thousand six hundred roundtrip in which he was going to drive without rest except for naps by the side of the road because nobody had enuf money for hotels—"Them Eastern hotels all red in the alley, ya gotta give everybody a tip. And in New York there's the Dixie Hotel and hit's expensive." Wandering around Eighth Avenue and 43rd Street on the river side with bags of new bought articles under their arms, Westerners.

---

100   Pott Street in New York City is nonexistent, which is somewhat surprising because Kerouac refers to specific streets in Denver, San Francisco, and elsewhere. He may have been thinking of Mott Street, which intersects with Pell Street (see p. 147 herein).

It was a reddish devilblack frowning night over the usual sun-descent into the maw's abyss of Berthoud Rocks—it was cold for October, it was 1935, they huddled by a forlorn flashlight—over burlap bags and oily motors and wrenches clanking in the cold ground—It was the eve of the big trip only they weren't startin at morning, they were startin at midnight. Everything was set. Packed, in the back seat high and obscuring the rear window the hopeless cardboard boxes tied with rope in which were packed all kinds of dishes and windowshades and shoe trees Old Cody had been collecting on Wazee Street in the dim hope that he would get to New York with Smiley and into that coldwater house and here was the beginning of his furniture. Then he pictured himself in the Bowery morning happily working on the sidewalk with a sheet of tin, making naval ratguards and twisting stovepipes among old Jew[s] with clothcaps wandering around in search of rags in the cold depression 7 AM—a dour and gloomy happiness filled the drunkard's soul. His little kid was all set to move, perfectly satisfied with any plans whatever just so long as they could get out. Because little Cody Deaver had already been everywhere and he likened none of it. He'd lost his father in El Paso and wandered by mistake over the bridge into Old Juarez, and had spent one night in a Taramare[101] dobe hut terrified by clarity of the moon and the howl of Fellaheen dogs of the dead in lost adobe alleys, while outside of town he saw moving shadows on the moon-sparkle-glassed dump flood flats—the thieves of Rio Grande—and on the hills, south to the Maguey,[102] moving men in dump heaps, gathering garbage and cloth—He'd lost his father under a ramp, writ by thugs with poems, and had sat by many tokay fires, many smokes, many sands—been lost in the wintertime, wandering in the alley—

Smiley, the man who'd been the first husband of his mother, and was now mysteriously showing compassion for the man who had run away with his wife—who was therefore Cody's might-fighter, or might-have-been-father, never spoke a word to the boy or looked at him, a thing which even bleary Deaver could understand—

Now they bent over the motor of the Ford, at about 5:30 in the evening, in Colorado, the first week of October—The last old barn was red—piles of

---

101   Kerouac perhaps means "terramare," an ancient habitation built on pilings and protected by a flood wall dating from 1500 BCE in northern Italy.

102   Maguey Bay is on the Pacific Coast in the state of Oaxaca, Mexico.

The Buddhist Years

dry boards were laid behind it, among dry weeds that were sparse and full of locusts—A hole in the back of the barn was your door to this vast back lot that stretched to the edges of the alfalfa land—barrels were there, old users of oil were gone—tires were laid around, thin ones of early Twenties models and earlier than that, thicker tires of later cars, one truck-tire from some lost and forgotten truck incidence—cartons, out of which the original merchandise was hastily and tremblehanded yanked, and used, and the boxes thrown where they lay now eight years later—A dry dusk wind is blowing cold dust from the mountains and also swirling and soushing in long land heatblasts from all Eastern Colorado, Kansas, Nebraska, Iowa, and God knows where beyond—The ground was swarming all summer with the hop and skip of locusts—They made molasses with grasshoppers and fried em in brown honey and served em up to Tantrum Saint John in his Baptist Saint Church—The ground was dry and whispering with the crackly rustling of a thousand blades of straw stuck at intervals in the alkali white. Cracks in the ground from the dry sage twig bushes—everything brown. There's the old Model T wreck truck a ways off from the Model A—while Smiley and Deaver bend over the hood discussing the motor, and Cody watches, you can hear the wind sing sadly in the dashboard of the old truck and thru the woodboards of its floor—all rusty and laid out no more for use, just wood slats for roof—incredibly erect and skeletal in the yard, like you'd almost use it one more time to get to the field—What is deader than an old car? What is deader than one who used it? It stands there haunted by old dead-now usages, the people of its hopes—a rusty skinny gearshift handle, no cap—dry wood spokes, as dry as the ground, cracked like it—old ferruginous mud guards clanking like cantankerous old dancers in an Autumn Jig when you touch them, have a funny sad ring and ring when you press and quiver on them—Piles of tarred poles [...] that were meant for postholes and new wire but the new wire never came—Beyond, like a Benton painting, the hay mountain with old dead wagon at its feet and only two wheels left, wild old dead skeleton plows alongside—This was the equipment of Wade White who was born in Big Kincaide North Carolina in a log cabin in 1852—long before he planned to use such a plow [and] said wagon, he had seen similar rusty tools lying around the backyard of his father's cabin—No one will ever know the extent of their mistake. There are still old covered wagons, not Prairie Schooners but the little narrow Mormon ones, in the backyards of

Wasatch Utah—The backyard faces infinity. "West of Idalia somewhere," sings the poet.

"Now I bought that thing from a cow eared dogcatcher in an old inn in Big Springs Montana—and drove it down here wearin all his son's rabbit feet on the front bumper, made about, oh, twelve miles to the gallon—So I figured something was wrong." And you see the rough furrowy frozen back of Smiley's hand as he fiddles with sparkplugs on the oily dirt of the motor illuminated brownly by flashlights and given a faint Satan tint by that eyebrow sunset burning to bare the naked fear of the earth from Indian and Human alike. The earth is an Indian thing, but the waves arc Chinese.[103]—"But it's fixed aright and if the rear end falls out somewhere past Shelton Nebraska then we'll just have to hitch hike back, is all." And Smiley straightens up, and presses lips together, and looks at Deaver who's too soaked with drunkness of 20 years to've heard most of the meaning, 's been muttering in his own mind in reply all the time, but says, now "Ah, that's right."

"So I'm goin in the house now and get a little rest and I'll be down to get ya in the shanty about ha past eleven—So hear."

"Okay Smiley."

Poor incapable Smiley was a lot more capable than Deaver; maybe this was the point of his pity, and his wrath of pity. Once old Cody'd run off with his sticklegged young bat—maybe he was returning the favor, young bats get to be old bats.

"What? ya never got jived by a tilt tongued and dont mean silt woman?—and ben thrown Maggie and Jiggs rolling pins of call down?[104] A r g c h ? where d ya fish that champion up? Kiss the wine, forgit the wife." This what Cody Deaver could've very well told him if talk was left on his numbed wino tongue…gagged of all his hopes when he'd throw up white liquid on streetcorners of the West, Sauterne and no food for two days. Eat, drink 'n' be merry, winos of the world! "Kiss the wine to kiss the wife." Kiss both of em, I say.

* * *

---

103 See OTR 268: "The waves are Chinese, but the earth is an Indian thing." This sentence does not appear in the 1951 scroll version, so it's original here.

104 Maggie and Jiggs were characters in the comic strip *Bringing Up Father* (1913–2000). Jiggs was a lower-class Irish immigrant and Maggie his scolding, Irish American wife who tries to make the family more upwardly mobile.

The Buddhist Years

AT ELEVEN O'CLOCK there's Ole Smiley put-puttin the motor up in the White backyard, cigar in mouth, slouched rainslung hat low over brow, suitcase in back for the big trip—On his cheek the familiar mole which, when Little Cody'd first seen it, he thought to be sign of a certain special tragedy that could only be understood by staring at it, the tragedy also that even the child could see in the man's dark forsaken eyes, that seemed to say, insofar as they avoided his so much, "At one time the world abandoned me to the dogs of eternity but by that time I had abandoned it myself and now it's too late both ways—ahead of me I see just dark night and there aint no going back, no one'll ever know where Smiley died"—In his father's eyes the boy saw lost white clouds of hope swimming in a blue emptiness, like the emptiness of ruined cadavers, fallen plaster, piles of crap in old houses, cellar doors leading to underground weeds, weak, watery, red rimmed eyes showing the tenderness of a baby, which went along with the little, incredibly timid voice "Co - dy? Co - dy? You awake in 'ere? S'time to get goin"—"Dam I know I had an extry stick of gum in this pocket—now where is the wha da I got no fall it—" trailing off in shadows of selfmumble, so that when little Cody came to his side he seemed lost in thought and unsurprised again, as tho forgetting they had to go—An empty Autumn wind on a gray day blew across his lustless eyes—The bacon of red nose in between, not a big nose but a mangy eaten nose and as if weather scuffed by a thousand snivels in a winter alley, butt flopped with peels, sad, tristerous as some saint's nose or even a Virgin Mary nose of some sad plaster statue rising from a pedestal on a lake—for drowners signifying salvation, for yet-to-drown: meekness—His peppery hair dripped over his brow, he had no hat, he had the look of someone being shpatted by pigeons and saying nothing—Whatever love Cody Junior felt for his father, buried in tears, found its way out at moments like this (as he gazed) out of an insupportable hopelessness in that longsuffering patience with the fumblings of the damned, saying to himself "O why does he do that when he knows we gotta go and he knows he just said it himself and he *knows* I know—"

These were the two men who were now to drive him, eight years old and old, across the unknown land to the unknown city, as cold wind gathered in the loin of old October, the heap eventual snow, the gestation; snowmen with seeless eyes—ice buttons—sad flies—

On the porch of the big house warm light cast its glow over the wicker chairs, heads moved within—Cody had never been in there but he could see the difference between that settled, secure, even mellow-gold light and the bleak tarn of things stretched in the scruggle of the Ford's headlamp spraying across the alkalized land—What unutterable bleakness the boy saw in one isolated movement of one dry weed in the illumination of that poor craplamp—"If no cop stops us we'll make it all the way to N.Y. and back without that lamp but hell I gotta stop somewhere and get a bulb"—"They'll think we're a motorcycle from afar off," says Old Cody with his rare, pleased, feeble grinnies, like the smile of icy despair—Smiley swings his railroad lantern into the place under his knees at the driver's seat and coughs to go, hat bent to it, gunning the motor—"Come on, gentlemen, get in—and we'll get this old Extry Train underway and see if we can get a straight shot for a change—No sense waitin aroun fer the reception committee, I've already told em goodbye—Well" as all settle in the front seat with formal solidity, eyes straight ahead, "so long Denver—hello New York—"

And yet for Joe White sitting in his inherited big house, behind lace curtains, it was a sadder Autumn yet, than that one in little boys' breasts driving east at midnight (with oil cans to sleep on and back fences to look forward to)—that chill, of middleage ghastly, that filled Joe's heart as he sat idly looking at some pages of the *Rocky Mountain News*, passing an evening at home (drinkless he hopes) with Sis Sara and Granmaw, and E. Dan's there (upstairs) (wife and kids gone back to school)—In fact he saw and heard the old car put-puttin out there and looked quickly thru the lace, a gesture little Cody, still intent on looming in thought the better warm curtains than the improbable worst of country kins, saw, from between the big bodies of father and fellow-uncle, enemies as far he knew, some old wife holding them together, in the chill of the night, that sudden head of rich Mr. White watching them pass on the driveway outward bound—thinking, Cody: "Now he'll set back and say 'Thank God they've gone, I can get some peaceful newspaper readin around here'" but Joe White actually thinking: "Hah? They're all packed and off. Midnight just like Smiley said. Look a tha old fool roamin off in the night—He'll be back here in two weeks full of aches and pains and broke goin off drivin that old drunk and his poor kid clean to New York and back by hisself—Smiley always did things the hard way. Ah, God, the despair on the fence I see there—in the moonlight and half-light—

The Buddhist Years

131

when am I gonna die? Granmaw's asleep in her chair—Granmaw Kemmerer, cant hear, speak, know of anything and I sit here with her, tick tock—I'll just go up to Dan's room and bring him a Scotch and soda—I can mix *myself* one—and thereby lies a tale—The curtains move like iron in the window of my home."—And he sits back to the paper, listening to the Ford disappear.

Meanwhile Ma is waving goodbye at Smiley from the door of the saltbox house. The kids Freddy, Louise and Tony are asleep, the starlight shines in at their windows, falls on pale moon faces leering in the tangled dusk of pillows, sheets, being phantom shapes in the crocheting of coverlets, the dreary counterpane, the sweet chair, the corners of their rooms invaded by phantom warriors of a lunar Rome long gone from here, on their sleepy lips the inscription: "Voila, les Anges infantilieséz sont trouvez leur sommeil de ciel imitéz—eux autres, dans leux *dices*, les crottons noires se change pas de raison nombrez, et on ne vuez seulment pas le noire sur l blanc—l'homme qui leux jette leux bonnasse de Nirvana, leur 5 et leur point, a des bons yeux fatiguez et les pardonnes et te pardonne aussi, et pardonne par defaut tous la vie entiers infernelle."[105]

A dog barks out by Colder's home, between that house and the back of Smiley's house, stubblous old Fall field waiting to be shoed by the horses of mud Spring, shoveled for a shack, be parked on by tractors and trucks, made to flower a green meaning. Star lit now and beyond, beyond cottonwood trees in the yard as ever now receiving the Plain's imprint rush kiss of oceana wild west roar in its a-thousand-and-one leaves be lipp-littered to twit about the night in that one vast how-song sushing the baby sleeper to the sleep, old as Old Bill Cody and Thundrous Horsefoot before him, to advertise a prairie—that golden tree that Old Wade White had loved so much when he'd bought the alfalfa farm in 1893, saying "Cottonwoods are used to having culvert killers in Cody Wyoming—and in Cold Hushamush Ole Coulson when that jilt rushed Badlands Girl Missouri rusk rosh river aims its spittin at the Spring in places around—but here a cottonwood over my home'll be no noose-holder, just sing me to sleep every night, like old trees of North Carolina long ago." As pretty a speech as a man could make around his trees—beyond that tree, and the fence and Colder's house, you

---

105 "Voila, the infantilized Angels have found their heavenly sleep imitated—them others, in their *dices*, the black boogers don't change their mind often, and we simply don't see the black on white— the man who throws them their goodies from Nirvana, their 5 and their point, has kind tired eyes and he forgives them and forgives you too, and forgives by default the whole of life infernal."

saw them there, like humps of old snow larked on a flat plain's horizon but rising from the ground with a starry haze and only half lost on the blue black horizon with her sparklers—incredible that you could see little parades of lights winding on the roads up there, travelers in a time machine elevator.

The Old Ford puts the land of the three White domiciles behind its pharting rear—faces east.

* * *

SMILEY IS WEARING a typical brood blackheart westerner's greatcoat Mackinaw, with huge plats of design like the ravings of Indians, the material rich, thick, colorful, looking beside Cody Deaver's tattered nameless topcoat like the sheriff and the culprit bum going to the jailhouse together in Tonto Springs New Mexico—Smiley has his black slouch hat that he uses to railroad, sometimes young brakemen'd gape at him in the dark of a countryside siding seeing him come back with a lighted fusee and a red and a white lamp muttering and cursing in the dark, the huge of his shoulders in the Mackinaw like ruined shadows in the night and the eerie unnatural fusee glow but most of all, suddenly, they see the black slouch hat rain-battered and ram busted by at least 20 years of wear on railroads and in his fields and on lonesome trips around the West in old jalopies…that, and the nose underneath it, the dark unhappy face, the young brakemen'd had their fits of fear to see it as now little Cody Deaver saw it, bent over the wheel, the brown glow of the headlamp thru the jiggling windshield and the poor almost blood-dim dials of the Ford sending back a faint illumination for a large distinct shadow—his pants thick, long, wearing street shoes but with his rubbers on, his pipe and tobacco stuck on the windshield and to which he kept reaching all the time, at least once an hour, for a big rich fulsome light…the very smell of which at first amazes Cody it is so indicative of a goodness in this secret man's nature he couldnt have guessed at, without its savory bonfire passage through the catchers and feelers of his nose-organ—but later, in memorial habit, becoming the symbol of Smiley's own fragrant bemuttered dissatisfaction with everything…hour after hour purshing that old patoota through the country, hour after hour the sharp flare of his match at bowl, wooden matches coming in enormous boxes that rattled like October and pea pods of the dead giant, veritable timbers of matches, that he scratched on his ass and flared up, to throw a frightful flame at nose, hat, pipestem, leering…Deaver, who sat next to him, in contrast calm, wore the tragically

The Buddhist Years

muggled, eaten, burned, beaten, puked-upon, many-times-sewn (by Mrs. Smiley herself) (in moments when she felt something had to be done for the bum and the boy) but a coat so old, the sleeves now beginning to drip like Louisiana moss, the hands that depended from the sleeves looking as tho they had been dipped in acid, dirtied in garbage cans, chewed on by dogs of ravage, washed in a cold sediment of winter and despair and drunkenness in an alley and finally vomited on and washed and vomited on and washed, then caked by February dont-care—these the hands of Cody's father, like the long, sorrowful coat, with its pieces of stuffing coming out that he kept pushing back in surreptitiously, and the whole shape of it giving him a woeful air (that he had without the coat in a lesser, unbeshrouded degree)—wearing, horror above all horrors in the mind of little Cody, those special white stockings and black weathercracked once-city shoes that all bums seem to wear, on land and sea; stockings bought at Army Navy stores or secondhand clothes stores, worn on ankles that are always somehow as white, as worn-looking, lifeless, sick, and that you see sometimes on the thin ankles of passed-out drunks in the street, the dirtiness of the stockings coming up the shriveled little hope bone to the inevitable scabs and scuffs and injuries of the fearless damned... from top, where he had no hat but just that same sad hair, the wearing of a hat being for Cody, had he done so, or thought of it, the epitome of change— something he could never have done, even if you gave him the hat he would find it impossible to wear it without blushing, as tho the tragedy of his head and thin unhappy hair must always be exposed unprotected and unblushingly even purely naked and confessional—let the sun confess to his scalp its own secret formula for flaring success—you couldnt imagine Deaver with a hat, coming down the road in the long ragged coat with those black once-black now-gray shoes and slain white socks and the awful pants usually with a big safety pin tucked at the fly where fumblings have taken place under the influence of two quarts of wine and a desperate need to get at urination, resulted in the tearing off of buttons and the tearing off of whole seams from the sewing—so if you saw a hat on him, you'd take him for a secretly sincere degenerate hurrying to his work, evil, but without the hat you just know it's an old boy who hasnt outgrown the young boy who wanted overalls every Sunday and a place to lie down and chew straw of stem—sitting in the front seat, coat collar up, hair askew, but erect, formal for the big trip, nodding and uh-huhing the interminable now droning drive-talk of lonely Smiley who was going all these miles out of the goodness of his heart with a man and a boy to whom he had absolutely nothing to say and no reason to do it—so talking to himself, much a la Bull Baloon, to keep the hounds of despair or shades of regret from his line of vision as he drove on—Little Cody himself, in the back seat, sitting on the spare gas can over which'd been draped canvas and an old piece of seatcover, wearing the white dirty little wool cap that he drew down over his ears whenever it got really cold, but usually that he wore back, letting the brown locks of hair flullff over the front and down his brow, and the football red turtleneck sweater his father'd bought him in a moment of opulence in a secondhand store in El Paso Texas years ago for 40 cents, a tremendous bargain, once-worn by Indians on reservations apparently and judging from the sheepskins in the store…the wool cap, the sweater, under which he wore a little blue workshirt with frayed collar and top button tied, tight, to keep the cold drafts of Autumn out—an undershirt with ten thousand holes from too much washing in the sink for too long— and his shoes that were boy boots going up over his ankles but now flapped at the front sole, altho the top of his feet and ankles kept dry and warm—he too wearing the white thin socks the sight of which his father's scabrous drunken ankle made him sick when he saw the man passed out in the shack at the Whites, on a blanketless mattress stained with rain and drinkers' involuntary urine—Dressed thus, the Ford rattling and crashing to prove herself, they drive out of Denver to go meet the others in New York.

Later it gets cold and Cody Deaver Jr.'s layin there with his head, cap-on, wrapped in a white thin gauzelike cloth that cuts out the wind but at the same time the child is bemused looking at the passing stars of out-window (with their faint edged-in telephone wires riding it) and occasionally sitting up from cramped position around burlap piles, twitting one bare big toe against another as he's taken off his shoes to keep warm—bang, out of the tucked around cramped position he looks up as suddenly the car fills with light, bright, from overhead, it's a gas station outside Denver and Smiley's buying gas—the old and ancient Negro sitting across the road on a log by the railroad track is looking intently and trying to wonder [what] it is he sees raising and rearing its hooded white head in the middle of the night in the back of a shroudy car that's maybe some broken down old hearse or sumpin.

* * *

The Buddhist Years

AS ALL THE COLD WINDS BLOW up from Mumpjump Mississippi—Armageddon in the Dark Air.

* * *

BY MORNING THEY WERE IN ALL GRAY NEBRASKA, under bleaky skies that made no sense except to show gray cracks of hope over the Plains, might be sunshine by afternoon but cold wind says so what—

> Where seldom is heard, a
>
> Discouraging word
>
> And the skies—

And the skies, the American skies, and the hoboes below, and the old Fords, the old Pontiacs, the old cracked geezy Chrysler Pantheon of Time, the REOs of old crack top table Nevada, the Chandlers of antiquity Marine, the Riots of yore, the Graham-Paiges[106] of Who-Wa-Saw Time (oowadiddy), the proppy old clink seat upclutch skinny pot pot trucks that old hopers and old sinners like Deaver and Cody Smiley McParroty Cigar[107] crapping along the hi-way, sat in and jiggled for, eyes ground to the wheel instead of wheels rolling on the ground and eyes in the rumps of horses and of oxens tame showing silhouettes of animal flesh to the gray raw Rockies to the Western Hope from now which the three adventurers hastened, as if America was washing back on itself disappointed by discouragin words—There's your song, your lone prairie, your bush jiggling in the windy wide open—The kid in back bouncing, the two men stiff in front but by now Smiley's got fair tired and has his eyes droopin in the road, pouts, head-nods even, so Deaver he keeps peaking, worried his driver's gonna fail and run the heap in a four-inch ditch and knock the wheels apart and throw people and ratpack suitcases clean out—Indians may bite the dust, but white men dont even sit in it, or wanta skid on it face first—car goin 25 miles an hour—Spanish grandees by the side of the road parading in regular beat, the telephone poles of olden—

They come to a town and get [...] gas—Cody boy runs to the toilet in back of the awful old shack that passes for a filling station with Wallace

---

106 Ford, Pontiac, Chrysler, REO, Chandler, and Graham-Paige are all present or former American car companies.

107 While Kerouac is mixing in resonant nonsense in this paragraph, Parrot Cigar was a brand circa 1930.

Beery[108] scratching his fat waterfront arms and in undershirt of early morning just-out-of-bed blowing disagreeable fogs like everywhere in America the kid had seen the same of people sleepy faces coughing, spitting, the disgusting sadness of it as tho life was not hospitable (a hospital for the poor) but a malign and cold influence to make the hurry out of bed and find the iron sandwich, that is, jump out of the warm sheets of true mind dream and go off in the wide cold void to some kind of odd labor or service meaningless in itself and completely imaginary (stickin straight out of the head like stovepipes, the ideas of this Mind-made world), among others irritable and shiny, go get money to buy food and pay "rent"—As tho food didnt grow on trees, like it did in gardens—Cody couldnt understand, he didnt [know] what a good piece of pie tasted like or what a soft, comfortable bed might be—He'd slept in clank bottom gondolas full of old singers of epics about the rivers and the swamps of antique New York and New Roses and New Lancaster America—ah hem em HEN, hums the blues man—in Arizona dawns ("that's real cold," says the palefaced hobo with a strap on his back)— among the bawling cattle cars—by siding banks full of corrals and old tires layin around with last week's rainwater in em, and holes—seen the men gettin off the sand coughin and spittin to their dreary new day but a day with that crack of hope in the sin of sky, rattle [of] old-headed forlorn autumn (all over) everywhere—Gold, Gold, Go, Go, sings the bush-tree to the jackass—

The proprietor of the garage accepting his bucks, hooking up the gas line, coughs, spits, scowls, and walks off huge and baggypants[109] and selfbelieving and for nothing—

Cody's return to the car, he sees his father and Smiley White seem to be *talking* for the first time—they're inside, ready

"What in hell you talkin about for now?" Smiley's sayin.

"I aint even talked to tell you. I had no ways of knowin what you think."

"That's awright, you dont *have* to know what I think—All you've got to do is sit there and drink your wine, I'll get you some wine just this one more morning and then you better straighten up because boy you gotta do

---

108   Wallace Beery (1885–1949) was an Academy Award-winning American stage and film actor. Beery played the part of Bill in the film *Min and Bill*, a 1930 comedy-drama that Kerouac also refers to in both OTR 251, 253 and DB 223.

109   Kerouac was engaging in wordplay here, as in writing "baggypants" both the "b" and a "p" have an upward and downward stem, so alternatively this word is the spoonerism "paggybants." It's unclear which version he wrote first or which he preferred.

The Buddhist Years

a little drivin on this trip not that I'm sayin *much* drivin—This aint no trip to sell flyswatters[110]—I'm takin you out to where you can yourself and from there on you gotta dive into yr own ocean—It's what we all of us do—If you wanta talk about Henrietta you've gotta realize you aint even got the sense to mumble and fumble and form your words."

"Henrietta didnt want a leave you—" attenuated sorry Deaver.

"Hm, hm," shakin emphatically no, "it's no sense talkin about it now and now it's not a matter—any-not-er hell, boy, s—t, damn, *hold* on, we gotta get outa here—It's not required for you to be suddenly *talkin*" he cried banging the wheel with both hands and concluding and starting up the motor. ("Here we are 200 miles east and now you start.")

("And boy I dont want to make you feel badder than you do, reassured")

Cody saw the drop of his father's face, the blue-eyed vacant misty look he had in space, forever fixed there, eyes really beautiful that nobody ever looked at except in moments when eyes showed all—and because *his* eyes didnt matter—cold ferret eyes of little skidrow guys who hang around the stove all day, had pierced and glanced to his soft ones, and made him sink long ago in the sea of "discouraging words"—There were plenty of discouraging looks that had come with them, much unnecessary crafty tight self-defense— and as now, much deserved coldness from a maligned man *Bleak necked to Help*, as if were Smiley, sandwiches of pure iron anywhere—Meat?

"We'll just roll along and be there by and by" says Smiley, pacified and almost made mournful by Deaver's apparent effort—

* * *

"WELL, SMILEY, I wish I had 16 beautiful girls to offer you for this," says Deaver not wishing to be funny, as he accepts the bottle-of-wine money from Smiley and leans to start running—They're parked at a Plains liquor store.

"I would appreciate it if you offered them 16 years ago, old son of a bitch, ya cant pour piss out of a boot but you say the wrongest things, every time—Go ahead, man, I'll wait."

Never mentioned Cody Jr., who, if justice had art and therefore injustice too, would be the desecrator of future daughters and be just as worthless

---

110   See OTR 196 and UK 188. In OTR Dean tells Sal about a Depression-era experience where his father and a fellow alcoholic sold makeshift flyswatters for a nickel. In "Old Bull in the Bowery" Kerouac repeats the story with Bull as Dean's father's companion.

as his old man now seen rushing off with a lope of backlegged heels to his winestore Gra-Ha.

> "Better be jocund
> with the fruitful
> grape, as sadder
> after none, or bitter,
> fruit—"[111]

—all night long the sadden dreamer—What made the dream? Dream, what made man? Rubicund Josies with rosy cheeks were in there waiting on Deaver, handing him a paper bag; "It's all that darn juice on the shelfs," thinks Smiley contemptuous of alcohol, saying "Ugh!" when Deaver got back in and uncorked his bottle and up tilted the snor to his snorter, disgustingly— sleezing and thwapping to taste his wine and thump it down the hungry gullet, to where the shivering nerves of the belly waited—

"It's stealing thru me like wildfire," he says, presently, and Smiley contemptuously looks to see the expression on his face change, which it doesnt, just eyes shine—

"It smells like stove polish—shoe polish—*some* thin's wrong with it," says Smiley.

And on they drive into the afternoon.

"I'll nap at nightfall," says Smiley. "We'll all sleep awhile by the side of the road."

"I'll roast them hotdogs."

"Where?" ("Where ya drunken fool ya dont even know we aint got stoves" Smiley thinks.)

The bum is glad. "I'm make a fire—"

"By the side of the road?"

"Yeh."

"With what?"

"With *wood*. Pieces of wood, and little pieces of paper or dry grass, and matches—I'll cook up them hotdogs and we'll eat and *then* sleep."

"Ye, *you'll* sleep with your bottle not done—All right, you handle this."

Cody, in back, is bouncing continually with the car, alternately glad to watch them and disappointed in the whole world—due to confusion in his mind about where he is, like Thoreau's Politician who is thrown

---

111   See p. 68 herein.

The Buddhist Years

into confusion by wanting to do his duty and at the same time retain his popularity,[112] real duty being to your self your only refuge

Atta Dipa

Atta Sarana

Anana Sarana[113]

"No other refuge"—no other lamp being for his understanding of whether he's gonna be discouraged or glad, in his realization of himself, his True Self, his True Mind in back a that, empty perfect—empty perfect and therefore feeling perfect—

But little boys do suffer, and old men too.

"When are we gonna get to Indiana?" is the only thing he ever dares ask, as, having asked it at first, and evinced laughs from the grownups, both his awful Driver Uncle and his father, he kept repeating it to show he knew how to establish his position as the clown-simple kid in the car, and solemn, serious, heartbroken performing this deed.

It'd be later, after castings of the iron spinet in his soft eyes, he'd regain to old hatred hardness learned from God knows what old life before— since children cant be expected to grow into adults without previous preparation and eerie education in some other garden human, mad, male, ant or otherwise—

"And we're movin on, yes we're movin on," sings the road singer.[114]

* * *

SMILEY, WHO WAS A WORKING RAILROAD CONDUCTOR, unlike Bull Baloon who usually boomed as a bum brakeman and showed up at some yard office looking for work with muddy news for Mississippi in his rain-and-wine face, showing any sensible leathersleev'd trainman he'd be fit alright for work as a rear brakeman under some Sober Sensible Regular Man *but*—Smiley, not a poet, was pulled up short near Kearney Nebraska by a blunder at a crossing at 4 PM that made him redfaced mad—"All he had to do was shove to clear the crossing—did he?" meaning the old baggy pants Comedian Conductor with red bandana out on the turnaround switch who had a cut of cars shoved to where he thot they cleared the road crossing but

---

112   Kerouac seems to be referring to Thoreau's essay "On the Duty of Civil Disobedience."

113   These are words spoken by the Buddha just before his death to his disciple Ananda: "Islands unto yourselves / dwell as refuges unto yourselves / seeking no other refuge."

114   Kerouac may be referring to "I'm Movin On," written by Hank Snow and first recorded in 1950.

(Engineer and Brakemen not caring or at least not noticing) in his zeal to get home soon and get all the cows in quick, "We'll wrap up this ole local the quickest it's ever ben done"—signaled to cut off the frozen turnaround and drop the crummy on a lead and pull two for industrial—"That dogeared son of a bitch" holding up transcontinental auto traffic just because he thinks the put put put of his old switch pot s' filled him with some idea he's God of the Railroad and dont hav ta think—if you think I'm gonna wait here all day for the mistakes of others you dern fool your lardass is making *you* mistaken cause I'm goin right up this mainline and cross—" which Smiley did with the old car, bouncing 20 yards up the side of the track and over on a sand path and back to the highway, in the clear.

Smiley, as tho his youth had been spent in a blur of ecstasy, drove on with pouted mouth to think of it—

"Brother, can you spare a dime?" sang Cody Deaver sometimes, one of his favorite songs.

Smiley felt better when they parked OO AA at the side of the road after 5:00 and could slump hat-on-eyes over the wheel as Deaver and the kid got out and started a wood fire at the edge of the Kearney Nebraska sand, with nothing but steel rails and drear solitary bushes behind them.

"Say, we oughta have a good picnic here."

"Curl up in the back of the car, Smiley," advised Deaver kindly.

"Nah, I'll wait till I eat a bite, then you know what, Cody, I think I'll curl up in this blanket Louise told me to take—it aint cold, and I can sleep right there on the side of the road till 7:00 with nothin but[115] a passin car to break my dreams."

"I get all kinds a them dreams too—" tries Cody, amazed, because Smiley hasnt called him "Cody" for a year, always talking and referring to him uniformly without resort to his name.

"I dont wanta talk about dreams," minces Smiley going off into his thing of his own, his sleep, and snores in five minutes while Lil Cody was glad to get firewood for his Paw's hotdog fire, he can smell them now—

Gray night falls as the fire reddens deeper.

"Cody," says the old man, looking at his son over the embers, bottle of deep dark wine in hand (California Four Star brand) (4/5 emptinow),

---

115   Again here (see fn. 108) Kerouac drew a "b" and a "p," so alternatively this word is "put" to reflect Smiley's pronunciation.

The Buddhist Years   141

"always ya can find a quiet bank side with trees moving very softly and very slowly in the evening—wont nobody bother you there—Years ago with yar mother, I done that—loved her—she was wild—why one time in Bakersfield California, boy, we sat on crates together back of the bum's moon over those Southern Pacific tracks at the yard there—Lord, time has come along and et that lovin pure away—Left no mark—I dont see no mark nowhere a what I loved—" […][116] and he drowns his dry wine and Smiley's still asleep and for a moment, father also asleep, little eight-year-old Cody Deaver is the only waking man in the great sighing openspace of Zacatecan Arizonan Kansas and yer Heaven—so listens wide-eyed, mouth open, for sounds of silence he never heard before, and it whispers to him, jackrabbits dream—

"I understand," says Cody, thinking inside.

* * *

LITTLE CODY DEAVER sat by the dying fire beneath the enormous emptiness like a little Mexican on this vast earth. Little Cody, who'd panhandled for his father and spoken for him in night courts as the great teeth of officials bit thru his face of innocence and childliness, sometimes with that impossible tied-together hat his father'd made for him (a wool cap that went over his eyes but with a sun visor tied on by safety pins, "Cause when you out in the open all day you gotta have a shade over your eyes so's you can see far and tell what's goin on")—Cody who'd played with rubber tubes at the bow shadows of great Orient shipping in Embarcadero Frisco while his father and mother stood, among hundreds of winos, back-to-wall, slugging in the Howard Street parade—Cody who'd slept in put-together cartons that by dew were made musty ere morning moved his eyelids, and felt that pain in the ribs from the world's inevitable secret dank, and sometimes from his little urchin lips you heard an unknown moan, like the moans of seven-year-old beggars of Mexico sleeping with bandaged hands in front of cinemas at 2 AM, no top hat millionaires to take them in and lay them in golden baskets, and no Guardian Angel standing by with bandaged celestial hand and heaven moans but the Invisible Angel of Emptiness in the heart of the heart of mind's cruel Ignorance—Cody Deaver Jr., hair over his eaten collar, soot on his nose, perfect purity in his eyes, wanted to know now of his

---

116   In writing this section, Kerouac was clearly drunk, and at some point he ran a line down most of three pages, marking the semi-legible scrawl for deletion.

stupefacted father at the embered side of their evening fire if "we gonna have a real place with sinks and a stove?"

Smiley was asleep in his blanket on the sand, it was 10 PM now—

"'T' s' near South Dakota Rolfe where's we come from here, we all had pitchforks, Kiota lowing. I had a Aunt Mandy in Popple Bluffs, had cans of pork and beans by the case—" Dozing off—

This was his answer—

So Cody bethought himself and never let his head fall but looked directly ahead eyes impervious to the sight of the vast haze plains there, cars impervious to the grassy sigh, the cold on-coming, his eyes fallen, understanding what was going to happen, once in a while looking at his foot and fixing a tape bandage inside his shoe where because no socks he'd built a blister. Under the black sweater full of holes his shirt felt damp. He bounced his old tennis ball in his hands. They called him Dopey in the gangs of little Negroes and Mexicans who played in the street at Welton and 27th near the gas tanks of Denver, "Dopey" because (with fantastic hat and always the tennis ball) he preferred to play alone and (as now) talk to himself, preferred to think his own thoughts behind their fires (the Depression's hole of hunger in his belly making him feel dizzy) and they could see his eyes brillianting in the darkness, a little boy frightening and prophetic and himself frightened by the Phantom of the Opera of our real childhood, the ghosts of wind that hid among the redbrick warehouses of Market and Wazee and came out at night wearing black rags for gloves and stole the little winds that come out of open boxcar doors—the whole scene so damned, dirty, you'd expect the foreman of the firstfloor dustghosts soon to come out with his pocketbook broken in a can if you should ever ask him "Can I sleep inside for the night?" Lost Indians forlornly with hands a pockets passing under the corner lamp, among blown bits of paper, going to shelters of plank and cardboard somewhere in the night beyond—Stars shine in bits of broken glass with the same merciless automatic perfection as the shriveled message of "Nobody Cares" groaned by the wind—

But now, Ah but now, little Cody and his father had found some key to joy's innocence in this trip's purpose—it'd all been whipped up in the poor blah blahs of cold corners—"We'll cook our *own* steaks on our *own* stove!" It was worth all the tears Cody had shed in haystacks dirtied by the horses of sorrow from Nebraska clear on back to Oakland Row; all the nights

The Buddhist Years

waiting in the wind praying for the toot toot of the engineer of the chaingang freight meaning it was time to rise and get on and roll on maybe to warmer mornings; worth all the mountain stars swelling like cold diseases as trees yelled at him and his father near creeks, malignantly crashing from every leaf; worth all the great wheels working underneath them like gigantic beasts haggard with fright walking arm-to-mouth pushing in the whitenesses of the fog the empowdering monstrous weights of steel that screamed on the track with a "squee squee" that made the cold jaw shiver, the dog of their try–sleep in coats in the night, heads on iron.

Worth it all—"O boy, now we gonna live together alone and at night I'll read the funnies to Paw and he'll fix up some pork and beans and maybe we can get a lamp." He covered the rip on his knee with hands joined, enjoying his dream. Worth all the times, that Golden Lamp to Read the Funnies By, he'd seen his father reading old pulp magazines found among the crappiles, shoes, bottles, plasters of ruined shanties under viaducts, or the times he'd seen him (impossibly mistaken Sage of Old wandering in meditation) walking half-unseen among immense six-foot weeds in boardpile yards, gruesomely his very blue Irish eyes showing in a muggled dark mask, with white underlip, a cover of a magazine dangling from his hand, so that people up on the viaduct could look down and see this real impossible poorman rolling around like an old ball in disaster and all the time he's actually thinking: "If I can find another paper bag to reinforce my bag—it wont make no difference if it's already been wet—if I could find *three*! Yonder's a baby toilet seat cover but I aint got no use for it" (complaining)—Forty years old but looked 60, snobbed even by hair-heavy greasy maned Indians who hid in the cellars of abandoned houses afraid, because of his incredible and apocalypse-prepared futility—worth it all.

At eleven o'clock all three were snoring, Cody on his father's leg, the fire died down to pink ash tips and an occasional car arriving from far off across the flats with a traveling wave of brown light, passing the parked gaunt Ford, disappearing into own infinities the Three Sleepers now in void sleep well understood.

* * *

IN NEW YORK they were met by Old Bull Baloon.

In the second letter that had explained everything Bull had said to come on an 18 Pott Street address. When they arrived in New York Smiley began drawing up to every curb asking pedestrians for 18 Pott Street, an address (off Chatham Square in the Bowery) so out-of-the-way none knew. "Dad blast the damn town"—As for Cody he was scared of something for little harmless reasons of his own like an infant in a large bed that doesnt belong to him, mortified by the sight of dirty ash cans leaning against one another in a long row in front of a movie theater, and Negroes with big hats passing by spitting in the evening streets.

Like windows cut in cardboard, and the cardboard against a low diffused horizon light which is the movie set Manhattoes,[117] Cody expected New York to be big black buildings undersupported by golden light, with little smokes that come out of hidden pots or vent-holes, and the big marble floor with potted plants inside the windows (like scenes of old Asia), women in gold printed on the windows like plaques of golden banks, like on restaurant menus of old newspapers he'd found on the ground and scenes in the Cameo Skidrow Movie when with his father he'd sometimes gone at 10¢ apiece to see afternoon doublefeatures sending out roars of gunfire and screams of New York into the sidewalk loudspeaker streets of lackadaisical Depression shoppers in calico dresses yawning to get it over with, in the drowse—It was a vision of old New York from myths and otherwise.

All impossibly lost in the city, Smiley and Deaver were. On Fifth Avenue someone said "Eighteen Pott Street, you got *me* mister!"

"Go down this way," said Deaver slackjawed sitting stunned and stupid in the car with his tongue between his teeth in innerest, and Smiley looked the other with the same stupefied astonishment. They turned the car in the middle of traffic in front of Lord & Taylor's, to think, to turn. Down Sixth Avenue they made a triumphant funeral to the hazes of blue traffic smoke below. There were policemen who tried to explain just how to get to Chinatown, and they didnt understand. "Aw mystery" was the strange expression escaping from Smiley's lips like saying "Aw hell." It was only when an old bum on Lafayette Street told them with motions and actions how—a veritable old clown in rags, sick as the devil agitating himself in the dirty wind, late in the day his big sunken teeth enduring life hard in the redness of seven o'clock Autumn and other old boys all lined up behind him

---

117   The term "Manhattoes" appears in Herman Melville's *Moby Dick*. Kerouac uses it here and once again later (see p. 145 herein) to refer to all of Manhattan although it specifically refers to the southern tip of the island where the Dutch first settled.

The Buddhist Years

with murders in their pockets and their hands on it. "Not when ya git to the corner of the three hockshops, hear me pard?—The corner of the *two*"—Old wood and iron was the platform [...], to which he retreated, to Cody like a mummy of the city being replaced in a niche in the cavernous cave street for the night, during which rats would sink. And apples cry.

"You reckon he wanted to play fool?" mentioned Smiley idly as such time he found his Pott Street and even No. 18, and there he was! Old Bull B! standing on the sidewalk, cigar-a-mouth, with a gray fedora hat and a dark gray overcoat that flapped in the wind, yakking with his big toothless mouth, with a Chinaman, Yao Shieh.

The boys in the car gasped; it was something new.

* * *

YAO SHIEH WAS DRESSED in an old gray sweater, and old pants, no hat, gray hair. He owned the queer loft upstairs, second floor, with big curtains in the show window where years ago someone had exhibited an inside neon showing perhaps the solitary beautified beautician's wig with rouged doll sorrow and campy coy lashes, in swarming night you saw the gold altar of her hair lost in inky regrets of American advertising as old hopers once sold on the *papiermâché* sidewalk. It was now a place for cards, on old boxes from his store, where he lit an old bulb once in a while and played cards with his friends. There was a rolltop desk filled with ancient bundles of receipts and dusty account ledgers, no longer important Chinese newspapers, lost doctrines in the void gathering dust, and in the black corners were bags of rice, boxes of dried fish, barrels, noodles. On the floor he had put old blankets on cardboard for anybody, as like sometimes a man turns drunk and might as well flop where he is, an idea Bull wasnt wont to make uncommendable sometime soon.

The old Chinese Yao Shieh; in Butte Montana long ago he'd run a famous little chow mein diner where there'd been stools spun back from the departures of such satisfied eaters as Wade White, Old Bull Baloon and old John McGranery who with slitted eyes contemplated hole cards for a half a century in the halls of gambling land. Bull and Yao Shieh and McGranery had participated in one famous game with a slew of carpenters, copper miners, and a visiting big league umpire that had lasted and blazed so long some flowery genius could have written a whole tome in the time it took to tell the winner of that phantom stake. Yao Shieh'd also worked with

Bull at a lucrative handprinting business outside several New England and New York racetracks turning out Clocking Green Specials with the ink still wet for the edification and amaze of departing bettors with empty pockets, the first four races all picked on the button. Nights afterwards spent playing cards in the barns with dour grooms and old trainers with faces like Casey Stengel.[118] Later they'd sojourned together in (Culiacán) West Coast Mexico in the days when Old Bull wanted to forget the alcohol and take up an opium pipe, at which time also Yao Shieh ran a restaurant, featuring tacos and rice, and other great games beneath the evening bells took place. A patrimony from China, property from a wealthy brother, had brought Yao Shieh to respectable days and now he owned one of the finest Chinese grocery stores on Pell Street and this loft was but one of his several holdings in Chinatown. "When my time haw come," said Yao Shieh, "I not be sod, I occident," nodding swiftly, gleefully. He'd once explained his religion, the Tao, to Bull, who understood. "I have hunchback uncle China say 'don be useful people seek to use you.' You unnnerstan thot, Haw Bull Baloon?"

"The more you're used, the more your blade gets dull—"

"Thass Tao!—an then, using use you the blade get doll and no-good, but s'not becaw of *Time*, becaw of *Using*—"

"Rusty time'll eat your little ears out, Yao m'boy—Lay me down a bet here, we're not here to count Mother Frannery's chickens how they peck and chuckle under the gray trees. Raise you two."

"Gray trees how chickens? You soluvbitch, I raise *you* two!"

It was night now as Smiley pulled the old car to the curb on 18 Pott Street and Bull, acknowledging the arrival with an imperceptible shift of the corner of his speaking mouth and a rising of his tone to howling nasal official speechese "—and here the lardass big top conductor of the Chicago Burlington and Quincy Railroad has finally BOOT his gut bones to another part of the farce flat, yesndeed—" stood waiting in the October wind that was starting to rise like a phantom in the streets, belly out, hands in coat, head back, like some old county politician caught flat without stale and spittooned office in the streets of man and in his whiskey eyes wet and blue you see it makes no difference anyhow; sticking out his freckled hand with

---

118   Casey Stengel (1890–1975) was a major league baseball player and manager. In the 1930s, when this story is set, Stengel managed the Brooklyn Dodgers and Boston Braves. He was far more successful during the 1950s, when Kerouac was writing this, as the manager of the New York Yankees, winning the World Series five years in a row, 1949–'53.

The Buddhist Years

its cirrhotic and nicotine splotches of sorrow like splats of chewing tobacco and Old America, saying: "As a long time Naval officer and I'm almost too old to be remembered, I am even prouder of the great pleasure of being here in New York today to say Aye Aye Sir and under this great memorial monument of over fifty-five million men that died in the enemy submarines which I see before us now offering you as a token of our esteem this day in honor of John Paul Jones this one pint bottle of old Red Eye, dedicated to the orphans and mothers of the United States of America writ in golden letters of history for our children's children, to my knowledge of the disasters of full Arlington Cemeteries gleaned in parks of San Francisco—termed as harmless," language which, if not grim reminder of the sneaky cold bath of life ahead for all of them, man and boy, dour old or young, unknowing, at least made everybody laugh and Smiley pushed his hat back and smiled at last.

The meet was made.

* * *

"WELL, LET'S GIT TO GITTIN," said Smiley, as he stept out of the car, stretching, tired, and wise, old—

"How 'bout a drink, boy?" proposed Bull with big face.

"You know I dont touch that stuff no more—"

"All's the more the pity—"

"Stick to yr own rows—I'm weedin this one."

"I got my own hoes—hang yoursen—"

"What are ya, rhymin?"

"Not two timin."

The night was like 'Your Love For Mother,' ink black.

The Long Night of Life

Chapter One
My Discovery of the Dharma

"The long night of life is over." When I hear these words in the silence of the night and my Essential Mind[119] shines with an empty brightness that seems to come from all numberless directions on the universe like a vision of paradise older than the earth itself and much older, infinitely older than mere human visions of paradise, I know that because it will soon be true, amen, thus it is, *ainsi soit il*,[120] Om, it is already true.

And what was the long night of life anyway? It was birth, the cause of birth; it was suffering, the cause of suffering; and now it is enlightenment, the cause of enlightenment. And this enlightenment consists of the realization that birth was the cause of suffering, and suffering was the cause of enlightenment, and enlightenment is the cause of the destruction of suffering which now frees me from this long night of life.

I was born on March 12, 1922, in Lowell Massachusetts, of simple French-Canadian folk. My father was an insurance salesman, big, jolly, goodhearted, handing out cigars around town. He believed in goodness and got mad when he saw badness. His temper, based on a trustfully Christian sense of justice, eventually got the better of him and he died 24 years later of cancer of the spleen. They say the spleen is the source of anger, and so I suppose the cancer grew there and multiplied on itself as he raged in his mind, like a demon god hopelessly snared in a net of injustice which he would seek to destroy, ending up destroying himself before his time. Even when I was young I would say, "But why get so mad? They're dishonest but

---

119   "Essential Mind" is a phrase used most notably in the *Surangama Sutra* as a form of enlightenment that Buddhists strive to cultivate. The Buddha's disciple Subhuti states, "In this life while still in my mother's womb, I already realized the pure emptiness of Essential Mind and gradually, as I grew up, I progressively realized the pure emptiness of all the ten quarters of the universe, and there developed within my mind the wish that all sentient beings might also attain to the realization, each of his own Mind-essence" (BB 233).

120   "*ainsi soit il*" = "so be it."

you're not dishonest and all you do is make yourself mad thinking about them."

"I tell you it makes me *mad* to think of all the things that are going on— The hypocrites! The liars! The crooks! The flatterers! The self-important fools! The destroyers! I tell you this was a good world when I was a boy!"

But it wasnt at all. His father Jacques Kerouac was a farmer in the howling plains of Quebec, he had ten children, the diet was mostly potatoes and the peels were saved for potato soup. This was the result of the wars between the French-Canadians in canoes and the redcoat British with their cannons. Deeper than that it was the result of the original destitution of the Indian people of the New World by the invasion from West Europe. Deeper than that it was the result of the sin of the Indian himself, his greed among neighbors, his slaughter of harmless animals for meat, his murderous rages due to pride, his concupiscence, his attachment to the bloody wheel of life and death. Deeper than that it was the result of Nature herself, her voracious scenery, her upheaval and madness, her chaos of storms, destruction, birth, suffering and death. Deeper than that it was the result of the Four Great Elements, Earth, Water, Fire and Air combining at the beginning of creation in an ignorant mass of warring details that produced and destroyed one another and provided for the continuation of production and destruction. Deeper than that it was the result of Ignorance appearing like waves on the perfect calm of emptiness, giving rise to illusion, to the shape of things, to the incontrovertible law of things that is their suffering and destruction.

Deeper than this the Cause was Mind, the Universal Essence of Mind, which nevertheless since beginningless time has ever remained pure and undisturbed by all this, because it is free from illusion, free from Ignorance, free from the shape of things, free from birth, from suffering, from destruction, free from the apparition of men in this tiny ash called earth, and free from all their conceptions concerning cause, birth, life, personality, injustice, destruction and death.

I had a long way to go in this long night of life, when I sought to explain to my father why he shouldnt get mad. And in trying to convince him we warred, and I got mad myself, and he died, and I died with him in my heart.

My mother was Gabrielle Levesque. She was from French Canadian people who lived in Nashua, New Hampshire; but her mother, while pregnant, took a trip to Montreal, and due to a big snowstorm, Gabrielle saw the light of the star of her pity there, in 1895. A twin was born with her but died; and a few weeks later her mother died. Twelve years later her father died. In 1926 her son Gerard, my brother, died at the age of nine, a sad angel wrested from her arms. And then her husband died. Everyone died on her; like the noble Nanon of Balzac's "Grandet"[121] she went on cooking, scrubbing, working; like the noble   of Proust's "Remembrance" she did not sleep nor undress till the dead were in their graves.[122] Like some devout and ancient saint of Orthodox Russia, to this day her sleepcouch rattles with the rosary bead in mid-night. She burns candles for the Virgin Mary. She has holy water for the storm. A giant crucifix hangs on the wall of my tiny room, where a couch is provided for me with clean sheets and a dresser full of clean, mended clothing. From the time she was 14, when an orphan living with her father's sisters in Nashua, till this day, with a few interruptions provided by my father's efforts and mine on one occasion, she has been getting up at 5:30 AM to go to work in the shoe factory. "I never had anything," she says. "Some women get up when they want, spend the day doing nothing, or causing trouble with the neighbors, and when their husbands come home at night they complain they want this, they want that, they havent got enough. I'll never have anything till the day I die. Everything I ever had slipped through my fingers—my mother, my twin sister, my father, my son, and my husband." And she yawns, because she never gets enough sleep, and goes to bed on her narrow couch while other women stretch in big beds in large homes in the neighborhood, and I hear the rattle of her rosary beads. Sunday morning she goes to church and gives donations and lights the votive candles. And the only thing I can say to her is, "It's established in the law of things."

Which is all too true.

From the moment I was born of her in the upstairs bedroom of our house on Lupine Road in 1922, to the moment I went to the library in December 1953 and took a book called "Sacred Books of the East" and opened it accidentally to "The Life of Buddha" and saw these words: "O worldly men! how fatally deluded! beholding everywhere the body brought to dust, yet

---

121   *Eugénie Grandet*, an 1833 novel by Honoré de Balzac.

122   Kerouac left a blank, not remembering the character's name, but he most likely was referring to Francoise in Proust's *Remembrance of Things Past*: "During the two weeks of my aunt's last illness, Françoise did not leave her for an instant, did not undress, did not allow anyone else to care for her in any way, and did not leave her body until it was buried" (*Swann's Way* 156).

The Buddhist Years

everywhere the more carelessly living; the heart is neither lifeless wood nor stone, and yet it thinks not 'All is Vanishing'"[123]—my life was a puzzle, suffering was my constant activity, and the knowledge of death was a knife in my throat. Now suddenly, on seeing the words "Repose beyond fate"[124] I realized that I had all this time lived in ignorance and struggled and suffered for nothing. Not in these words alone, but in the many others I studied, and the unfolding thought I lent them, till finally when New Year's Eve came and people were raising drinks and wishing one another good luck in the coming year, I realized that I had crossed the ocean of suffering and was now on the shore[125] because their meaning of "good luck" no longer applied to me. In that instant I knew I had a long way to go in attaining perfect realization of this freedom, that I would fall back many a time into bondage and doubt, that I was only a beginner but at the same time sweet certainty manifested itself in the thoughts of my mind, a calm fearless insight into the true easiness of my goal, inevitable and prophesied somewhere, and I smiled with happiness and wished them "good-luck" with my tongue and in my heart I was wishing them the Dharma—the only good luck there is.

---

123   Kerouac is quoting from LOB 37. In the actual text, "All is Vanishing" is not capitalized and ends in an exclamation mark.

124   "Repose beyond fate" does not actually appear in the text of LOB; it appears to be Kerouac's own, invented phrase—i.e., his takeaway from reading it. The prospect of freeing himself from mental anguish, escaping his fear of death as well as fate's vicissitudes, was perhaps Buddhism's foremost appeal in late 1953 when Kerouac's career as a writer and love life were stalled. That said, the following passage, which contains the word "repose," is a likely candidate for what inspired "Repose beyond fate":

'Depressed and sad at the thought of old age, disease, and death, I have left my home to seek some way of rescue, but everywhere I find old age, disease, and death, all (things) hasten to decay and there is no permanency;

'Therefore I search for the happiness of something that decays not, that never perishes, that never knows beginning, that looks with equal mind on enemy and friend, that heeds not wealth and beauty,

'The happiness of one who finds repose alone in solitude, in some unfrequented dell, free from molestation, all thoughts about the world destroyed, dwelling in some lonely hermitage,

'Untouched by any worldly source of pollution, begging for food sufficient for the body' (49–50). Further suggestion that Kerouac invented the term, which he also uses elsewhere (e.g., SOD 3 and GB 152), is his "Author's Note" to WU, saying that the text "contains quotations from the Sacred Scriptures of the Buddhist Canon, some quoted directly, some mingled with new words, some not quotations but made up of new words of my own selection. [...] The purpose is to convert" (5–6). And we can see him further playing with the phrase when he writes "FREELY RELAX BEYOND CONSCIOUSNESS,—??" and *"Retire beyond happiness"* (SOD 234).

125   Kerouac's words here echo the *Maha-Prajna-Paramita-Hridaya* (a.k.a. the *Heart Sutra*), in which the Buddha declaims, "O Transcendent Truth than spans the troubled ocean of life and death: safely carry all seekers to the other shore of Enlightenment" (BB 86).

By what miracle was the Dharma revealed to me? By some hopeless walking to a library across a railyard in the winter sunset? By some hopeless, idle thumbing through a dusty book? By mere words imprinted in lines across a page? By bleak thoughts bent over them? No. By virtue of the Buddhas of old who made their vow to reveal the Dharma, which is only its name and means "The Established Law of Things," long before books were printed, aye long before men and gods and long before the propensity of men and gods to give names, oh long before creation and long after too. It was the manifestation of the universal essence of mind revealing itself to itself, as before and before, as now and now again, as after and long after indeed. As Already.

And would this miracle of the Dharma be revealed to a man or to any form of living being anywhere in the created universe, if he were a piece of empty space devoid of birth, suffering, and destruction? So it is because I am a living being under punishment of birth, suffering, and destruction that the law has been revealed to me. And it was already revealed from the beginning, but the veil of Ignorance was over my eyes in the long night of life and I did not know. Now that I know, I know that I always knew. And with this knowledge comes the realization that I truly dont know when the long night of life began and if it ever really began or ended.

* * *

Chapter Two

Birth

As far my present body is concerned, its birth, genesis, and continuation of suffering began on March 12, 1922, at 5 o'clock in the afternoon. But now, 32 years later, I often sit in the trance of meditation and there comes to me the eerie sensation that it all happened before and more times than numbers, this birth, suffering, and destruction. Deep in dreaming at night I wake up and realize that I have just been dreaming that I am a bug crawling over a barrel eating "peach meat" and the only thing that occupies me is the eating of this "peach meat." To paraphrase Chuangtse, am I a man dreaming that I am a bug, or am I a bug dreaming that I am a man?[126] How can I really know? I may wake up tomorrow and realize that I'm still a bug and had a

---

126   See WCI 643: "Soon I waked, and there I was, veritably myself again. Now I do not know whether I was then a man dreaming I was a butterfly, or whether I am now a butterfly, dreaming I am a man."

The Buddhist Years

long dream that I was a man. Or supposing I should wake up and realize that I am a Buddha-Beyond-Creation and had a long dream that I was a bug dreaming that I was a man? No science on earth, with its measurements of the combination of the Four Great Elements and their interactions in force, can discover it.

But the measurement of illusion, which is called "maya" in wise old India, revealed a babe and the birth of a babe and its body and he who is known as "I" was born. Why this caution to say "I"? Nagasena said to the King: "Resulting from my hair, nails, teeth, skin, flesh, sinews, bones, marrow, kidneys, heart, liver, abdomen, spleen, lungs, intestines, mesentery, stomach, excrement, bile, phlegm, pus, blood, sweat, fat, tears, serum, saliva, mucus, lubricating fluid, urine, brain in the head, and sensations, perceptions, predispositions and consciousness, there is that which goes under the term, designation and name of Nagasena. But in the strict sense there is no individual in that matter."[127]

Like characters in the Great Movie the family of Leo Kerouac bustled around the birth of little Jean-Louis. He was soon nicknamed "Ti Pousse," Little Thumb, for his plumpness. He had a dozen other names, endearing *patoiseries* like Ti Cul (Lil Ass), Ti Loup (Lil Wolf), Ti Mechant (Lil Bad), Ti Pette (Little flatulence), Ti Ange (Lil Angel), Ti Cochon (Lil Pig), Ti Ti (Lil Little), Ti Ange D'oree (Lil Gold Angel),[128] Ti Chou (Lil Cabbage), and Tourlipi (Lil Runt).

But thinking on my birth, which leaves me no images but the obvious crystal reality of the baby's mind beginning the long and exhausting task of discriminating all the sights, sounds, smells, tastes, feelings, and thoughts of his new dream and arranging them in a false conception of what is self and what is not-self,[129] a conception unentertained in his possession of mind before, my thoughts lie sadly across the visage of my brother Gerard. While I was being born some relatives took his picture on the back porch. He joined

127 Kerouac is loosely paraphrasing (undoubtedly from memory) from the *Milindapañha*, a conversation between Nāgasena, an enlightened Buddhist monk, and King Milinda of Bactria, located in present-day Pakistan. Kerouac encountered this text in BIT 130, one of the texts listed in his "Bibliography" in SOD 8.

128 Although Kerouac translated "Ti Ange D'oree" as "Lil Gold Angel," "D'oree" in New England patois suggests "golden" rather than "gold."

129 In the *Surangama Sutra*, the Buddha states to his disciple Ananda, "The notion that your being is your mind, is simply one of false conceptions that arises from reflecting about the relations of yourself and outside objects, and which obscures your true and essential Mind" (BB 124–25).

his arm around little sister Caroline's arm and together they sat, in the late afternoon sun of March, on the railing.[130] He was wearing the clothing of the little French boys in New England in the Twenties: highbutton shoes, long black stockings, short pants to his knees, and a shirt buttoned at the collar and such a mournful shirt to me now, looking at the picture, like the shirt of a prisoner, or the shirt of a Russian saint in a cell. Each item is precious to me, in the possession of my eyes is the appearance of he who was my first Teacher. The gleam of his high buttons in the sunlight, the mystery of his very being and the being of bedraggled shoes he wore, and the dolor of the long black stockings, and the poor littleboy needs all palpably evident there and yet he needed nothing in himself. His face is piteous, it is the ancient face of life as I know it on this earth; in it is a great sadness as though he knew everything and foresaw his own death and divined the unhappy law of life. Soft brown hair falls over his brow, he holds his head gently considerate of the picture taker. He holds Caroline's hand firmly into himself; she looks frightened. The sun is sinking in the west, over the Merrimack River, and so the shadow of his nose obscures his east eye; but the other eye is a Kerouac eye, in it is my father's rue, my mother's love, my sister's innocence and my own disinclination to commence and continue with the beastly existence. There is also pain, regret, weariness in the eye and the little ring underneath it, caused by rheumatic fever that ravaged his body. His ears stick out like little boys whose faces havent filled out. His mouth is set in an eloquent position as if to speak and the words will be sad and perceptive, as if he will just say, "Aw," or "Ta tu fini, matante?" ("Are you finished, my aunt?") or "J'veu pas faire en" ("I don't wanta do this") in shame and embarrassment. His modesty, sorrow, and palpable compassion reminds me of many a trustful portrait of the Lord Jesus; it has that same expression of regretful pity. Soon it will be 1926 and he will be buried in a rainy grave, all this, this combination of understanding racked in flesh, disemburdened of its combination and the flesh for worms! But the understanding that he was a little lost phantom in the ancient light that created him, where went that? When was it ever born?

In old October, 32 years after this picture was taken, I went back to Lowell on a secret trip to see this house of my birth. Nothing had changed in the quiet little city, new covers on top of old forms here and there, such as the superhighway over the dump which no doubt contains the remains of

130   See fig. 1.

The Buddhist Years   155

my mother's first washing machine or even the rusted chassis of the old car my picturetaking aunt had owned. It was gray dawn as I walked from the bus station to Centralville across the bridge; somewhere in the mass of roofs I saw, was 9 Lupine Road of hallowed fame in my pitiful dream of life. At 7 AM I stood before the house, looking up at the porch. The same dark brown slats were there, lining the railing and the ceiling of the porch. The same old weatherboards, brown as an ancient dream, covered the house next door, which are seen in the photo of Gerard and Caroline. But now I saw my first sight of life!—The porch light globe, because undoubtedly I was wheeled out on the porch in the baby carriage from the beginning, in April, May, drowse-resounding afternoons in June, and left there, on my back, to get air, alone. What did I stare at in that brown sea of ceiling-slats but the one object, white, fluted like a pumpkin, nailed there like a moon first seen in the empty sky-night by a fledgling bird? On seeing the fluted globe, in an instant too swift to grasp, and forever lost, flashed the primal memory of the world and of all worlds. The fluted pumpkin shape, unforgettable discrimination of the shape of things, reminded me of my pre-birth bliss in the unborn. The compassion of Gerard who no doubt rolled me out on that porch was inherent in the globe, in the brown wood. I walked around to the back door that leads upstairs. The first sight of the hall again flashed, old misery and old compassion were in the faded woodsteps so worn by feet that they seemed powdery white in the general brownslatted gloom. I went up and looked at the kitchen door that used to belong to the Kerouacs when I was one. It had a glass pane, painted green, a lost memory that now returned, like dreaming of the recapture of a lost memory; older than rain the flaked greenness of that glass. I stood in the silent hall, prepared to say I was looking for somebody should the neighbors notice me, and stared at the green pane. It roused the great memory, the first memory in my mind, of a rainy gray day. In the vision of this memory I see gloomy closets, wet overshoes, damp raincoats, doorhooks, the brown light of the kitchen at dawn, people talking in the room like giant phantoms gnashing in a self-believing and self-created gloom Inside Mind. There seems to be voices calling me from beyond existence, beyond the rainy grave, crying, "Go back, go back," unseen Tathagatas in space who've previously warned me in a bright starry night at the lip of earth not to come to birth; reposeful spirits far in the middle of the void, sitting, singing, saying "Do not do it, choose not" but I am an eager spirit-eye seeking to enter the dense world-ball because the lights have fascinated me.[131] Now in the rainy gray dawn I repent and feel damp and wish I had taken that brighter advice from the center of darkness, from the realms of emptiness. There are angry words in the kitchen, troubles, sentient complaints, faces contorted in suffering. I cling to the image of the face of my human brother as to pity. Its paleness is the source of my hope and pity, the rain is ignorance and mistake and pain, the suffering victimization are the faces. I want to go back, I cant go back. Years later, in narcotic ecstasies, I had again this vision of the pity and understanding of my brother's face in the seeing of the face of a later brother who was also my Teacher and protector. For always I was helpless little Ti Jean, gloomy, sad, imbecilic, waiting to be saved, scared, unwilling, submissive to the pushes of sentient fate, on the verge of fears always and intrinsically.

Poor blind gods who have stretched their arms and rayed forth this gray epiphany called world, as futile as driving rain in the sea.

* * *

Chapter Three

The Castle

At the age of 30 I conceived of a castle in my imagination and placed it on top of the hill where I was born, and set it as the scene of the source of world evil, wherein all the evil forces in the world were gathered in one common task: the freeing of the Great World Snake which lay coiled under the castle. This Snake, like a worm in a rotten apple, was the Snake of World Evil and it was to be loosed by the Wizard of Evil, Faustus of Nittlingen returned to life, and used to conquer the world. Opposed to this master plan was Doctor Sax, a caped figure in a slouch hat, whose vow was to destroy evil, and whom I conceived as the friendly shade of my boyhood who at first used to frighten me when I was alone in the dark and saw closet doors ajar, or hanging coats, or the midnight window rattled. Now he was revealed as the Enemy of Evil and my friend.

---

131   This passage precedes one in VOG, written a year later, which it closely echoes:
It is the long night of life. And think. The morning he [Gerard] was born somehow there was gray rain and damp overshoes and rubbers in a dreary closet and a brown sad light in the kitchen and angry smirch of bepestered life-faces, and somehow from somewhere out, in the center, Counsel coming to him saying, "Dont do it—Dont be born" but he was born, he wanted to do it and be born and ignored the Counsel, the Ancient Counsel—" (68).

The Buddhist Years   157

As I walked up the hill that gray October morning revisiting the scene of my birth, I looked up to see what was really on top of the hill aside from my imagination. And there I saw, as I saw the fluted globe and the green door of rainy birth, for the first time since infancy, a castle indeed. A gloomy stone mansion of 25 rooms, shrouded by pines, with turrets, gables of granite, gray, overlooking the city and Lupine Road like a distant vision. "So this is where I got the castle!" In the little thinwheeled wickerbasket babycarriage they'd wheeled me about these streets, and up from my pink bundlings and wool blankets I'd looked and perceived that gray phantom on the hill which must have become as natural to me as the mountain for the mountain-born boy. What thoughts must I have entertained concerning that gloomy vision of granite and silent windows, those pines, that sloping lawn all bleak. How wise the child must be! how old his mind in the dimply cheeks! to know a castle when he sees one, as though preserved like the castle of the Gandharvas,[132] like a seed in the mind and knowing it to be what it is! And to know that evil underlies it, coiling, not only the evil of the rapacious New England that raised it on the blood of the slave trade but the evil of the castle reaching as far back as the Elephant King of Antiquity. And to know that the evil must necessarily be in and upon the hill of my birth, and be my fault! To know indeed that as all things are mind-only so they are One Thing, and the castle is myself, the evil is myself, the snake is myself, the Wizard and the Hero myself, and myself a dream.

I remember now that Gerard took his sled and went sliding on the castle slope with the other children. The scene is white snow and black pines and sleds winding around the trunks and joyous cries in the keen dusk and smoke of winter. Something hoggled and mournful abides in the air, I cant tell direction, there are four gloomy tree horizons, vast numbers of excited people raging in the snow, dogs barking, I'm apparently lost in the void. Then I hear that Gerard was hurt banging into a tree and went home crying. Caroline makes me lie belly down on her sled and pulls me home. The little snow packed on the sidewalk sings me little songs of her kindness; she doesnt have to drag me, pull and struggle to please me, but she does, and my eyes hang watching the passing of the little snow under the sled, the kindness

---

132   Gandharvas are celestial beings, divine performers (singers, musicians, and dancers) in Hindu, Buddhist, and Jain mythologies. They are often depicted as dwelling in an imaginary, castle-like city in the sky.

of that little snow, the occasional scrapes of grit that drag the sled down but Caroline tugs and on we go to the smooth. Both of us are bundled in glad winter-misery, sniffling and snuffling, going home. This kindness, this serious mystery, sliding and scraping and shooting sparks, the hobble of the sled as she steps along blithe and loyal to our golden goal in the kitchen where potatoes are burbling on the stove and making steam in the windows. But I know, looking down at the kindness of the little snow, it is my fault Gerard got hurt and cried—I know the evil of that castle ground.

* * *

Chapter Four
Gerard

Gerard was always getting hurt and he was always helping others. We moved from Lupine Road to a cottage higher up on the hill, on Burnaby Street, a sad little name the pronunciation of which to me is like infant delight and something toyly sorrowful. Here, when I revisited 32 years later, I could no longer remember which cottage tho the sight of one or two haunted me; but what I did remember was the meadow at the end of the little street which led to a grove of pines and the forest of Dracut beyond, a sight misty, primal, like the beginning of the world and the sad meadows of my dreams that always have long red sunsets on them and something about old cars driving on lonely roads to the gray lake of time. It was on Burnaby Street Gerard came home one day with little Beaupré, a schoolmate, and begged my mother to feed him because he was hungry. I remember the gray yard, the organ music of the church in my thoughts, and the bread and butter and bananas my mother gave him.[133] He was a tattered boy with a dismal face. I'm proud of my memory which is total with respect to events that took place when I was in my right mind, prior to drunkennesses and blackouts of tangled maturity, and on this last trip to Lowell I did see Beaupré now grown huge in a workingman's sweater, anxiously hurrying down the void. Not a sign there of his remembrance of the face of Gerard who was once his tearful protector and must have looked big to him who is now four times the size of what the grave received of Gerard. The fruit of the seasons swells and bloats, blank nutriment is the cause; all the bread and butter and bananas in the world will have led the tattered needy kid illumined in a moment of moral light to the

---

133   This episode is recounted in VOG 4–5.

The Buddhist Years

darkness and huge gut enriching more the worms when the grave receives her poor Prince Ignorance.

Gerard fed birds, picked up stray cats, and rescued a mouse from a trap in a fish store and took it home and bedded it down in a box. He cried because the birds were afraid to eat out of his hands.[134] He lay on the floor with his cheek on the linoleum watching the cat slup up its little saucer milks, singing, "Ti Fou, Ti Fou, oh comme t'est fou!" (Little Crazy, oh but you're crazy!). We petted the cat together, he showed me how, I was with him day and night, I looked up to him for pity and light, as I looked up to my mother for love and food. I gazed at my sister with a stupid little face of happiness. My father was the King bestowing dark affections down on me, as from God in Heaven.

When Gerard was in school I played alone; at first I ran my ghost-remembered vehicle over the kitchen floor and over the rumbly transom of [?]; then pell-mell down the sidewalk, a little bug racing under the enormous emptiness. In the mornings of rain I could not see the mist beyond the meadow but I knew the trees of eternity were blearing there, Ancient Indian faces formed in their gloom. In the dirt road construction sands and oil cups smoking, and boards in the grit. When Gerard came home from school I saw his black stockings, pitiful coat, and tenderly smiling face. He brought me good things.

We moved from down the hill into the thickly settled French Canadian neighborhood behind the parish buildings of St. Louis de France Church. The street was narrow, with wooden cottages, backyards, washlines. Beaulieu Street rang all day with the cry of schoolchildren. It was because Gerard was sick and could hardly walk that my father moved us there. In the mornings he and Caroline had oatmeal and crossed the street to the parochial school. You saw the boys on the field on Boisvert Street wearing short pants and long black stockings, and the little girls in black with white lace trimmings, playing, and beyond, by the redbrick walls of the school, the black robed nuns with their flaring snow-white *capuchons*,[135] bowing like ravens in a field of happy sparrows. The church was just a basement with a gravel roof and two concrete crosses. At the end of Boisvert Street was another school, a

---

134 For the story of saving the mouse from the trap (and its aftermath), see VOG 8–16. Regarding Gerard's effort to feed the birds out of his hands, see VOG 19–21.

135 The nuns' headwear. In English, "cornette."

non-parochial public school, and the little Catholics were not allowed to fraternize there because these kids were said to be devils. Gerard and I and sister Ti Nin believed they had tails.[136] "Les Anglas," they were also called (The English), a term without meaning but deeply deriving from the ancient conflict between French Canadians and English Canadians in Canada. Finally it became "Les Irlandas" (The Irish) though, somehow, "Les Irlandas" were also Catholics, but that was through no fault of the Church's.

---

136   See VOG 24.

The Buddhist Years

A Dream Already Ended[137]

Version 1 (Untitled)

A dream already ended. All you see before your eyes will not be here in seven million million aeons. Gone already therefore. How can you believe in all this? There were adventures I had when I was nineteen that I thought I would never forget; now I see them through the wet blur, the dismal prism of lost memory, deceived memory, dying, decaying, unimportant memory. Mornings when with Sebastian[138] I rode to Boston in backs of trucks, legs crossed over the plaster bags, smoking Saroyanish cigarettes of our early idealistic belief together,[139] watching the black tar roads of New England wind back away from us, and Sebastian still with sleep in his eyes saying solemnly in his big deep voice, "Zagg, life is awfully real, awfully earnest, really," and taking a big drag. The red sun of my boyhood in New England rising over the green landscape, the fluted tunes of birdies in the mist, the slashing of my shoes across the wet grass towards downtown Moody in the dawn as the mill whistles blow across the river of my birth and destiny. For I have to say "I," and I have to say "my," throughout this book, for the sake of identification, which, dear reader, is a discriminated, arbitrary idea, alright, arbitrary idea, that will find its end of course on the other side of this sideless, non-othersided, timeless, unchronological, un-logical, mad dreamlike eternity. O this fault-sour sea of mournful samsara suffering; on this ball globe earth, our morbid selfbeliefs, wild eyes; I see lawyers haggling over nothings in the morning, their hair is combed, their briefcases neat, their eyes puffy with the midnight oils, their quiddities do hang heavy on them;

---

137   This phrase, that life is a "dream already ended," is Kerouac's own, and he frequently repeats it. See SOD 55 et seq., VOG 6, 111; SGE verse 51; DB 25, 119.

138   Sebastian "Sammy" Sampas was one of Kerouac's closest friends during their teens. Sammy died at age twenty-one on March 2, 1944, during the Battle of Anzio, Italy, in World War II while serving as an Army medic.

139   William Saroyan (1908–'81), the novelist, playwright, and short story writer, was an early influence on Kerouac, especially because Saroyan wrote about his experiences as an Armenian American, opening the door for Jack to embrace his own ethnic background. In VOD, Jack credits Sammy Sampas for introducing him to the writings of Saroyan as well as Thomas Wolfe (61).

their skins which once were shiny tidings out of windows, now, like robbed taverns, defunct and void of sheen, pasty, the candles lit and met at both ends they ate; the bushels of grain emptied into the granary of their belief in this world; this gray, drizzling world. When I was nineteen, O God America, the belief I did bring to it! The black yesses I wrote on the page; the black eyes in bars I got; the mainstreets received the imprint sorrow of my believing feet.

From the center of my living death I bring you these messages of emancipation and awakening from the dream of living.

Hark.

Version 2

A DREAM ALREADY ENDED

And now I know that life is a dream already ended. There is nothing to do but be kind. Death is truth. Death is the Golden Age. Life is not worth living. Life is suffering. You're done up at birth only to be done in at death: in between is the valley of darts which we go around smilingly calling life, and believing in it. We dont even know that it's all a big dream that in seven million million years will be utterly passed away from the face of the void. Nothing will be left, the weft will be unwoven, it will be seen that it was only a dream that we thought it was being weaved at all, and as in the beginning there will be imagelessness and silence. This is the sweetest thing I know. It will be a sleep in the golden dream again, deep within the womb of Mind. The world has already come and gone, and everything in it. How can you stand there and tell me that since in seven million million million years all this will be completely gone, it isnt gone already? Do you have to wait to understand the truth? It's a dream. The reason it lasts so long is because it is the huge dream of universal self-illusion and seems completely solid only because you're not small enough to walk right through it, through benches, bellies, iron walls, which are just put-together molecule universes that any microscopic intelligence can roam around in. "Concrete objects" are emptiness in essence flowing to accommodate the molds of form that have been imaged from the phantom dreamer which is the Universal Mind[140] with its surface rippled by the wind of Ignorance. When your own individual mind puts out a dream during sleep,

---

140   The term "Universal Mind" appears repeatedly in the *Lankavatara Scripture* (BB 300 et seq.) in contrast to "the discriminating mind" (BB 279 et seq.), which relies on false appearances. See also TCB 195–97.

The Buddhist Years   163

and the phantom of self-illusion which is "you" walks around in self-invented places and scenes participating as anxiously as in "real" life, that too is an empty dream but a much shorter smaller one, changing in one night to vanish forever. The dream of the Universe, of what we call "life," is your little night dream multiplied I dont know how many billion times, is much stiffer, takes vastly longer to dissolve; takes aeons and aeons to change and vanish forever. So it's all over anyhow. Suddenly on Sutphin Boulevard one night I saw people on the sidewalk in one vision imprinted on liquid; I sensed mysterious dreamy emptiness, as if they were apparitions in a ball of water; the ball of water was in the center of the intrinsic night; it was a big fantastic joke very unfunny; the people looked ignorant, sad, tragically involved in a watery grave. They had no selves, no selfhood; it was only an illusion of theirs, temporary and crackable at death-time. I had no selfhood so couldnt honestly say that it was "my self" experiencing this vision. Nothing was alive, but only had the appearance of such; it was the living death, *mortem vitalem*; shadows in a dead dream Zombie-ing by with seriously ninny expressions. I dont mean to be cruel but ignorance is pathetic, must end, because people eventually will be the first ones to awake from this dream, to notify other forms of sentient life, perhaps other ignorant shadows in other ethereal planets, and thus will end the universe gently and peacefully everywhere. On Sutphin Blvd. I didnt see people walking on the street, I saw figures in a strange dream floating around, in no particular place in space, and already it was passed away in time. The world is a shattering dewdrop. I saw trees as watery umbrellas of living pain crawling out of the ground; automobiles I had to double bangbang my thoughts to see them first as ore in the ground then mined, smelted and hammered by phantoms in a huge selfbelieving hassle that kept on going just because of ignorance, so now they sat there staring in steel, with license plates, windows, sad face-like grills in front. These too shall be heaps in the slag dump of time, to be ground into finest dust with the selfsame dust of men and earth. This dust has no universal selfhood of its own, it is only emptiness shaped as dust in a dream. I saw it all vanishing, vanished—all come and gone—my thoughts with it.

"What'll I do now?" I asked my poor compounded flesh.

I had nothing to do but rest and be kind.[141] I looked around and saw the pathetic ignorant world crawling on and on, saw how sad, what compassion

---

141   The phrase "rest and be kind" also appears in SOD 212, 323, 407; SGE verse 30; PAS 138; DB 63, 80, 142, 146.

must be given to it. Because there was pity and sorrow in me, which I recognized and saw, there was compassion at the heart of the world in the center of mind's essence.

At my side at all times I have my Buddha books, in which, especially in the shortest and the greatest book, the *Diamond Sutra*, I wasnt surprised at all to find that it had been taught 2500 years ago in India, in agreement with my own infant suspicions, that life is only a dream. A short vague dream encompass't round by flesh and tears. "A charming dream," as Genet says, but a painful dream for naught.

"Though the sentient beings...to be delivered by me...toward perfect Nirvana..." (says Buddha)..."are innumerable and without limit yet, in reality, there are no sentient beings to be delivered. And why? Because should there exist in the minds of Bodhisattva-Mahasattvas (Masters of Perfect Wisdom)...such arbitrary conceptions of phenomena as the existence of one's own ego-selfness, the ego-selfness of another, selfness as divided into an infinite number of living and dying beings, or selfness as unified into one Universal Self existing eternally, they would be unworthy to be called Masters of Perfect Wisdom."[142]

Buddha is saying this to 1250 monks in the morning in the Jetavana Grove. They have just partaken of the daily meal, which was begged at the doors of Shravasti by all of them, from Buddha on down to the youngest Pratyeka.[143] They're all wearing yellow robes. The ancient cities are raving around the world; catapults are being hurled at the walls of Jugurtha in the morning; Ionic marbles gleam; European hunters are strapping thongs around their ankles; the Spring and Autumn of Chun-Chiu and the Seven Powers cover strange China, and you hear a baby crying in the afternoon of the world, flies drowse, merchants pass in the street; twenty dynasties sun themselves in hottest Egypt; Nomad Chichimec have reached the dry Zacatecan plateau, Tlaloc the Rain God is holding the archaic symboled feather in one brown hand sprung from raw Americas with a million pristine names; the king of Benares trembles to hear the drum of life even as the Saoshyant is being prophesied by the maniacal prophets of Rameh;

---

142   Kerouac here and in the quotes that follow is loosely quoting from the *Diamond Sutra* as published in BB 97–102. He considered his alterations of the actual text "transliterations."

143   "Shravasti" is a town in the Uttar Pradesh district of India, near where the Jetavana Grove was located. A Pratyeka is a buddha who enters nirvana without teaching others, as opposed to a bodhisattva. Kerouac misspelled this word, writing, "Pratyaka."

The Buddhist Years

Alexander has yet to hit the Persian Royal Road, yet to believe in his self and call it Great, yet to be born, swell in size, suffer, decay and die. People have sweated, dropped blood to the ground, and departed forever and new ones have come and sprung up and done the same thing, and still the vicious wheel goes rolling new ones out. Expressions on the faces of human beings are the same serious, selfbelieving, stupefied, dumb glares in the morning; a father is beating a child over something; a warrior is boasting on his sword; a woman is lying for a bracelet.

"Only terrestrial human beings think of selfhood as being a personal possession. Even the expression 'terrestrial beings'...does not mean that there are any such beings. It is used only as a figure of speech...All things... are no-things." The Tathâgata sits crosslegged. Tathâgata means He Who Has Come and Gone. Fully awake from the dream, unfooled, the Buddha, the Awakened One, not interested in anger, greed, free from all delusion, desire, from sorrow and from little delights that come and are as soon gone, holds out his arm with fingers pointing downward in some mystic *mudra* and asks: "As you are looking at my fingers, are they in an upright position or in a reversed position?" He wants Ananda to understand evanescence and false-imaginations in this dream; the Prince of Gorakpur born 563 years before Christ, abandoner of the Maharajah's Palace, cutter of his own hair with a sword, self-exiled mendicant of the forests, he upon whom lotus blossoms rained on the night of the mysterious radiance of the Highest Samadhi, ready, waiting, already victorious, does not cling to this or any illusion of mortal mind. "If you take...as many Ganges rivers as there are grains of sand in the river Ganges, and as many worlds as there are grains of sand in all of these innumerable rivers...you will find...every form of sentient beings with all their various mentalities and conceptions, but not one of these...is to be held as...an arbitrary conception of phenomena. They are merely thought of. Not one of this vast accumulation of conceptions from beginningless time, through the present and into the never ending future, not one of them is graspable...Because all the mind's arbitrary conceptions and ideas relating thereto are like a dream, a phantasm, a bubble, a shadow, the evanescent dew, the lightning flash."[144]

---

144   (a) The Buddha's final statement here, that "the mind's arbitrary conceptions [...] are like a dream, a phantasm, a bubble, a shadow, the evanescent dew, the lightning flash" (BB 102) is one that Kerouac frequently repeats. See SOD 53 et seq., DB 172, DA 42 et seq. (b) It is here that the typed version ends. What follows is from the handwritten version. See note on pp. 258.

Being a 'modern' man laboring under the delusions of the 20th Century I see my vision of Beginningless Time's Endless Splitsecond in the swarm of the moment of Saturday afternoon everywhere in the world, the excitement of market day, late, when the sun turns red and the last lettuce leaf is being swept from underneath the stall and the least, last little child is crying in the sadness. Ah mothers of the world! pick up your little babies and bundle them in your shawls, birth is evil—your littlest angels are your biggest mistakes but it's too late for anything but sympathy. Pity is the only reality; it obtains from the womb of Mind Essence that emanated all this thought of dust.

There was a Mexican boy whose father had one leg; it was Saturday afternoon in Mexico City, they ran a vegetable stall together. Country people, big straw hats, sundark faces, big brown eyes, crucifixes around their necks. At sorrowful dusk I came padding my broken shoes through the littered *merced* watching all the merchants closing up their stalls, the poor wrapping up their shawls of peppers, their baskets of tamales now sour, one old woman who'd been sitting all day in front of one orange (and never even sold that) now wrapping it up carefully for tomorrow. The scene like scenes in all the Fellaheen markets of the world, from Bombay to Hong Kong, from Karachi to Cadiz, from Mongolia to the dismal mountain villages of Chile; essentially like market scenes in the materially rich West, like the 5 & 10 at the close of day, country stores in West Virginia, big Macy's in New York and all the feverish last-minute activity, the disheveled counters of greed. The little boy had to do all the work, his father was incapable. There were no brothers and sisters. He was taking orders faster than he could comply: "Take that board! Not that one, the other! Pull that rope! Pull! Bring the baskets here! Hurry! The truck is waiting! You're a lout! *Cocino!*—all can do is eat! But you cant do a day's work! Lift that thing!" But the boy, 10, 11, is so tired he can hardly begin to budge his work; he's been up since dawn working constantly; children need sleep, greed doesnt excite them as much as it does adults and so they need more real strength to carry on; false fevers energize them not. The old man is hopping around on his crutch screaming at him. Nobody notices, the whole market is a scene of maddened closedown; the sidewalks are all juice of fruit and vegetable, slimed by feet, garnished with banana and mango peels; the stars of Holy Mexico show sweetly in the unnoticed sky above the rickets and roofs. The expression on the little boy's face makes me stop cold in my bemused 5-mile walk, when, often, I'd have a 36¢ bottle of

The Buddhist Years

cheap champagne and be drinking it as I walked, talked to myself, enjoyed the blue ink deep neons of Spanish night, pondered the coffinmaker's window as I swiftly passed. He was on the verge of crying and in no position to cry; too old to cry, too young to die; his face a fixed mask of fearful blubbering grief that he'd been thrown on this cruel merrygoround and made to be shouted at, wearied, filled with pain in arms and legs; nobody to swoop down and save him from the maniac reality that, even if he suspected it was a dream, cruel and insane, nevertheless he couldnt run away till his awakening, for which he cried and prayed inside while weepingly conducting furious labors beyond the capacity and strength of his years. I wanted to step up and call a halt. You might as well stop all Mexico, all the world, as stop the greedy father with his ropes and toys and wagon hitches. "A day's work." As if you had to grimly, proudly kill yourself to produce one pot of beans and a head of cabbage for the whole family per day. Like old Negro farmers in North Carolina I saw one day, winter, no work to do till Spring plowing; the woman is in the attic window with the boy, watching the men. They stand arms akimbo looking around for something to do; they see a couple of big rocks by the wagon path; they hitch up the mule and pull the wagon to the rocks; they push and tussle and get the rocks up on the flat; they cluck the mules and slowly meander down across the field; they drop the rocks over there; it's bleak December and gray. The men think they're men because like children they've found something to play with but they call it "a day's work." Pretty soon they'll be beating the heart out of the boy because they've earned the right now.

It's better not to look. My little Mexican sufferer, wherever you are now, and maybe he's kneeling in an old Spanish church and filled with understanding of his own, cling not to the delusion, greed and anger of this world and of your fathers; just rest, the brief dream will end, be kind, dont avenge yourself, the wheel's got to stop, has truly already stopped.

"Any good pious disciple who undertakes the practice of concentrating his mind in an effort to realize Highest Perfect Wisdom, should cherish only one thought, namely, when I attain this Highest Perfect Wisdom, I will deliver all sentient beings into the eternal peace of Nirvana. If this purpose and vow is sincere, these sentient beings are already delivered..."

A thing already ended.

Yet nothing but a dream...

"And yet, if the full truth is realized, one would know that not a single sentient being has ever been delivered. And why? Because if the Masters of Perfect Wisdom (the Bodhisattva-Mahasattvas) have kept in mind any such arbitrary conceptions as one's own self, other selves, living beings, or a universal self, they could not be called Masters of Perfect Wisdom. And what does this mean? It means that there are no sentient beings to be delivered and there is no selfhood that can begin the practice of seeking to attain Highest Perfect Wisdom."

Like water, like the reflection of the moon on the lake, like the reflection of an orange on water.

It's 4 o'clock Saturday afternoon in New York and I'm going down a dim hallway with my girl,[145] we've just come down from her top floor room where I've been sleeping and she's been jolting heroin all night and nervously reading, singing, wandering around the room while I recuperate from the drinking. It's October, always it's October in the great vision of Manhattoes, the shining river, the ships coming in from Hamburg, from Malaya, from Pernambuco, lonely seamen all eyes to hit the Big Port and make the nearest bar by nightfall. Great clouds that have massed like iron from the North pass hugely romanced in red at the edges over the Lost Eternal Skyline with its imponderable smokes and giant haze and dreamlike stillness on the earth which is a rock. The Apple, the capital of the modern world, the high shelved fantastic megalopolis of America, the New Rome: all over America the red sun falls, more golden to the West; your Manhattan is the prime huge beast of comprehension connecting with a million wires, a billion invisible waves, a thousand sun-silver rails, arterial cloverleaf ultra roads, gossip of ten million tongues to the rest of the vast sad land where October raves. Football games in stadiums (Ann Arbor, Yale Bowl, Los Angeles Coliseum)—October in the poolhall (Pete's, Remsac's, the Blue Cue)—October in the railroad earth (the Southern Pacific, the Chicago, Burlington & Quincy crashing across Kansas, the mighty Seaboard bashing through a Southern town where a thousand Negroes stand by the sun-haunted stores waiting for Saturday night to fall). I pass in the dim and dusty hall, bleary; ahead is a window with an iron grill facing west side piers. It's Thirteenth Street and 8th Avenue. Through the years of dust on the windowpane I can nevertheless see the sorrowful

---

145   The "girl" is Mary Ackerman (1926–2012) (Maggie Zimmerman in BOD). Jack's affair with her is mentioned in his letter to Allen Ginsberg in May 1954 (see SL1 409, 412).

The Buddhist Years   169

redness falling in the clefts of street, elevated highway, warehouse, wharf, the unbelievable river, the unbelievable sudden orange and black booms of ships docked, the unbelievable haunted other Jersey shore beyond, the clouds going off like dogs on their hind legs over the horizon. A tinge of rose falls into the hall, makes a wedge on the floor, you see the dust motes snowing in the shaft of afternoon. Puerto Rican mamas are hanging out their wash from third floor windows in the court without. I hear children screaming in the street.

I'm tremendously hungry for food and drink, I havent eaten since the binge began. We have no money. I'm carrying three beer empties. We're going to the Village to scrounge for money. On Washington Square, at the circle, it will be sad and soft and red too; leftists with guitars; night; the glitter of bars, the passage of friends on the Paris-like streets; more likely than not, by midnight I'll be drunk again and wont have eaten and the thought of this makes me weary of the fancy dissipated bohemian life I lead. I follow the girl down to the end of the hall, where we turn left to descend the stairs. There's an open door at the side, the kitchen of someone's place. I look quickly as I pass.

Sitting at a table covered with food and a bottle of red wine, leaning way forward from a pushed-back chair, is a gigantic fat man of 400 pounds whose girth from belt buckle to backbone is so extraordinary that even though the chair is three feet from the table his belly is touching the table as he leans chomping to his work. Completely alone in the green sad kitchen; a hanging bulb light; signs of a woman's hand in the arrangement of pot-holders, matchboxes, salt and pepper shakers, openers on the wall, towel racks and cute cozy designs. Red oilcloths on shelves. His neck so vast he has no time to turn and see us as we scuttle by his doorsill.

Oh all New York! The young men fixing motors in the street—the Canuck from Bangor Maine hurrying down Eighth Avenue with new shoes and a hotel key with the red plastic pad so's he wont lose it—old women buying turkey sandwiches in White Rose bars, going home with them in a little paper bag, in the streets of lost understanding. No end to it—and no end to the chain of thoughts and memories the sight of the fat man rouses in me…visions of the world, and of my spectral passage through it, dubious, ghostly, like a visionary flower in the air.

Remembrance of Mr. Gross who too weighed 300 pounds, who was a character in a short story about sad red sundowns I'd written when, at nineteen, I lived in a cheap room on Main Street in Hartford Connecticut, in October,[146] so at Saturday nightfall home from the lubrication pit (the dead leaves in it, and the oil, and the gas station smells and the wildness in the air of October, the purple pussywillow scent) I could see the dim and almost votive glow of the westering light in the deadwall of my window and felt such pangs of sadness and homesickness and growing fear of the hollow world. Mr. Gross. All about the conscious boy calling on him in answer to an ad in the paper for a typing job. Mr. Gross is not in his office, he's downstairs eating in the Star Restaurant. Huge, sweating, with glasses and rumpled vastcoat you see him leaning to his mashed potatoes stained with beets, his haddock stained same, his coffee and buttered bread, eyes bulgant, lost, in the Red restaurant of time into which the hero comes in search of him. "Mr. Gross?—there's a job in the paper...you advertised..." "Oh yes...sit down, my boy"—so the story telling of his huge grossness, the way he eats, suffers, sweats, the enormous patheticness of the little eyes—how they climb puffing to his room to sign papers, and all about his room: the cheap hotel, the redbrick wall burned by the Saturday afternoon sun, the hard white iron bed, the forlorn clock on the dresser, the one necktie hanging from the mirror knob, the place where Mr. Gross leaves his battered hat and where he hangs his tortured coat. When I was nineteen years old and my soul cried out to sadness like a French movie about America.

Seeing the fat man for a fraction of a second as I passed, hungry, thirsty, bleak, the incredible good sense of people who eat and drink on Saturday afternoon and the loveliness of what they eat and drink, the huge amounts, Gargantuan Spreads, the lugubriousness of the need, of this life, and that light falling on all Manhattan, all the world Around...The least speck of dust in the least gutter of New York at this magic exciting hour enough to make me pray—

Mr. Gross—and Pa. My own huge father, long dead, who on Saturday afternoons too bent to elephantine repasts at the kitchen table...the sadness of his eyes, of his dumb tenure on this griefish earth.

Pa and I are riding in a coach of the Eternity Railroad. It's Saturday night, we're traveling from Shmosh to Cross Posh in the world (from Lowell

---

146   The story that Kerouac describes here is not included in *Atop an Underwood*, and I have not discovered it in the Kerouac archive. That said, the "fat man" in this story and "Mr. Gross" are clear precursors to "Mr. Groscorp" in VOG 121–22.

The Buddhist Years   171

to New York). The windows are streaked with dust, we can hardly see outside the red and green lights of the railroad but coalsmoke permeates the old green car, coal dust covers the leather seats, railroadness and gloom sits with us in the night, no one else in the smoker coach except two deadheading brakemen, asleep. I glance out the window and see pines of New England. It is a dream of my life, my essential dream. Pa's thighs are thick, he drops cigar ashes on them, brushes off with his hand, coughs, is telling me something while I dwell on thoughts of *him*, his tremendous innocent seriousness in all this gloom. I wonder if my father realizes how old I am, and if he knows why, that, being not *a person*, without selfhood, egoless, substanceless, if the Lord took me to death immediately there would be no me to take there so that now, in life, I sit in the Dharmakaya Mind Essence Truth digging all things and especially "myself" as naught and should "I" die it would be not the dissolution of a compound entity but the return of Pure Truth to the Pure Truth Bodilessness from whence it sprang embodied—for what reason a body? a self? Pa doesnt concern himself with all these ideas. He's talking about a book he read that's really great. "By gosh, Jackie, that guy really knows people and what makes them tick—" His cigar ashes fall in his lap. He coughs hugely. "Uch-u-pla-pla!" and brushes them off somewhere.

[Separate one-page journal entry dated June 19, 1954]
Saturday Afternoon   **NOTES**
(A Dream Already Ended)

Visions of everyone on Saturday afternoon—beginning with the big fat man of W. 13th St. bending to his food & wine at 4 P.M. as I pass in hall, one quick glance, as red sun soaks West Side waterfront I see thru dusty hallway window—bringing us to Pater Duluoz & the dolorosa vision of him in Manhattan on Sat afternoon wandering around to Times Sq. (Lost Father Chapt.)—visions of Eternity Railroad, he & I in train at night—*Port of Shadows*[147] we saw together, how we saw it—how in childhood I saw movies with him—(as in deleted Boston Chapter)—Time he escorted me to Columbia & the vision we had of NY—

---

147   *Port of Shadows (Le Quai des brumes)* is a 1938 French film starring Jean Gabin, Michel Simon, and Michèle Morgan. Kerouac describes seeing this movie with both his parents in "Ozone Park" (see DP 163).

"The Universe is empty…"

The Universe is empty throughout, in and out,
All that there is, is Ignorance
Why there is Ignorance, and why mind essence manifesting
It, therefore why is there a Universe,
Is like asking why there are horns on the hare's head
      It's empty and imaginary
      Life
      But what are you gonna do
      Sit like a lump?
      Meditation on mind essence
      Was the enjoyment of the saints
      And may be mine too
      On days when it is my enjoyment
      But if my enjoyment now is in a can of beer
      In a good lunch
      In a good girl
      And if I want work I enjoy
      Like writing what I like
      Modern prose wildbooks
      Like 225-mile freight runs
      Across the Tucumcari Desert
      Or living off beautiful blondes
       Or taking sudden trips to Mexico
      I knew my body is an empty spectral
      Giant, has no substance, no self,
      No nature of its own, and is in the air
      A visionary flower, gnashing to attach,
      But I breathe in and out, I am dualistic
       I cant escape my sentience

The Buddhist Years

And the 3 Gunas of Light, Infinite Energy[148]
What to do
 Commit suicide?
People stop enjoying
That's when they get moral
And start precepts
There is no enjoyment in New York
For the Porto Ricans who enjoyed life
Without money in Porto Rico
And dont enjoy what they have to do here
To earn money to enjoy life with
So steal, this is your Crime Wave
 Enjoy life, eat, drink & be merry
Live a full life, a lil of everything,
Dont bound yourself constipate yourself
With moral restrictions & precepts
Enjoy till your old age when enjoying ends
When Sheol closes in[149]
And the smokepuff, You, is gone forever
Until then? Enjoy dont be dismayed.—

---

148 The three gunas—sattva (consciousness), rajas (activity), and tamas (stability)—are the forces that control the physical universe.

149 "Sheol" in the Hebrew Bible is the abode of the dead similar to the Underworld in ancient Greek mythology.

Dharma Fragments

1.

THE DHARMA

The Mind itself is not fantastic, but what rises from it.

The Mind is in an eternal state of pure emptiness, it never had a beginning, never will end, like the sound of hearing in a silent room when you realize that No-Noise is eternally pure, empty and unbroken but all noises taking place outside the room are impure accidental fantasms imprinting on the clear hearing surface-calm of the ear sea, as the winds of Ignorance ripple the mirrored emptiness on a lake. Hearing itself is not fantastic, only what it hears is fantastic, improbable, troublemaking: sounds, The Mind is pure, holy, continuous, endless, but the thoughts that rise from it are impure panicky passing things, limited and mortal, such as the Four Great Elements of Fire, Water, Earth and Air, and the Six Senses of Ear, Eye, Tongue, Nose, Body and Discriminating Mind, a combination of Four and Six telling you all you need to know about how the world is made. The whole world rises from the non-fantastic Mind, completely fantastic. Yet we spend every day working, worrying, hurrying, ~~coping, trying, dying,~~ disappearing and reappearing, raging, gnashing, ~~killing, lusting, politicking,~~ ambitioning to degrade what we take to be selves of others, stealing, groveling and sniveling and all because we took the fantastic emanations from the empty center of the world, which is silent universal mind, to be the real world. It's only the false mind-made world working in that combination of Four and Six. The real world has no combination and is no less empty and is the Mind itself, unmade, unborn, everywhere peacefully causeless. The Dharma.

This very teaching of the Dharma is also false, like the world, because it too is mind-made, it is like a finger of falsity used to point at the truth of emptiness. Just so, this unreal world of seemingly real miserableness is nothing but an apparition of falsity used to direct all of we sentient beings ultimately to the truth of perfect emptiness, which is Nirvana, or Heaven, whether now or in kalpas and epochs to come.

The Buddhist Years

This is the faith not only of Gotama Buddha but that of the Buddhas of old whose lost ancient path through the woods of the world Gotama only rediscovered when he sat under the Bo-Tree vowing not to get up till it should come to him the long forgotten way of saving all living beings from their miserable delusion of life and death in all the Ten Quarters of the Universe, 500 years before Christ the ~~Saviour~~ Hero of the Western World.

About a thousand years ago, when Yuen-tso translated a sacred manuscript written by the Sixth Century Master Chih-Chi, in China, he wrote: "As we look outward upon the world, we see corruption everywhere— people hankering after amusements, seeking to gratify their own selfish comfort, trying to rationalize their prejudices, deliberately blinding their eyes to their own enlightenment. How few there are who comprehend the way to practice meditation! Instead of studying this book, they keep it hidden away in a bookcase and their labor is in vain. But again I bring the teaching to the 'engraver of wooden blocks' for another republishing and I hope that everyone who reads it will profit by its teachings. Moreover, I hope that everyone who reads it will practice its teachings and gain thereby a personal realization of its immeasurable treasure."[150]

2.

Buddha is an Indian word meaning Awakened One. Buddhism teaches awakening from the dream of living things. The founder, who is called Buddha, was a human being born Prince Siddhartha, and was the son of a Maharajah of the Gotama tribe reigning in a great palace in the forests outside Kapilavistu, Gorakpur, India, five hundred and sixty-three years before Christ. When Prince Siddhartha was twenty-five he suddenly became depressed onto death. "Why are we born just for suffering, decay, old age and death?" he asked, and turned away from the delights of royal existence. His father instructed beautiful girls to dance and distract him with enticing postures, but he sat out the day staring through them; and at nightfall they lay in a great sleeping party throughout the hall. Prince Siddhartha saddled his great horse and rode forth into the wilderness to retire from the world, as was the custom in those days. He left behind Suddhodana his father, his beautiful wife Yasodhara, and his son Rahula, and a life of power and

---

150   The quote is from BB 438 ("Dhyana for Beginners") with only one change: the word "meditation" substituted for "Dhyana."

leisure, to go and seek self-realization of Noble Wisdom in the woods of India. Finding a ragged mendicant in the forest, he desired his old robes and exchanged his royal garments for them. Then he took his sword and cut off his beautiful blond hair. Then he ordered his servant to take his horse back to the palace and inform his father the Maharajah what was being done. Then he wandered off into the woods in the beggar clothes, seeking the holy men for instruction.

3.

Being a Tathagata
transformation
you yield yourself up
to all beings
for the sake
of their emancipation
by practicing
continual conscious compassion
because all things
and all creatures that tremble at punishment[151]
are different forms
of the same
Solitude of the
Lovelight of Compassion
and therefore
are already in Nirvana
now.

* * *

Being a Tathagata
transformation you
yield yourself up to
all beings for the

---

151   Kerouac is echoing a line from the *Dhammapada*: "All men tremble at punishment, all men fear death; remember that you are like unto them, and do not kill, nor cause slaughter" (WCI 336). See also WU 77; SOD 211, 323, 328.

sake of their emancipation.
No more desires, discrimina-
tions nor ego. You
practice continual conscious
compassion,
which *is* Noble Wisdom,
which *is* Reality,
and all creatures tremble
at the fear of punishment
In the Solitude of the Lovelight
of Compassion—

4.

"Someone may enquire why I was led to write this Commentary.—
My first and main purpose was to save all sentient beings from
suffering and to bring them to eternal happiness. I had no desire
to gain by it worldly fame, riches or honor.—I felt impelled to
present the Lord's Teachings in all their profound wisdom but
to explain them briefly, succinctly, but clearly and adequately."[152]

These pious antecedents, saints, who did not write for glory, should
be my constant models in this elucidation of the Dharma and the Eternal
Brightness that I am going to try to unfold for the sake of those proceeding
via a narration and interpretation of my whole lifetime in America, from
bawling babe baptized in the Catholic Church, through youth and dubious
manhood stained by crime, adultery, doubt, defeat, idiocy and proud poesy,
to the sudden discovery and realization of Mind Essence and the vast opening
up to interior radiances and holy tranquillity.[153]

These glorious saints of the East, pious beyond description, wrote for
no glory but the glory of their Teacher who said all things were empty as
he and they themselves. They should be my constant models in this study
of the Dharma for signs of its eternal Brightness in some of the scenes of
my life in America. I write of myself not only because I have not known a

---

152   The quote is from BB 360–61 (Aśvaghosa's *Awakening of Faith*), using dashes instead of ellipses.

153   Kerouac marked this paragraph for deletion, replacing it with the one that follows, but I have
included it because of its value autobiographically.

Bodhisattva-Mahasattva in this life, or at least recognized one on the road or in the street, or a Pratyeka or practicing Sage of the Order, least of all a Buddha, to venerate and translate, though if I have not seen Buddha in my mind he need not appear in streets and roads, for the ground is holy; I write of myself because it is in myself that was accomplished the beginnings of Self Realization of Noble Wisdom, and only there the story begins, the confession of the sins of self by getting in the Ganges of lifetime, the laying bare of contact with Buddha in mysterious samadhis of holy ecstasy wherein I have seen the actual light of golden waterfalls, swirling completed, prickling with silence, the million trillion eyes of all the Tathagatas watching across time that separates us from the void, where they sit, each cross legged and shining, on primal dewdrops, waiting for the fools and sufferers to hurry on back.

My first memory of life was of this. "Don't try it, life is not worth living," I was advised in the dark excitement at the lip light of the world—

BLAKE: "My mother groaned[154]

---

154   Quoting William Blake's "Infant Sorrow": "My mother groand! my father wept. / Into the dangerous world I leapt: / Helpless, naked, piping loud; / Like a fiend hid in a cloud."

The Buddhist Years

Ascetic Plans for the Future[155]

Modified Ascetic Life
For Temporary and American Responsibilities
FOLLOWED BY FINAL AUSTERITIES

1. No chasing after women any more—no hankering to lust & create sorrow & multiply desires & rage
2. No more drunkenness on alcohol, no more "sipping"—no sickening of healthy body, or temporary numbing of body blanking mind

1954 3. No false social life—no 'friendships' except associations in temporary movement

4. No more work—~~after 1 or 2 years SP braking to buy rose-shack in SJ for Ma &~~

1955 ~~money for car bum truck (temporary vehicle for Sketching America) & building~~
~~huts in Calif. & Mexico (temporary)~~

5. No more rich or/and expensive foods—elementary diet of saltpork, beans, bread, greens, peanuts, figs, coffee, (& later grow everything & pick acorns, pinyon nuts, cacti fruit myself)

6. Finally (after 5-Volumed LIFE) no more writing for communicating & after

1960 SKETCH books of Wilds no more writing or I art-ego of any kind, finally no I-Self,
or Name; no shaving of beard

1970 7. No possessions finally, but wilderness Robe, no hut, no mirror, begging at houses of
village

8. No communication with rest of world or family

9. Dhyana & contemplation ecstasy

2000 10. Nirvana & willed death beyond death

155　See figs. 3–7: photos of these pages in their original handwritten form.

ELEMENTS OF THE BASIC DECEIT

1. Search for Nest Place +	1. Search for Love	+	1. Ma
a. Mexico	a. Indian whores, 'wife'		No
b. California	b. "wife"		Yes
c. No. Carolina	c. None, "wife"		Yes
d. Lowell	d. None, "wife"		~~Yes~~
f. N.Y. L.I.	f. N.Y. girls, "wife"		Yes
g. Woods	g. None (except Mexico woods) + No		

2. Means of Saving Stake	Disadvantages
a. Railroad	a. No sleep. no Eastern work, or strange Texas
b. Seaman	b. Bribes, work, war, men
c. Writing	c. No money, art compromise
d. Others	d. Not enough $

3. Fears	3. Fears Specifically
a. Changeminding	a. Mexico—Alien scorpion land, far, no mom-joy meaning
b. No patience or stamina	b. California—No sex, overculture, dry season, expensive, far
c. Inability to work well	c. N.C.—No sex, strange snake land, Southerners, dullness, overculture, notoriety
d. Art Ego anxiety	d. Lowell—Dreary return, cold, notoriety, expensive
e. Loneliness	f. N.Y. L.I.—Overcrowded, expensive, cold, sinister, warbomb, TVitis
f. Basic Insanity	g. Woods—Inexperience, poison plants
g. Cowardice	
h. Appetites rule	

The Buddhist Years

Articles in Small World Bag

1. Camp kit cooking
2. $1.25 Peruvian jack knife
3. Bible, Shakespeare, Dante, Thoreau, Buddha, Latin, Finnegan's Wake
4. Corduroys, 2 Levis, 1 navy blue slack pants, swim shorts
5. Two flannel shirts, red & green, old black & white
6. Socks—workshirts (2)
7. Underwear—tops
8. ~~Suitcoat (wine), tie~~
9. 3 sports shirts, red, gray, tan & tie
10. New shoes, workshoes (old shoes)
11. Plenty pencils (3), lead, notebooks (few), PaperM. pen, thin paper, clamps
12. Pipe, pipe cleaners
13. Mirror
14. Lantern, bulbs
15. Razors, both
16. Work gloves
17. HBrush
18. 2 caps (earmuff & RR)
19. Toothbrushes (3)
20. Slippers
21. Raingear

22. Medical kit (ideal)
    •V10 form
    •Iodine
    •Bandaids
    •Anacins
    •Noxema
    •sulfadiozene
    •Penicillin pills }
    •AntiHistamines
    •Bennies   } In Mexico no
    •Goofballs   } presc.
    •Codeinettas }
    •Cotton & dressing
    •Water pills (halazone)
    •Serum snakebite
23. Hotplate
24. Railroad watch
25. Old pictures
26. Machete
27. Lamp, bulb, wire, ext.
28. Matches (big box)
29. Alkaline yellow soap (wash poison ivy)
30. Ginger for emetic (in woods)
31. Sleeping bag

WOODS

axe	(raingear)	boots	Medical Kit
spade	Gun—.38 Colt	seeds (all)	Harmonica (big)
hoe	meal or flour	Bull Durham	Rope & string
nails	salt	candles	Sleeping bag
fish hooks, line	sugar	flint	Blankets (2)
matches	saltpork	campcook kit	Magn. glass
	vitamin pills		

WITH TRUCK

Sacks of meal, of sugar
Sacks of noodles, rice
Cases of Nescafe
Cases of Salsa Pom'r
Sides of saltpork
Earthen jars and containers

The Buddhist Years

Necessary Plus Elements

1. Humility—"if he can be called humble who never aspires."
    TO BECOME PHILOSOPHER

Be Philosophic Woods Man with Small Pack & Shelter
- Man as Nature
- Pricot—believe in hallowed prostitution & orgiasm but not fatherhood & "responsibility"—intellectual bequeather like Thoreau
- Philosophic is Priestly
- Sketch America
- Roll philosophic wanderer

Signs will Come with the Times
- Wrong in assuming that you want to get married, from sex desire & love of kids—sacramental appreciation of married life rather— (woman interrupts solitude & work & is tedious to hear)
    - Keep getting moola, you'll get enuf ass—
        - Beethoven
        - Thoreau
        - Wolfe
        - Shakespeare?!
        - St. Francis
        - Buddha
- Have $ to hit woods in war

Meet next 3 challenges head on
- Including $125 permit and berth NMU
- or NWP railroadin
- or discipline of Tathâgata

MAZATLAN PACK

1. Blanket, blue bag
2. Raincoat
3. Lantern ?
4. Camp kit
5. Jack knife   Peru
6. Crepe soles   Levis
7. Pencils, leads, notebooks
8. Machete (no hacking away at nature)
9. Razor, Noxema, mirror, hairbrush, toothbrush, soap
10. V10 form, Anacins, iodine, sulfa, halazones
11. Swim shorts
12. Workgloves, cap
13. Mackinaw
14. Small books (Buddha)
15. Food pack & plastic wraps
    a. Salt pork, salt
    b. Nescafe
    c. Peanut butter
    d. Sugar
    e. Figs
16. Fish hook & line
17. Matches, Bull Durham
18. Harmonica
19. Rope with loop
20. Sketchbook (11) for cactus foods

RAILROAD SUITCASE

1. Watch
2. Workshoes
3. Sports outfit: corduroys, flannel shirts
4. Slippers
5. Books: Bible, Shakespeare, Thoreau
6. Underwear
7. Pipe
8. Hotplate
9, Reading lamp & extension
10. Manuscripts, ribbon
    a. Sax
    b. Mary
    c. Railroad Earth
    d. Subterraneans
    e. Dreams
11. Machete for Calif. woods
12. Clamp blackbook & white onionskin
13. Padlock(ed)
14. Machete to hack away at nature

The Buddhist Years

The City and the Path

THE CITY AND THE PATH[156]   April 21 '55

PETER MARTIN was living the life of a religious hermit in a hollow in the hills outside of Tenancingo, Mexico, a tiny village at the end of the road.

It was a pleasant forest, well situated at an altitude of about 6,000 feet, some fifty miles southwest of Mexico City. Over the hollow and down the hill ran a sweet little brook from which Peter drew his water supply, straining the water through a towel, boiling it in clay pots, and then storing it in bottles, because he had gotten dysentery from his first drink of it in the Spring. Now it was almost Autumn, he had spent six months living and meditating in his hermitage, which consisted of a grass sitting-mat under a tree and a crudely, thickly piled system of branches further off to which he resorted when it rained. He was living in accordance with the ancient rules of the homeless disciples of all the Buddhas of old.

In the *Dhammapada* the saying is: "Forests are delightful; where the world finds no delight, there the passionless will find delight, for they look not for pleasures.[157]

For six months he had gradually begun to ascend the stages to true apprehension of the emptiness of reality, divine by nature. Nevertheless he was still attached to the notion of his self and his meditations were often interrupted by a bug, a noise in the thicket, a stray memory of life past in the town and the city in America. And he had a dreadful fear of the scorpions that abounded throughout the ground. Although he knew that intrinsically the ground was really the Divine Ground, and that the scorpions were no more than the same thing as himself, that is, they were parts of the same Universal Dream, pitiful, subject to pain, their essence nothingness, just like him, nevertheless, of course, he shuddered at the sight of them and dreaded

---

156 "The City and the Path" is a continuation of *The Town and the City*, utilizing the same pseudonyms as the novel. Peter Martin is Jack, and Peter's brothers Joe and Francis other aspects of himself (or else Joe = Neal Cassady, in which case Pat = Carolyn Cassady; and Francis = Gerard had he lived); Galloway = Lowell; Alexander Panos = Sammy Sampas; Julian = Gerard; Leon Levinsky = Allen Ginsberg; Will Dennison = William Burroughs; Kenny Wood = Lucien Carr.

157 WCI 334.

the day or night when one of them would finally sting him with its murderous tail. But he had faith in his knowledge that there are some things much worse than scorpions in society and civilization, in ignorance and the world, things much worse than sand in your shoes in the marble floors of Progress. "Peter," a voice said to him in the night as he half-dozed in his prayer, "it is a dream and you've entered the Golden Stream of Awakening! Rejoice!"

Every month he walked into Tenancingo and loaded up his duffle bag with the same groceries, cashing a small traveler's check of $5 in the same store and then spending the change on ice cream and pleasantries in the Market Day Square, so that when he returned to his hermitage with another month's food supply there was no cash in his pockets. The travelers' checks, numbering ten, bought at the border, he kept in his breast pocket with his pencil and notebook. In the notebook he regularly wrote letters to various friends explaining the truths he was discovering during his discipline, mailing them on Sundays when he came into town. The walk was six miles, over a path and down a dirt road to a narrow paved road that gradually wound into the dense adobes of the village, a road he remembered from some ancient dream of life. Returning on those Sunday evenings with the heavy bag of groceries, which he balanced on his shoulder with a staff, was a hard and heavy job but he enjoyed it knowing the fruit of his sweat would result in a month of blessed contemplative rest. The groceries consisted of a bag of cornmeal (*maiz*), a bag of pink pinto beans, a bottle of vegetable oil, a bag of flour, some onions, potatoes, oranges (that lasted only a week), sometimes pineapples and mangos (also lasting a week and therefore luxuries), brown sugar, and the luxury that cost him almost as much as his staples: instant coffee, which the grocer always presented to Peter holding the jar in both hands. With these ingredients Peter was able to provide himself with a full diet: with the flour and cornmeal and chopped onions, he fried delicious cornbread in the oil; with the beans he made excellent pot beans a la Boston with a little brown sugar; with the cornmeal and brown sugar he had his daily breakfast of mush, the ancient meal of the North American Indian; then coffee, black, with brown sugar; after which he lit a 25¢ corncob pipe packed with Mexican rough-cut and digested his supper with as much contentment as anybody with a house. For iron vitamins he foraged around and found natural greens and boiled them with oil and salt, or ate them raw. He washed his clothes in the creek and dried them over bushes. In long afternoons he

The Buddhist Years

dreamed in the earth the ancient dream of Awakening. On special occasions when he was furiously hungry he quickly sliced potatoes and fried them in oil, peels and all, with salt. Water was his drink; he took to drinking it slowly and thoughtfully, dwelling on thoughts of thirst, as he had done as a boy in Galloway when he used to dream that he was dying of thirst in the desert and suddenly someone brought him a glass of clear pure water. Thoughts of women occurred in his mind with less and less frequency; he realized that most concupiscent thinking which had risen in his mind in society had been due to alcohol, for, whenever he succumbed to a bottle of mescal in the Village, bringing it back to the hermitage with a few bottles of orange pop, and getting drunk on mescal cocktails in the hitherto holy night of his previous month's meditation, on the following day he experienced strong and sickly thoughts of pornographic sexuality. The most beautiful brownskinned maidens walked around Tenancingo in their bright attire on those Sundays when he came in, and he tried to keep his eyes to the ground, with modesty and circumspection about a plough's length along. But when he did look, and found them so lovely and young, he sighed with a "Damn." Most of the time he succeeded in reminding himself of the truth, which was, that they looked better to him than they actually were. Highest Perfect Wisdom was his goal, Supreme Reality was his guide, Holy Enlightenment was his strength. But for a young man, and an American at that, the renunciation of beautiful girls, the sight of them, the thought of them, let alone the possession of them, is almost impossible for any length of time, that is, for a normal American brought up in the usual American surroundings (called *Macho* in Mexico) of glorified pseudo-virile sexuality: the gangs on streetcorners, the college crowds, the heroes of the movies. Nevertheless Peter was striving to keep his behavior pure, in accordance with the instructions contained in the ancient scriptures, and he understood completely the reason for the advisability of chastity, which is, a quiet heart. "In the solitude of desert hermitage," the glorious Ashvaghosha had written in the First Century A.D., "nourish a still and peaceful heart."[158] And Peter knew there was no way to wake up from the nightmare of existence, while swilled in it; that a man led around life by the lust in his loins is not free. Knowing all this, still he had his relapses, the rising blood, and longed to be in Mexico City where the girls roam the

158 LOB 304. The actual quote reads, "in quiet solitude of desert hermitage nourish and cherish a still and peaceful heart."

streets at night. Then he reflected that he was better off in the woods. Armed with continence, unwasted vitality, and childlike solitariness, thus Peter sat in the forest absorbed in discipline.

He was absorbed in discipline and in the ecstasy of meditation, known as Samadhi. Samadhi was only possible after the initial sitting-down and stopping of thought, known as Dhyana, the practice of meditation. After breakfast, for instance, the thought would rise, "I'll wash my clothes and then Dhyana." He washed his clothes, torted it dry, flung it over bushes, and sat down with legs crossed underneath in the soft mat of grass, leaning against his rolled-up coat against the tree trunk, and fell instantly into the "dreamless sleep" of religious trance. First he began with the prayer, the Heart of the Great Dharani, which goes:

> "O thou who holdest the seal of power,
> Raise thy diamond hand,
> Bring to naught,
> Destroy,
> Exterminate."[159]

Or sometimes he would simply say, "O thou who hast always held the seal of power, hast always raised thy diamond hand, hast always brought to naught, destroyed, exterminated," thinking of his father who was long dead and buried in New Hampshire, or of Alexander Panos long dead in World War II, or of anything to which he'd ever been attached which was now extinct, destroyed, exterminated, following the law of things born that they may die. A wave of peace would always sweep over him as he realized, again and again, that all things come to an end; that all compound things decay; that things begotten from a cause, die from a cause; that in reality, however, it only appears to be so, and there is nothing but emptiness and a dream.

> "O thou sustainer,
> Sustain all who are in extremity.
> O thou purifier,
> Purify all who are in bondage to self.
> May the ender of suffering
> Be victorious."

---

159 Kerouac is quoting from "The Great Dharani," which is included in the *Surangama Sutra* (see BB 273). This quote and the two that follow are accurate except that the text is in all capital letters, and where he uses periods, the text has exclamation marks.

The Buddhist Years

189

These gentle words assured him that though his form was wretched and impure and would not last, still there lay hidden in the center of the universe, in the heart of emptiness, like a wink of an eye, Compassion; pity and tenderness for all living creatures large or small, which sometimes he thought he could see in the little benign winks that cosmic particles make, that he had trained himself to distinguish from the imaginary blossoms in the sky, when he looked. "O thou sustainer," sometimes he'd pray, "thou hast always sustained all who were in extremity; O thou purifier, though hast always purified all who were in bondage to self; thou ender of suffering, thou hast always been victorious." Nothing could be truer. And the prayer concluded:

> O thou perfectly enlightened,
> Enlighten all sentient beings;
> Thou who art perfect in wisdom and compassion,
> Emancipate all beings
> And bring them to Buddhahood, amen.

"Thou has always enlightened all sentient beings," he prayed with an inward shudder of gladness, realizing that it was all a dream a long time already finished, just as he had realized long ago in childhood afternoons of insight when he used to sit by the window in his mother's house and watch the clouds of lost human hope float, lamblike and heartbroken, across the purity of the perfect blue. Inward dazzlements filled his heart, so that, opening his eyes, he was surprised to see that it was a dark night out there in the world which he had been falsely taught was the "real world." Everywhere, he saw men buried in ignorance, women too, the regretfulness written on their lips, because they did not know this and should it be pointed out to them they would be angry. Tears came into his eyes remembering his mother, so suffering and hard-working, her long life of devotion to her children, even at this moment waiting at home for him as he sat in a foreign land on the terrace of the earth remembering the Light. And hopeless sadness made him shake his head, remembering his Pa, George Martin, so furiously shouting across the spate of days then stuck into the earth like a peg, forgotten, the eagerness of his face beneath the ceiling bulbs of old, the yak of his midnight enthusiasms, the vast sorrow of his thighs and the cigarsmoke falling on them in smoky old coaches of the railroad on brown nights of life-travel, then gone, a puppet of pity, a fleshy ghost, a man you saw there selfbelievingly and heartbreakingly walking forth with the perfect accommodation of some liquid spectre in a magical action inside Mind shining in void night for naught.

Then Peter would become mindful of Jesus Christ and see his gaunt tormented visage as if bending over him sadly in the Fellaheen dark, and he would understand the different spirits, the different symbols, the different words; the special relation between Jesus and his father and the fathers of his father, the long woe of all the Martins reaching back down the cave of the world; the sad Good Fridays of his boyhood, the rainy misery, his little brother Julian's Catholic funeral in 1926; the old church at Tenancingo where, every Sunday, Indians from the hills trooped, heads bowed, bare footed, their baskets outside just as in Galloway they would leave umbrellas and overshoes in the damp alcoves, all in one accord praying to Christ the Redeemer from the Dark.

"Adoration to Tathagata,

> Sugata,
> Buddha,
> Perfect in pity and intelligence,
> Who has accomplished,
> Is accomplishing,
> And will accomplish
> All these words of mystery.
> Svaha! So be it! Om!"[160]

The magical prayer concluded, the words and symbols denoting that which was hidden throughout the world, like the mystery in the rose, like the jewel in the lotus,[161] Peter, edified and calmed, would fall into his intuitive trance and keep it up for an hour, or hours, without moving, sometimes without thinking, completely relaxed, like someone just waking from a dream in the morning and reflecting on its illusion of reality, like the moon

---

160 Kerouac again is quoting from "The Great Dharani" in BB, only this time more loosely. The actual text reads: "Adoration to Tathagata, Sugata, Buddha, of Perfect Wisdom and Compassion, Thou who hast accomplished, is accomplishing, and will accomplish, all these Words of Mystery! SVAHA! So be it!" (273).

161 "The jewel in the lotus" is a reference to "Om mani padme hum," the Sanskrit mantra particularly associated with Avalokitesvara, the lotus symbolizing purity and wisdom and the jewel symbolizing skillful means, thus the achieving of enlightenment.

shining on a perfect pool and the fool thinks it to be the real moon but the wise man is there to remind him that it is only a reflection of the real moon.

Meanwhile dogs barked faintly in the village six miles away, the wind of Mexico soughed gently through the pines, night sighed, the stars fought throbbing wars, some were golden red, some were flint hard bright; they rained down the trees off the wall of eternity, they illumed the brow of the Americano who was renouncing the world.

* * *

ONE SUNDAY MORNING IN OCTOBER Peter was suddenly awakened from his perfect sleep by the peep of a bird; he raised his head quickly, looking around, just in time to see the horizon of the earth and the sky above it move swiftly, like surreptitious stage property. And in his head there flashed the thought:

"It's all the same thing."

And gazing on the horizon of the earth, which he now saw as no different from the sky, he remembered all his past life and [the] eerie sensation of many other past lives, the endless sadness that he had undergone, his kind, his brothers, his kin, all because of pitiful ignorance and the false deception of space and sight.

"O little bird, O little bird, you foolish little bird—you're bound and determined you're gonna be a bird!" he laughed, and tried to go back to sleep. Faintly from Tenancingo came the breezeruffled bells of golden happy morn of Sabbath, the bellropes were being swung, tinkling was in the air, the sparkling breeze. He suddenly saw everywhere the perfect crystal clear emptiness of his enlightened intuition. His brain swam through unconscious words: "It's Saturday morning in China and I see the fantastic blossom sparkling in the emptiness, intuition smiles brightly everywhere, *amen the jewel in the lotus*, the transparent crystal clearness of the world, the brown mountain in the blue sky was just a childish dream, the angel is standing in the void with arms outspread crying *"It's light up help-help time!"*

Totally happy, mistrusting such elation which he knew would be followed by foreboding and heartache, if only a little, he got up and rolled up his sleeping bag. Over the trees he heard the voices of Indians passing on the road to the village with their baskets of oranges, their mangos, beadworks, freshly made tamales, new straw hats piled on crown by crown like a pagoda on their heads. "I'll go too, I'll go to church and kneel with them. And then I'll sit on the park bench and watch their children play and give them centavos for little candies of mystery. And I'll be bored," he thought in his dreary inner world-heart, remembering the other Sundays, all the Sundays of all his life in New England and New York and everywhere. "I'll be bored because I'm a junior disciple not yet free from the intoxicants, and I cant understand that the ecstasy is always already in my mind. And so I'll be bored and time is a burden on my back."

He poured water out of a jar into his cookpot and then put the match to the kindling in the campfire rocks. When the water was boiling he had already washed. He sprinkled salt into the boiling water, then sprinkled yellow cornmeal and watched as the starch boiled to the surface in a brothy wholesome fragrance. Then he stirred. When the cornmeal was popping little volcanoes of mush he poured brown sugar on it and removed it from the fire and waited. Then he took his trusty wooden spoon and began slowly eating the hot repast.

An idea came to him and he began writing a p.s. to a letter addressed to Leon Levinsky. "Leon, p.s., to prove to you that the self is false, which of the two men has the true self as they walk away from the lake, one east with the reflection of the sun following him east, one west with the reflection of the sun following him west?"

He tore the pages out of the little notebook, folded them, put them in the envelope, and addressed it, Leon Levinsky, 432 East 7th St. New York City. And suddenly he wanted to be down on the Lower East Side this Sunday morning, walking with Leon Levinsky in the crowded markets of Orchard Street and Delancey, talking about poetry, about life, about the Dharma, about Will Dennison, Kenny Wood, Francis Martin, all their friends, the girls, the thousand interests; he had a vision of Levinsky, forefinger up, explaining with a giggle some mysterious Aramean riddle like "Dead Eyes See" or "If the trees had eyes I would have eyes." Peter wished he could be there and suddenly he wished he could be everywhere else. His entrails stirred with excitement as he thought of California, his brother Joe Martin living in San Jose and working on the railroad, his children and his wife Pat, their happy Sunday morning breakfasts; San Francisco, the City, Chinatown on Sunday morning, the delicious pan fried chow mein to be had for 45 cents, the wine, the lonely streets of white leading to the blue bay, the lovely girls with short haircuts passing by, his friends hurrying to hotel rooms with

The Buddhist Years

wine and jazz records, the Filipinos on the corner with Sunday new hats of pure pearl gray. "Think I'll go, think I'll go," the little refrain ran in the lonely hermit's head. He realized he'd been lying on the ground with chin on hand for an hour, lost in reveries of life. "If I was a piece of empty space I'd be perfectly enlightened and I'd never run off into thoughts like this and I wouldnt even have to practice solitary ascetism. I would be a perfect Tao cloud, floating, dissolving, returning to origin in nothingness. But I'm foolish Peter, hankering after life."

* * *

Alternate start to last section:

ONE MORNING IN OCTOBER Peter woke up from a perfectly dreamless sleep, because a little bird suddenly began to trill on a branch nearby, and with amazement he realized that it was all the same thing. Flat on his back, raising his head, he saw the horizon of the earth and it was a fantastic dream. The whole thing moved, shifting quickly like stage property. "No, no," he thought, smiling, thinking of the bird singing its self-existent song, "there is no bird, there is no bird-ness, that bird is pathetic, poor bird." Himself, the bird, the earth under the empty sky, and all life, it was all a secret mistake in the Mind. It was all the same thing, the perfect inexistence of his dreamless sleep and now the existence of the bird and the world and Peter Martin suddenly, all the same thing and a lightning flash. He didn't know whether to laugh or be sad. "God," he said under the enormous emptiness and went back to sleep.

And in that brief sleep he had a dream

On The Path

On The Path

Aug. 19, 1955
Mexico City

All life is suffering.
The cause of suffering is ignorant craving.
The suppression of suffering can be achieved.
The way is the Noble Eightfold Path.[162]

It was November. I had just concluded a love affair with a girl who was so pretty to me she had driven me mad and sometimes sex-mad,[163] as men will get with women that ravish them, in my case dark-eyed and dark-skinned lovelies of the lazy woman's world afternoon—the very belated touch of her fingertips was a thrill. Having got so enamoured of her, she perceived it, and looked for something harder to get: all women are essential Napoleons.

I woulda drank poison in some of the lousier interviews. But I came out of it feeling like an old and lousy man whom no girl would ever cleave to again. The purpose of the rout of the Waterloos is to make a defeated man.

It was November and I lay in my room contemplating painless suicides. The most painless of all, not to commit suicide but to go on as though I had. I stared at my wall angrily. Wearing an absurd Korean prisoner of war hat, earlier bought to wear to work on the railroad to get money for baby. The cold winds rattled my window. I sulked and decided to do nothing. I was convinced something would happen "from outside."

Idly I thumbed through Thoreau, procured at the library. Interested I was in the thoughts of a hermit in the woods. He is magnificent. "I know nothing my neighbor does that is not vicious," he might have said, a plainer, more outspoken Yankee than female Emily Dickinson who would put it

---

162   These are Buddhism's Four Noble Truths.

163   The woman was Alene Lee (1931–'91): Mardou Fox in S; Irene in BOD.

this way, "I know nothing my neighbor might do, that in my buttercups might—furor—"

What's the sense of all this literary allusion? I walked across the Long Island Railroad yards in the Autumnal night. Shadows of boys danced on boxcars. I drank wine behind cuts, on cinders, sitting on old tie-piles in the sandy dusty bank. The red light of a nearby warehouse elevator ramp swarmed with mysteries. The stars were clear.

That "something from the outside" came at once. Thoreau talks of Hindoos, philosophies from the other side of the sunrise where you put a stop to everything and everything stops with you. And he alluded to mysteries of silent profundity. Afternoons I crossed the railyards, slowly, and went to the little library with granite and round windows and giggling high school pretties at four. I took a book on Oriental Philosophies and Religions.

At home at night in my sweet and quiet room I perused the news about the Indian Bhagavad heroes, the *Zendavesta*, the *Koran*, till I came to Asvaghosha's *Life of Buddha* (translated by Samuel Beal) and there I stopped.

"Rest beyond heaven," in effect it said. Buddha says you dont have to struggle to go to heaven, all you have to do is rest beyond heaven. There is no heaven, and no no-heaven either. All that is to be done, has long been done. Saved, sweet hero. Sufferer, your suffering is stopped. All life is suffering. So ignore life. The cause of suffering is ignorant craving. Grab no more at pretty girls. The suppression of suffering can be achieved.

"What?" I thought, always thought it was impossible. "Suppression of suffering" is possible. Thought after thought, torment after torment, night after night of human loneliness when it rains on a cold night—fears—all poof! "They dont even exist—They are illusions of the mortal mind."

"Get you to a quiet place in the woods, sit down under a tree, stop, realize, and slip into Nirvana from whence you originally came, perfect like you always suspected you were."

I was dazed. I got out Lin Yutang too.[164] All books. For the first time since I was a kid in my mother's house, I sat in my room reading seriously deep into the night. One night I took benzedrine to heighten my excitement.

---

164   Kerouac is referring to WIC, edited by Lin Yutang.

I hung on the paragraph about the Five Defilements[165] and experienced my first flash of "enlightenment."

"Go away, stop, purify your mind. Remember that everything that happens has a form, if you ignore form it doesnt happen; ignoring form, you dont go through the process of discrimination, of *picking-out*, of thinking-it-out. Not thinking it out, naturally there's nothing to grab. Not thinking of roast beef au jus, your mouth doesnt water. Not grabbing means not aching and aching to grab. Not aching to grab, not suffering decrepitude and decay. Not suffering decay, you never change. Not changing, you never were one way or the other and can never change to something else. Everything's all right inside. Always knew it.

"Go away," said the silver book to my mad salvation-haunted mind of those first nights in 1953, "purify your mind of its store of defilements and the result will be like water in which all the sediment has settled, clear and pure, as original."

I read the *Surangama Sutra*, the little of it in Lin Yutang's book, then went to the NY Public Library to get the rest, emerging with a stolen copy of Goddard's *Buddhist Bible* under my belt and walking jubilant down the waterfront, safe from all harm.

"It's a sin to steal my books but my purpose is to absorb this, then I will return it in five or ten years."

All the instructions and disciplines were there. I began to make plans to leave New York City and head for the open country where I could meditate undisturbed under trees. In America, with my stolen *Bible*, covers sliced off and covered with soft leather and held in by rubber bands and holy and as soft as a foodstuff to my reverent touch.[166]

---

165   See SOD 104:

THE FIVE DEFILEMENTS

1. Individuation of "form" (which is but fantasy)
2. Erroneous views about form
3. Developing desire for form
4. Grasping at desired form
5. Imaginary conflict of form—weariness, suffering, growing old, decrepitude. O topsy-turvy mind!
See also SOD 81, 253, 254.

166   This story belies the frequently published account stating that Kerouac stole his copy of BB from the San Jose library while staying with the Cassadys several months later, in early 1954. Over the next several years BB serves as his primary Buddhist text.

The Buddhist Years

CHAPTER TWO
I Head West

Meanwhile I'd stopped drinking, a very difficult feat for a lush. New Year's Eve came and my mother persuaded me to drink in the year with some dry martinis before the TV set, which I did, ending, at midnight, hilarious laughter watching the drunken celebrities and announcers and the general raff-like goof of the world, poor world.

I knew I had made it.

"Happy New Year and good luck this year," my mother toasted, referring to my inexistent incomes and careers, also to my unhappy love affairs, my poor health, my unshakeable melancholy really ecstasy sitting in a trance of spastic anxious actually silent unconcerned near- catatonic thoughts all day. "Ti Jean n'est pas toute la," my mother thinks, "he's not all there, poor child grown up into beastly sicksad man of 32." But I knew I had made it. As she wished me luck, I saw the raft arrive, and I stepped off on the other shore— the long-sought othershore, across the Holy Stream, to perpetual safety and, as I didnt realize at first, the perpetual burden of compassion for all living beings, with its reward of Light.

My first visions of this Light came during my first practice of meditation. The book advises: "Sit ye down, in a room, in a field, anywhere, where it is quiet and no one to disturb you, close your eyes very gently, let your breathing slow down to nothing, in and out, slow, serenely breathing, serenely feeling, let the silver magic silence grow out of you like a halo, or dome into you like an outer-halo, soft, easy, tender, in love with all existence whether good or bad, sick or poor or rich or well, no difference, let it come in, it's all One Thing, Yourself, the Essential Mind of the Universe, in all ten directions up and down and in and out—like a man caught reading a page with his eyes wide open and motionless and he doesnt even know there's a page anymore. Pure trance.[167] Like a monkey I felt inside myself instinctive ideas about how to instantly sink in a trance—I all faded away, everything fell, peace. I felt I could communicate it to others.

The thought of the girl I had loved was like a past dream.

* * *

---

167   The "book" that Kerouac refers to here is most likely BB and specifically the "Dhyana for Beginners" section from which he quoted elsewhere (see p. 176). This apparent quote and several others, though, seem Kerouac's inventions, and in Jack's text there is no close quotation mark.

Late at night while my mother slept I sat on my bed, legs folded, back against pillows (because of my curvy spine, Schmorl's nodes, and my general thick thighs I couldnt sit unsupported at first), eyes closed. I looked outside the window at the snow and I knew that though my eye-organ said it was snow, it might just as well be elephants for all the accuracy that conveyed. I thought of Helen Keller, the perfection of her Rosy Hope before the evil teacher drew her out to the darkness of our world. I was conscious that no one had ever thought of HK that way,[168] but I didnt know yet that it was because of a stubborn and universal ignorance prevailing in our conditional world of cause and effect. Cause, birth; effect, death; condition, suffering.

During the day I was very testy, very Anti Christmas-y, intent on thoughts of loathing for the world. Though I read the *Diamond Sutra* where it said "Do not fall into the error of either accepting or rejecting," I rejected the poor sad conditional and illusionary phenomena of the world not realizing that bubbles are neither real nor unreal.

I cursed over my thick thighs which wouldnt bend; I staggered out of meditations with pinprick deadlegs, smiling with secret fear, thinking: "the Holy Saints forget their legs—they dont consider their legs as private property."

I rubbed my poor sore legs.

I sneered at Christmas Television and stared through the Christmas tree my mother'd so sweetly and in such eternal loneliness put up, not realizing that her own journey thru the centuries' uncountable suffering was as helpless, dark as my own. At first I yelled angrily at her the first teachings of the Way—

"Wasn't brought up that way," she said. "To us, real is real—You've got to work for your living—enjoy what you can—Then you die."

"And you die," I yell in the middle of her humble pots and pans, "and then you come back lookin for more, not any more enlightened than before—"

"I dont know those big words lighten—"

"*Enlightened*. You become awake to the fact that it's all a big ignorant dream, and that all the powers on earth and education are behind it—"

---

168   See TC 156, where Peter and Francis Martin discuss Helen Keller: "'If you didn't have eyes and if you didn't have feelings and senses all that would be still out there, but you wouldn't know about it...' 'That would be sort of nice,' murmured Francis faintly." See also SOD 7: "A note on Helen Keller: [...] (She doesnt perceive the discriminating phenomena of the mountain, which swims before our eyes, her eternal and Tranquil Mind perceives only Rosy Pure Essence without shadow or shape)"

The Buddhist Years

"Whattaya wanta do?"

"I wanta go away and do nothing in the desert."

"Why?"

"That's how you find the Holiness—it's bright, it's empty, it's your own mind, you can save yourself by doing it yourself, you stop, stop—"

"Why?"

"To understand that it's all the same thing—all poor sufferings—make people know how to stop all this—it's all in their heads—*Heaven*! You go to heaven."

"Why dont you go to heaven when you die?"

"When you die is too late—If you dont stop now—You gotta stop right away."

"Well," she'd sigh, "I always said you missed your vocation. You shoulda been a priest."

"I don't wanta be a priest—I am *not* a Catholic—I'm a Buddhist."

"Buddha, Buddha, weyondonc—"[169]

"I want to be a monk in the desert—"

"Go ahead—make your trip—You'll starve to death—"

"It's all that continual eating of food all day long—"

"Dont you like anything anymore? And why did you act so sassy when your sister was here?"

I'd brooded and busted around and made them sad refusing to escort them to the big Macy's window with the kid (nephew)—instead sat home and cried over St. Luke in the Scriptures—still continually believing in my Christmas Star and in the eventual Safety and Love of all creatures.

My mother understood, in a way. It didnt matter. I decided to hitch hike to California and make it on the road, put my beliefs on the road, go find my Nirvana for myself, not yet understanding the subtler laws involved in the holy pursuit of Highest Perfect Wisdom.

For instance, I made a list of essentials for a pack, to camp on Mt. Shasta, by a pristine mental Amitabha Lake[170]—not realizing anything but

---

169 Still a common expression in Québec, "weyondonc" is the phonetic rendering of "Voyons donc," used to express surprise, amazement, or doubt and meaning something like the American "Come on!" or "Oh, please!"

170 Amithāba is the primary Buddha of the Pure Land sect, a branch of Mahayana Buddhism focused on afterlife in the Pure Land, a beautiful natural paradise free from pain and want.

my own mad and sad void-rippling little obsession beneath the endless and unimaginable skies of Imaginary Eternity.

The pack included a raincoat, I figured it would go good as an underneath mat for damp camping. I bought it in the Bowery, $5, but it was too cheap, cloth inner lining, soggy, and belt and Dragnet Detective Murderer epaulets, making me look, with my essential winter muffcap, like a degenerate in the road.

As many times, nights, before, in this rocky or soggy or marshmallowy adventure called life (for some I suppose it is clearer and harder)—I picked up my quaint personal eccentric pack (army blanket, rope, crazy appurtenances like Noxzema for desert shaving) and kissed the mother, who must have been my mother in a million other lifetimes she's so familiar and so sweet by now, and went out in the dark night, the cold night—wearing railroad gloves (brand new) to keep my poor-circulation fingers warm—headed for the meaningless but perfectly frightening void.

There he goes, leaves his home, like Buddha—leaves his good home, the prince, sadly lamenting the end of his youth and the onrush of old age—anticipating death already—victim of time—human-eyed and concerned and alone and humorless—good education, good man—earnestly fumbling, hitting the road for the path—I saw myself walking off the road (or truck highways) down a secret forgotten path through rocks and bushes into trees, rediscovering the Law of Old.

Even the details are unfamiliar and have faded, and around the map I've gone, and it's all in the mind—even now I know that—even then I knew that—

Headed for the Western Road with about $50 and faith in my Lord.

FIRST TWO RIDES

Arrangements were (grim faced) for me to run Neal's parking lot in San Jose, for butter bread and beans. So I had a job ahead of me though I secretly knew that inside six months, somehow, I'd be begging door to door and longbearded with my begging pot.

I took the bus to Washington at icy midnight, walking off at dawn towards the Virginia bridges. En route ate Cream of Wheat breakfast (with toast) in busy lunchroom where I walked out without paying. Buddha gotta watch his pennies, Christ gotta eat. It was pale, dirty snow, the George Washington monument, horror everywhere.

It was rush hour to work, ten thousand automobiles automaton-like passing, eyes to the morning east. No room even for me to walk on the bridge. I crossed on the grass on a curve. I was sorry I had left my quiet and comfortable room at home to go goof in the real mornings of the world with ideas in my head about the inexistence of anything.

Resolutely I stared through the cars and they werent there. Behind the bleak red terror of the railroad tracks, where engine puffed steam into Ice Dawn Hole, I knew was the Shining Pure Land, so I alternated between fear and inside secret belief.

Fear and belief—Then a car stopped for me and I ran for it, thinking, "I will convert this man by my telepathic silence conveying holy peace forever."

But he was a talkative one, a salesman from Alexandria, talked about real estate boom, Washington, laws—took fatherly interest in my education and background—didnt give a damn about real or not real, delusion, illusion, shmillusion—had wife and kids, proud to be talker, felt that life was 'doing him alright' when all's said and done—good quiet man, maybe a Bhikkhu, a secret saint of India reborn in America with no arbitrary conceptions of anything, completely un-ignorant in his perfect Ignorance. At intervals I relaxed the knot in my belly and closed my eyes and sank in, and he quietly drove, and I radiated immensely bright messages—"All is well—realize your own essence of mind—be quiet—there—sleep—sleep with me—in God's Ecstasy—in—the pure snowflakes—in Transcendental Empathy—in Universal Brotherly Shivering Joy—rest."

He got no such messages but the message indescribable. There was coffee and toast in his gray mornin hat. When he left me in the highway I stood alone in the northern cold contemplating the back of his car, smiling. Twelve miles south, near a Howard Johnson. I went in and had coffee. I looked weird. I combed my hair.

Everything was happening everywhere in the world with the same lack of intensity and the same general melted-candleness of time.

I got my next ride from a Negro truckdriver (talked a little about jazz) whole long silences with grave thighs bouncing to the truck were pure indication that my radiating silence was working in on him. I blessed, I prayed, I instructed. He took me to Richmond.

It was warmer, noon. I was shaky all over from the truck. "In search of peace I'm going through hell," I realized, and then I was in the middle of nowhere.

DOWN TO SANFORD

Next ride was a Richmond plumber who had ulcers, I found out why. "Always did wanta go to Florida."

"Why dont ya?"

"What? They only get 1.69 an hour down there—we get 1.89 here—"

"You got ulcers because you're worryin about that 20 cents," I didnt dare say, saying instead: "Quiet down your belly, sit still, think nothing."

"Hell I'd go mad thinkin nothin."

"No you wont—it'll heal your belly"—"everything's already all right," I coulda said—He was a funny old goat, talked of laying women (him 65), talked a lot—wouldnt believe me—But when I got out of his car I felt good. "That man will remember some of this."—"I let him into ancient secrets and he seemed surprised." He dropped me off at the James River Bridge where I converted my $50 into travelers cheques.

Warm sun. Ride right away, from a car dealer. "This new car just got in Norfolk. Brother behind me. Way behind. We drivin the two cars down ta Sanford."

"Where?"

"Sanford, s'where I'm goin." In North Carolina, deep down on Route One.

I thought "Ole holy Bhikshu is makin time now, halfway into No Carolina in one day." Not realizing, the Law of Old works its own way for its own illumined results.

It was dark in Sanford, almost, so I got a room in the railroad hotel. Railroad hotels, when you find em, always best place to sleep and rest. Always cheap, clean, quiet. Always near railroad. Only noise is the slam-by extra special Be Jamboreeing old number firstclass Freight-Train, with caboose red at rear, when the 3-unit Diesel balling that pack down the track comes air-whistling electronic wild baughs by your open window at night, when dew's on the roofs of the chickenfields—that's less disturbing than bawdy parties in the next room.

The Buddhist Years   203

With the leftovers of a halfpint brandy brought for my midwinter New York cold, I sat in the bed celebrating. Slept. Dreamt of Eddie Fisher—Eddie Fisher the young Jewish crooner with a brunette girl for me, whom I feel.—Wake up with the taste of her lips.—Holy Man has man-dreams. "Wow," I think in the night in the Sanford North Carolina sad southland hotel room in midwinter still, "you cant get away from life. Sit and meditate too long, your legs hurt. Away from women, your all body hurts and swells up. You got big boy propensities to get rid of 'fore *you'll* be a saint"—and I know it. And I grind my teeth. Maybe drink, finish the bottle. "Aw, and I left poor Ma to herself, again, she comes home at night with a smile on her face—" the long long story of Jacky Duluoz the kid from Lowell who became a football player then defected to writer then got married twice and stayed poor and spent what little riches he had, and sad, the saddest longfaced brooder-in-rooms in America (as perhaps fitting for young American writer type) but also gay crazy fool with the drinkers, fighting his way like *borracho* Mexican drunk through the haze of that dubious gift called Mortality we all enjoy this Christmas. "Spiff, spaff," I'll make it to my California dryland blues, burn woodfires by the track, cook up cornmeal mush, brown sugar, and beans—saltpork—I can take care of myself like an Indian and spend all the day meditating on Buddha's truth."

And I curl up my legs, closing window so as to hear the silence, which shushes at once in the walled room,—and lean against pillow of recent sexy dream—lights out—fall, hands a-clasped, into instantaneous ecstasy like a shot of heroin or morphine, the gland inside of my brain discharging the good glad fluid (Holy Fluid) as I hap-down and hold all my body parts down to a deadstop trance—Healing all my sicknesses—erasing all—not even the shred of a "I-hope-you" or a Loony Balloon left in it, but the mind blank, serene, thoughtless. When a thought comes a-springing from afar with its held-forth figure of imagery, you spoof it out, you spuff it off, you fake it, and it fades, and thought never comes—and with joy you realize for the first time "Thinking's just like not thinking—So I dont have to think any more." And you think no more on the lilypad lotus of the bed in a paid hotel room, but then comes the jolt of "reality"—"I've got to leave here tomorrow and move on—how can I stop thinking?" Then you know, you hate to admit, "I get up and I walk out of here, without money, without anything but whatever clothes I chance to put on, warm but not complete outfit, just the rags and the tatters of shame, and go in faith that my supper will come."

I picture myself leaving the raincoat, the pack—the packet of travelers checks—walking out into Route One at Sanford, going forth in faith with no hope. With a smile. Suddenly turn aside and run in.

Can't do it.

Gotta compromise.

"No—I will stay as I am, be a saint anyhow—with my clothes, with my money—Later I'll give up everything and go to India—on foot over the water—"

NO RIDES

You cant disturb the serenity of the ego of the saint-believer. I saw saints in that early meditation, as in others. The swarms of wild whitelights you see in the blackness of darkness, so you dont know if it's darkness or bright, must be both—Transcendental Sight of No Objects—I saw each of them, without numbering, a waving saint—sight of which manifested to me via mental lights by big Decider of my Fate—Lord Karma, Supreme Reality.—What difference to me that a damn old train's crashing by, years later I re-harken and remember the noise—"Ojos, forget to listen"—Sitting in my room, mild, gentle in Non-Thinking, till thoughts fought through and defiled the mind again and I returned to "practical concerns" in the very trickery of this universal illusion.

The millions of piteous and interesting images of light swarming in the closed eye, that's where I wanted to go.

"Will come to you like it came to Pa," I thought.

"All I gotta do is hitch hike to California and sit under the stars at night and all that I ever lost will come back to me—This I believe."

So in the morning I cut out, went for big breakfast of sausages and grits and eggs and toast and syrup and jam and even asked for homefries, fortifyin for the road. Felt good. Combed, handsome in my sidebooth mental selfmirror. "Okay." All good. Felt like strong traveler. Felt respect of others seeing me. Paid bill and swung out. Little cold sniffle. Buy Benzedrine inhalers for that. Stand by road. Pointed South. "The snowless Southern road, or I'd freeze in Wyoming." "Tryna get to sunny Californy—"

The Buddhist Years

Boom. It's the awful raincoat making me look like a self-defeated self-murdering imaginary gangster, an idiot in a rueful coat, how can they understand my damp packs—my mud packs—

"Look John, a hitchhiker."

"He looks like he's got a gun underneath that IRA coat."

"Look Fred, that man by the road."

"Some sexfiend got in print in 1938 in Sex Magazine."

"You found his blue corpse in a greenshade edition, with axe blots."

Gay college students driving by. I spend, boom, the entire day from 8 AM till hot 4, and no ride outa Sanford North Carolina.

By which time, eight hours on that road with everybody staring angrily at you, cops included, I'd come across a lot of forgotten pre-Buddhist gurls, and growls cursing disapproval, and swearing.

"Ah Jack, now it's all done—where's your line of merit, measuring, those people aint real, that they dont give you a ride or DO give you a ride is sumptin goin on in unreality—reality isnt rides—reality didnt leave New York and aint goin to California."

My feet hurt, cold—too. I tried to console myself on the road. The road to the path. "There's the path, right there—right here in Sanford—that yard, that glen of leaves, that sunsplash, that forgotten memory, that old road home—"

I combed my hair and removed my muffcap and still no rides. I blasted them with back fire, "Ah you're only two guys, whattaya men or mice afraid to pick one guy up"—"Oh you bitch, all the women in America have the cars now"—Remember, too, rueful memories of early hitch hikings as romantic moonlight harmonica youth of clicketyclack railroad fence blues—"Now I'm just a gripin ole miser"—Weary, weary, I was going through all this in the search for peace.

Late in the afternoon I walk down the long hill south side of Sanford and go up a long rise, and eat an ice cream, and am standing staring at a mysterious pleasantness in the grass by the road reminding me of other lost lives I must have had, car stops for me. Big tough trooper on vacation, I think—because I had my railroad lamp hidden under my coat, at my feet, and he Hawkeye watched when I bared it—if it had been a machete, I think I woulda got a clap in the kisser pretty hard.—Seeing I hid no weapon, he talked. "See that house," as we fly by, "whole family of six went out driving last Sunday, all of em killed in a head-on crash. Just goes to show you. That there house is just as empty as the day it was finisht." I watched that sad house on the hill, under the dream. He drove fast. To Southern Pines. He reminded me of old boyhood hero who boxed in my father's gym, Armand, the rocky sorrowing face, the glittering instantaneous eyes, almost laughing at you for some secret reason—so overwhelmed me I made no attempt to transmit message of truth, by now too tired. Too human with too foot feet.

Southern Pines where he leaves me off is a paradise of warm tranquil sun and thousands of sighing little pines. "Why should I go any further?—"

The Buddhist Years

The Little Sutra[171]

THE LITTLE SUTRA

All living things are already Buddhas of perfect love and intelligence because they are No-Things. They seem to arise, abide, and pass away, but their Essence was Undisturbable from beginningless time and into the infinite present and into the endless future. "The Buddha perception and understanding is inherent in every sentient being." Argue no more.

As to other shore, this world, enlightenment, ignorance, who ever told you it was anything but a dream? Ignorance and Enlightenment, like Existence and Non-Existence, are the same thing. The reason why I said it was "unreal" was not to confuse you with the ultimate (therefore actual present) teaching that things are neither real nor unreal. Does it fit the case to question whether a bubble is real or not?—since it is impermanent, infelicitous, and devoid entirely of ego selfnature, the question of its reality or unreality is child's dumbshow. The inside of a bubble is neither empty nor non-empty. Though we may say Ignorance is the pencil that writes, and enlightenment the pure empty page the perfect potential light of which allows and makes available dark writings, nevertheless, the light that is everywhere, Essence, the Golden Silent Oneness of Reality is undisturbable whether there are pencils, empty pages, non-pencils, non-emptypages, ignorance, or enlightenment. So in your dream, "How can I be enlightened when there is neither enlightenment or Ignorance?" yes, there is no definite teaching to be made about the indefinable and the Unteachable, but to return to ignorant attachment to ego selfness after realizing this is like the stupid dreamer all drowsy and darkly fettered by conditions and thoughts who having awakened from the high cliff that he was afraid to fall off of, re-sleeps and re-finds himself scared again. This is the White Bullock Buddha Vehicle teaching of the Golden Central Stillness. The rest is illusion. In other words,

---

171   This ms. is part of Columbia University's Allen Ginsberg Papers archive, and it is specifically addressed to Ginsberg.

"Lucienesque Reality"[172] is illusion and Buddhahood is Tathata, Actual Is-ness, the cessation of Illusion. (In Reality there is no Illusion Anywhere.)

> Ripples on the sea (read my stanza, Chinaman)
> are no more illusion
> than the sea,
> but when the wind dies
> where do the ripples go?
> the ripples are the thoughts of your life
> the sea is Mind Essence
> beyond thoughts of life
> or non-thoughts of death.

Tathata, means, Essence, suchness; "gata," means, "farer, arriver," "He Who Has Arrived at Actual Isness" is the meaning of Tathagata.

As for your Chaplinesque Love, it is a lot of Lust. To be frank with you, I'm disgusted by Western Cupidity Hypocrisy. Why dont they come right out with it and admit the knifelike cock and the gashlike hole is what they mean by "love" and nothing could be less like love. The perfect love-filled imagelessness of Samadhi is "Not-Two"-ness. It's nothing but the Great World Snake.

Havent you heard what our Buddha of this part of the dream (world) said to a beautiful whore called Lady Amra? (who wanted to be a Bhikku)—"You seem well-talented as you are beautiful. That one, so gifted, should by faith be able to receive the law of righteousness is, indeed, a rare thing in the world…that a woman, weak of will, scant in wisdom, deeply immersed in love, should yet be able to delight in the holy path…(to his Disciples: Loathe and put away the form of woman")—[173]

Now if Chaplin ran along singing "cock cock cock it's cock cock-cockcock…cunt—it's cuntcunt it's cunt cunt cunt cunt cunt" and you had sung That to Jamie and Cathy,[174] I would be less inclined to disapprove over the camp of it.

---

172 A reference to Lucien Carr, who was dismissive of Kerouac's Buddhist ideas.

173 Kerouac is quoting from LOB 255–56, replacing the word "piety" with "the holy path." See also SOD 123.

174 Jami and Cathy Cassady, Neal and Carolyn's daughters. In 1954, when Kerouac wrote this, Cathy was six years old and Jami, five.

The Buddhist Years

When the time was come, it was a holy day, on the fifteenth day of the month, on the last autumnal plain full-moon night the Exalted One took His seat in the midst of the assembly of monks under the canopy of heaven. And the Exalted One beheld the silent, calm assembly of monks and spoke to them as follows: "Not a word is spoken, O Monks, by this assembly, not a word is uttered O Monks, by this assembly, this assembly consists of pure kernel.

"Such is, O Monks, this fraternity of disciples, such is, O Monks, this assembly, that, O Monks, there are among these disciples some monks who are Perfect Ones, who have reached the end of all illusion, who have arrived at the goal, who have accomplished the task, have cast off the burden, have won their deliverance, who have destroyed the fetters of existence, and who, through supreme knowledge, have liberated themselves."[175]

175   Kerouac is quoting from the "118th Discourse" (BB 74). See also WU 69–70.

The Blessedness Surely To Be Believed[176]

Version 1

Frontspiece

"An exhortation given to the exceedingly corrupt makes no impression, but, like a mark drawn with a stick on the surface of the water, it immediately disappears."[177]

~~The Happy Truth~~

The Blessedness Surely-to-be-Believed

PRAYER

I Bless all living and dying things in the endless past;

I Bless

all living and dying things

in the endless present;

I Bless

all living and dying things

in the endless future,

amen.[178]

> They do truly abide
> in ecstasy and extinction

Wherewhence   Whereall   Whereinall (Where-in-all)   Wherewhence[179]

---

176   This is another of Kerouac's often-repeated phrases. See SOD 369 et seq., SGE verse 18, DA 32, DB 102, DP 60, 104.

177   The quote is from "The Birth of the Buddha" (BIT 40).

178   Versions of this prayer appear multiple times in Jack's published work. See SOD 342 et seq., VOG 70, DB 123.

179   This is the end of the first page (title page) of Version 1. Two more pages follow with the final paragraph appearing at the top of the third page. Kerouac crossed out the next page with a big "X" (not obscuring any of the writing), and he did not cross out the following pages, so he seemingly reconsidered, and this version is worth preserving.

The Buddhist Years

The Ecstasy of Life and Death

ECSTASY FOR ALL

The Nature of Reality
Why Life and Death?
Happiness for Everybody

THE HAPPY TRUTH

To be frank, my human readers,
Three things you can be sure of: our life wont last, there will be physical and mental misery in it, and it lacks true realness at the base.
In what way does it lack true realness?

One, as a thing of time; because in time our life will come to an end, therefore it is already ended; a little more time and a few more years has nothing to do with the truth that life finishes at some time or other.

~~Two,~~ Our life lacks true realness as a thing of experience; if it wasnt for our possession of the six senses by which we see with our eyes, hear with our ears, smell with our noses, taste with our tongues, feel with our bodies, and think with our brains, there would be nothing experienced, no life, nothing felt, just an absolute untroubled blank, like empty space.

Life lacks true realness as a thing; its objects and phenomena are made of atoms and yet the atoms are empty right down into the middle infinity; the more powerful the microscope the more the forms are discovered to be empty; clearly, our life and the universe is an endlessly empty arrangement of ghost-forms that keep appearing and disappearing altho the inconceivably pure emptiness the forms are made of, wasn't, isn't, and will never be disturbed.

The happy truth is the truth to be realized deep within your own mind. All's well from the very beginning, all is blissful and perfect and delivered to the original source. First you've got to clear away the ignorance of mind.

Why? Why these living and dying things in endless time and endless space? The very asking of the question Why by existent beings is ignorance of mind itself. Empty space doesnt ask why. Look above at the endless skies, be mindful of the ten directions of space, try to think to the limits of the ten ways where the void goes off forever. There is no Why, except that our mortal mind has invented it.

There is no Why because there is no true realness in things and in the asking Why concerning their appearance. If you see the sun fall thru the leaves, *it's your fault*. It is only in time, and with our senses, and by virtue of false appearances of forms that are empty within, that things and life seem to exist and give our minds the illusion of true realness.

Time is not real; we think that because an empty form appears in our apparatus of six-senses, then disappears from our apparatus of six-senses, that there was a before and an after to [be] measured in between the two, called time. What is this false, arbitrary, made-up measurement but a toy thought?

Space also, is a false arbitrary division drawn in the emptiness to measure the separation of two apparent things that are not even truly real. The stars are imaginary separation. The distance from Tit to Tat is Nil. Tit tat.

Version 2[180]

The Blessedness Surely to be Believed

Jack Kerouac

[I]

Deep within your own mind, as soon as the ignorance of your mortal notions has been cleared away, mental ecstasy reappears as clear as a crystal and as perfect as open space.

This immeasurable happiness of your original perfection is already there because it has always been there. You've been like a person who thought north was south, and south was north, and was going exactly the wrong way. You believed in the absolute realness of the circumstances that contributed to your unhappiness without realizing absolutely equally that they were as real as they were unreal, which would have given you pause to reconsider the scenes of your grief.

There is a blessedness surely to be believed. Under stress of harsh circumstances, smile and think deeply, there is a sudden center of enlightenment that has nothing to do with what you're experiencing in life. That is so, because the experience of life with its shortlivedness and pain and dreamlikeness is one thing, and the rediscovered permanence of unending mindgladness is another. This beatitude, this gladness is indeed no thing but the essence of thingness. It is the ecstasy of form, the 'stuff' the world is made of. One atom—and all things including air are made of differently

---

180   This version begins immediately below the end of Version 1 with the title in bold face: large lettering copied over at least twice in blue ink whereas the rest of the text is written in pencil.

The Buddhist Years

arranged atoms—is made of the same common stuff as another atom. All things take place and act out their coming and going, their living and dying, as atomic forms in the same bright sea of the mysterious stuff of mind which some call the Mind of God, some call God, some call the Body of the Law of the Truth. All existing things and all that has not yet formed or has lost its form, partake of it and are perfectly it.

All appears magically as in a three-dimensional movie in a crystal bowl, and has no more substantiality than a movie or a dream, being but images, imageness made up of empty atoms. The more powerful the microscopes of we human scientists have become, the more we have seen into the unending emptiness of the forms that our eyes had taken to be substantial and real. It is neither to be said to be real nor unreal...words words. To invent the word "unreal," it was necessary in the beginning to have the word "real," neither of which makes sense. Real or unreal, it's a dream because it makes no sense to call a dream a "real dream" or an "unreal dream."

We all have our mortal mind, which is like ripples, and the immortal mind, which is like a sea upon which the ripples appear and disappear. Alive, our ripple appears; dead, our ripple disappears; but the sea of mind ecstasy remains, and, but, and therefore, you cannot separate the water of the ripples from the water of the sea, it is all the same mysterious stuff.

The blessedness surely to be believed is that we all are the same, and perfect. Every dog has already had his day.

II

It would be extremely hard to write a book explaining the essence of the world without boring some readers. That's why I want to approach the subject with stories and illustrations and the use of unusual phrases. This book is addressed to all the people in the world.

Question One: How do I know the truth of what I'm saying?

The answer is, how can I even claim that what I'm saying is either true or untrue, since the word "untrue" had to be invented after the word "true" and they are equally words. Since words are relative expressions, it doesnt fit the case to say "This is a true relative expression" and "This is an untrue relative expression." The fact that I'm saying what I'm saying has only to do with the vow to speak. This vow to speak was handed on to me like a flame from torch to torch by the religious heroes of the past, obeying in the awakened spirit.

The vow to speak-and-explain is an illusion that issues from the source of things, and all things are illusions except the source, which is the mindstuff. The mindstuff is in perpetual joy, undisturbed and serene, allowing ignorant forms to take shape and dissolve again while itself has never budged, changed, or moved, or altered one whit. It's like drawing a circle in the water, the essential liquidity of the water has never been dissolved, its potential to fold right back again has never been disturbed. Water is water whether you leave it alone in peace or thrash wars within it. So whether a religious hero vows to speak or not to speak, in the awakened spirit or not, the basic stuff is not concerned. A religious hero vows to speak to other living beings only to point this out to them. Living beings are not to take the mere *words* of the religious heroes as the basic stuff itself: the basic stuff is neither awake nor asleep and for that reason doesnt need to be awaked. The basic stuff is eminently pure bliss, and so are we in the central entirely of our minds when we become awakened from this dream of pain.

III

"dreary bliss" (Chapter in Red Dharma Notebook (8))[181]

IV

"consciousness" (Chapter in Red Dharma Notebook (8))[182]

V

I have been sent on a holy mission. It is to teach everyone that they're already in Heaven here and now on earth. It takes no great mental effort to know this. Just realize that everything you see is in your own mind, and Heaven is your own mind.

---

181   See SOD 371–72: Kerouac is likely referring to the section following the heading "SAMADHI OF JANUARY 1, 1956" beginning "The dreary bliss of eternity" and ending either with "amen" or the two postscripts. The SOD version is only slightly altered from the version in the Dharma (8) notebook (Berg 49.9): "Samsara" is capitalized, the word "groups" is twice changed to "groupings" (first lower case and then capitalized), and the phrase "nothing ever happened" is added.

182   See SOD 371: Kerouac is likely referring to the section beginning "WHY, TO ASK *WHY* is an act of consciousness" and ending "Buddhas neither appear nor disappear." This time also the SOD version is only slightly altered from the version in Dharma (8): "samadhi" is changed to "Samadhi ecstasy," the words "or imaginary judgments or decisive ideas of phenomena" are added, and again in all three cases the word "Groups" is changed to "Groupings."

The Buddhist Years

You say, "I am looking at this book; how can you say that this book exists in my own mind? All I have to do is call you over and you will verify its existence too."

But who said there was a difference between your mind and my mind? There is only one space. Different houses make different rooms, but there is only one space. In the same way different selves make different viewpoints, but there is only one mind. This is what is meant by Universal Mind.

Like space, your Universal Mind is perfect and unchangeable and illimitable and eternal and therefore blissful. In other words, is Heaven, Nirvana. For Heaven cannot be separated from hell nor hell separated from Heaven. Whether you call earth a heaven or a hell, it is inseparable.

The wisdom of *knowing* this is the path, but This Itself is Heaven, or, the wisdom of knowing wisdom is the path, but, what wisdom seeks to know, is Heaven.

Beat Generation

BEAT GENERATION   Tangiers March 26 1957

Silence is a diamond, it cuts through the fury of the generations, and when the generations are done, silence is still a diamond, and was ever so—

This story begins in 1951 when I tried marriage with a girl who just didnt love men[183]—so Lucien came one night and moved me out, I limped with boxes of books and manuscripts and finally my whole rolltop desk and I put it all in his car, parked outside in the rain while Lu sat yakking with my wife, coming to the conclusion, as we drove away, "Kerouac, methinks you tried to marry over your head"—"What you mean?"—"Boy, you tried to improve your lot with what I guess *you* thought was a fancy doll" (the inexpressible sadness of Lucien's voice when he talks like this and when he says 'doll')—"Ah Kerouac—" "So what do I do now?" I say, and Lucien shrugs, like a man whittling a stick—"You can move into my loft and stay as long as you want and I spose the Good Lord'll let you stay on earth long as you want but boy with that fucked up psyche of yours it is not an enviable thing to see—sad Jack" and laughing—So we drive to his loft on 27th Street near 7th Avenue and stagger up the four flights to his big dirty crazy loft where I pile all my books and manuscripts about ten feet high from desk top to ceiling and Lucien, getting drunk, says: "And I should knock all that down and there wouldnt be nothing left of you, boy"—Truer words never spoken—But I was in the way of finding that I could love God in a dew instead of furying ignorantly in the world and it would take another six years or more (1951 to 1957) to finally calmly make it—These events that I am about to narrate being the sequel of my adventures *on the road* with Neal, and even more hopeless and love lost and silly—but the way up the silver dove's ladder to heaven is a mighty sad and dirty ladder, boy—

It was about this time that Lucien and Allen, both wearing full mustaches, were deciding on the trip to Mexico, and I was to come along— but this whole story would have been entirely different, were it not for

---

183   The "girl" is Kerouac's second wife, Joan Haverty (1930–'90). The two married in November 1950 and separated the following June.

The Buddhist Years

Doc Perrone down in the Village, to whom I went for a shot of penicillin for my limp—"Jack, you're very seriously ill with this thrombophlebitis of yours—for one thing you've got to stop smoking—and not only that I'm sending you to the hospital" and he writes me out the necessary papers to have me admitted in the Kingsbridge VA Hospital that very night[184]—so I go reluctantly losing our "wild trip to Mexico" and that night, after lights out, lying in bed contemplating the ceiling and the silence of the sick sleepers, suddenly I realize: "God intended I stay and be quiet here instead of mad trips again and again to nowhere—I have nothing to do but rest and remember the folly of my life and maybe something will come of it and I be reborn in repentance and recall"—true, and that first night the nurse brings me a message from Lucien, written by Allen: "Leaving for Mexico tonight—be a good angel"—And I think how typical it is of my life that silly messages follow me everywhere making me look like a fag in the eyes of simple people and I think "I'm well rid of the whole generation"—the whole generation being Lucien (whose elbow was broken by cops who arrested him for screaming *sanctuary* in a Protestant church on Fifth Avenue a few months ago, who'd broken a beerglass in a soldier's face in my company and we got beat up by six hoodlums as our other friends watched and one laughed)—being Allen, whose misadventures included arrest for harboring robbers and their loot in his room, the madhouse afterwards, the night in Harlem in 1947 when he screamed at me demanding that I beat him up—being Neal, with whom I'd raced around the country like fiends looking for girls and pot and jazz, all ending in gray exhaustion and probably my present disease—being Huncke, always in jail, always greenfaced on Times Square—being Bill Burroughs, arrests, narcotic addictions, silly cutting off of his little finger in a hotel room, and about to shoot his wife in the brow[185]—being his wife, Joan, benzedrine addiction that blackened and dropped all her teeth, exposed her to polio, made her an alcoholic—being all these and many more—But it would take me many more years to quit them and find God in that dew, the dew on one leaf of grass in my little final yard, where I'd learn to delight in life and forbear sorrow and believe in joy.

---

184   Kerouac entered the hospital in early August and was discharged on September 12, 1951.

185   In the typed version, after "about to," Kerouac changed "shoot his wife in the brow" to "battle Arabs with knives in the alleys of Tangiers."

The ocean rolls on and so the night is drenched with rain—I lay there in the hospital midnight listening to the rain gurgling in the gutters of New York, off the rooftops, down the drainpipes, down into holes, out to the river, the rain, the rain, all humanity inside rooms with bent heads of shame ruing their foolishness, the rain silencing the fury, the mountains grimly rolling rain down, the rivers maw-ing to the sea, the sea washing, washing, on the shore, on the liquid Whitman shore of America whose beauteous song I want to sing, all over America on Saturday Afternoon the beautiful song I hear, the simple people—my whole life among the vain and arrogant intellectuals and bohemians and subterranean fools a waste, a foppery, a pointless buffoonery—I now come out and make this confession to the world and to my eventual son how foolish I have been, we all have been, this silly *beat generation* about which nevertheless the story'd best be told then put away—Because a greater day is coming, the day of the diamond silence which wont at all be *day*, or *night*, but paradise—And I dedicate this story to Avalokitesvara.

In my ward was a man named Kaiser who knew that he was going to die, he had leukemia—he was just an ordinary like some newspaper driver banging around 43rd Street in back of the Paramount, having a beer with the boys, raising the glass to thirsty foamlips, wearing spectacles, rednosed, simple—"Yeah, I wont be here long—my son[186] visits me on Sundays—That's the way she goes" almost cheerily—and as I write this Mr. Kaiser's long been dead and no more ships for him except the heavenly ship—My bed was over on the corner, with a view of the hospital yards and all the Bronx which I imagined to be Babylon on lazy afternoon[s] what with men and women everywhere reading newspapers and walking around and having arguments in rooms—In the peace and purity of the bed, I got to vision man essentially as someone with a hat walking around with a newspaper, is what I mean—Wash waving on rooftops, and the peculiar keen joy I felt on Saturday morning to see the American-flagged old fort (remembering George Washington)[187]—Mr. Kaiser would just amble up to my bed for a daily talk, nothing much, that I dont remember any more I accuse myself

---

186   The typed version ends here.

187   Fort Cockhill, located in Inwood Hill Park, built by the Continental Army during the Revolutionary War, is located west of Kingsbridge Heights, the location of Bronx Veterans Hospital (now the James J. Peters Department of Veterans Affairs Medical Center).

of the sin of neglecting poor time—in the hospital O God I should have scribbled holy loving notes about every one of those poor dogs—"How is she today?"—"O, the swelling's going down, I'll be able to walk soon"—"Well I hope so kid"—That's all. And across from me the poor old Jew (Rumanian) who reminded me of Seymour[188] and had *cancer of the brain* and also was dying, would moan then asking Jehovah why, remembering all his life in Rumania and America *why*—who saw I had an appetite and kept sending over his desserts and often his eggs or even whole dinners—"Go," he'd say with open palms, "I cannot eat it, I'm old and dying."—And the worst sufferer of all, old Italian fellow, who had the disease my own father'd died of, Banti's disease, all his food changed to water and swelled in his belly and he had to be tapped regularly (they'd stick a tube into his poor belly and let it piss out, which relieved him, nay *gladdened* him and gave him new hope so's he could return to his *Daily News* his softboiled eggs for a few more days, uddered out like a big sick Picasso nightmare cow, no more moo at dusk, the farmer's come and satisfied the pail—

When I was a boy of 18 just starting in to write, one summernight in long-ago Lowell, a moth came and blatted about my night lamp and I carelessly belted it, killing it, I found it dead in the morning by my old iron book-ends and felt the horror of what I'd done, writing a story about the moth (a "Hemingwayan" I thought story, 'dignified huge dead moth by the Karmak pillars')[189] but now as I was just writing about the old dying Italian a moth here in Tangiers came and tried to light on my two candles and was swiftly killing itself—so in honor of the moth I put the candles out, for must we repeat in this Shining Pleasure Ship called the world all the meat-dead dying again and again? In honor of the moth my holy candles burn no more but this story can go on.—

Another patient was a typical American character, the martyr of our culture, the ulcer patient, who smokes too much, drinks too much, talks too much, never sleeps, is nervous, greedy, mad, sad, full of bewildering anxieties and frustrated cravings up to here, who'd chat with me by the night light windows of the city, foolishly sad—"Why dont you relax?—arent you going

---

188   Seymour Wyse (1923–2015) was a lifelong friend. The two met while attending Horace Mann School in 1940–'41.

189   Kerouac is almost certainly referring to "The Dead Wasp," written in 1940 at age eighteen (see S-P 35–36).

to sleep tonight?"—"Oh man no, I'm too nervous"—with all his "when-I-get-out-of-here's" and "I-wish-I-had-ten-thousand-dollars" and similar yakking dreams that had worked down through his metabolism and yearned a knot of ulcerated pus in his living flesh—young fellow from Poughkeepsie, too fat too, who now, probably, is more miserable than ever because the river of joy does not flow for him (I guess no more than it does for me, for you)—"But make an *effort* to be happy!" I try to say to him—"No, no, I'm too nervous, I want too much"—"*What* do you want?"—"Well, I aint sure but gimme time and I can dream it up"—Whose grave's a restless image— Who went hunting and shot sweet birds in their Autumn wood, who did not appreciate the tender seriousness of his children, who yawned in his father's face, who burped over unnoticed meals, who will step aboard the gangplank of the Great Shining Ferry with his ashen sins engraved upon his skin, head-bent—"Surely God rewards us all," I think, seeing him, so plain and familiar a fellow-*guy* of America so fucked up and sad enuf to make you cry or puke, one—I see the twisted mouths of remorse leading off into infinite darkness, I hear the drumbeat of the funeral parade—"I *must* find the answer!"

The answer is always so simple and plain as I found one morning, just by leaning back glad on my pillow and reading the boxscores in the *Daily News*, just the name "Stanky" at the head of the New York Giants Lineup, making me think, "Ah, gray printed little name denoting a serious game of baseball and all the men with hats who went and dug it or read the boxscore in the papers, here is the peaceful everyday joy the ballplayer to his baseball, the worker to his job, the hospital patient to his little bed joys, the nurse to her chores, the President to his, the doctor to his tubes and scalpels, and the benighted poor Indian of old Manhattan (as he was) to his porridge in the gray drizzle"—Makes me happy, to think that life, and man, had an everyday simple even sweet regularity and mockfaced silence (no-comment), gladness, gravity—Which I saw exemplified in that sourpuss name *Stanky* belonging to a sourpuss little pepperpot shortstop who was making baseball history with his gut[190]—So that when the doctors turned me over and gave me a big shot of penicillin in the ass, it was all the gray activity under Gray Atlantic Clouds blowing over New York, the hot dog man to his hot dogs, the hospital patient to his bed thoughts (gained at the expense of needles

---

190   Eddie Stanky (1915–'99) played two seasons with the New York Giants (1950–'51) before finishing his career with the St. Louis Cardinals as a player-manager.

and pain, as Stanky gained his superb confidence on the field because of the horrors off the field in dreary street life)—But all the hats of the readers all over New York, seeing how he

	AB	R	H	PO	A	E
Stanky, s	4	2	1	4	3	0

had made his other day of swanky baseball keeping him in good trim—Yet now he, Stanky, is a hardware store owner in Peopaw Louisiana[191]—that's where the mighty marabuding Mississippi rolls, snake—(I see little Stanky running for a pop fly with his little ass out)—

"We'll take care of you, son, as soon as we can see what's wrong with you," the doctors said, and went upon an intensive campaign to learn the cause of my disease by pumping blood out of my veins every day, for study of prothrombin and general studies obtaining even from a horrible suck-up of me breast-of-the-bone marrow, which they extract cruelly by leaning on you with gentle words and yanking in a long superpowerful hypodermic that they hammer through yr bones the damn fools not realizing the cause of any disease is in God's Mind because everything is God—They study charts, Voltaire could tell you all about it—But so kind as they all stand around you and show you by their judged seriousness that society has good intentions and so you must forgive society, which is not out for your skin but only for the reward of your skin—

The visiting doctors watch as Doctor So and So kneads roughly in my leg—"Ah yes, hitcha surgical blace." Yes, they nod.—Like a bunch of fishermen around a boat—Yet it's all free treatment and their interest in my welfare is just as plain as the nose on your test tube, why should they complain if I

l i v e—?

Or weep if I die?—This boat cant hold that many, can it?—

When I was a kid I sometimes thought the world was but a show, put on to amuse me on my way to heaven, and I was the only one who was not yet in heaven and all the others were goosing me in—so sometimes when I turned my back, there they were, rigidly back in place, zipping back, fast,

---

191   Peopaw, Louisiana, does not exist. In the spring of 1957, when Kerouac wrote this, Stanky had moved from Minneapolis, where he had spent one year managing the Triple-A Minneapolis Millers, to join the coaching staff of the Cleveland Indians. He later spent fourteen years managing the University of South Alabama team in Mobile and died in Fairhope, Alabama, in 1999 at the age of eighty-three.

mum, mockfaced, pretending not to know that a minute of a moment ago they'd all been huddled there discussing me and laughing about me, gayly, absolutely without bitterness or strife, just angels discussing behind my back, till I turned around, then they snapped back into place, to keep on fooling me, so I wouldnt know that heaven was just around, because I had so much of more to earn—Good God, the earning ends sometimes soon.—So okay World, if I am the only one, you are the only One. Songs echo across the ages from the groves of India.

Now too I thought about it in the hospital, all the crutches and needles flying as nurses and patients zipped back into place as I turned, good old world going right along fooling me down the road—Me feeling like a little Negro Boy rushing down the southern highway to buy a popsicle at the corner crossroads store—Vast Oklahomas out there beyond the gray New York, and I could go fool around out there, working in mines in Butte, on construction jobs with big cats in the red sand of Mexico, on railroads in the Western night dew, which I did, after leaving the hospital—I began to think of Neal again, who was out west, standing by a mountain of black used tires in the mist of Colorado or West Kansas—I saw him ply the manure fork and skin horses in Arkansas (ugh) and all the bad feelings of my first night in the hospital were in peaceful neutralness.

For when people leave you alone, Joe, you learn to like the comforts of your sack and shack and back. And so you learn what old Thoreau knew, that God is in one pond, and on one flower, and raises but one speech in silence.—I was to learn all the secrets of the peacefulness of the hospital, in the woods later on, at night, under stars, under a tree, sitting thinking, stopping thinking, seeing light, more light, till all the night was bright with a swarming silver vision full of innumerable mist of shining Buddha-fish. Or any kinda fish, call em—

Hospital 1951, what a *drag* to look back on history of your own life (which is a History in itself, O archaeologists and grand historians of the world) and see the hopeless, utter awful hope within it, hopelessness, despair, gloom and general awful despondent bullshit of your latest dreams and latent balderbullshit balderdash crash the cat-is-gone feeling of stupid phooey death-in-life—(to put it one way)—I finally got my wheelchair and whee I raced around and had a ball, went to the toilet, took one-legged showers, chimed 32 tunes from the shower stall, and sang Frank Sinatra, nay *sank*

The Buddhist Years

Frank, with great renditions of "If You Are But a Dream"—towels, more towels, wiping up, big floppy pajamas, back in my wheelchair, back out to the ward where now the television had began to vibrate to the great winning streak of the New York Giants that copped them the pennant of 1951— Previous to my wheelchair privileges I'd snuck to the toilet every night anyhow, absolutely refusing bedpans, great gawd who wants a poor pretty nurse or ugly play with your bedpan ('full of the awful venom of our brunch,' I thought then, then 'not fit to add,' I thought, because what is stool, what is shit, but the very food you et with your big dreams of God as you chewed away, O beast of heaven)—At just this time too Frank Worthington the colored guy had begun to roam into our ward from his own, where there was no television, walking slow, bent over, hand on hip, "Artur-itis," he says, sings to the whole ward of twenty men in a strong blues yowl, "I got arthur-itis, and *neu*-ritis, and every kinda ritis—I'm *made* to be stand!—I got joints, locks, knots in my eyes!—I'm just comin in here to see what the New York *Giants* are making on the field—" —He rolls his wheelchair next to my bed, which is the nearest to the TV set, which is crowded about by other wheelchairs of watchers, smoke and talk, and at night the same for the fights, which I dont mean, sometimes I turn over and go to sleep on a dull fight then wake up at dawn, refreshed, rubbing my eyes, the bird is luting in the trees of the vast hospital lawn, where I'll go roll my wheelchair and watch the birds thrashing in the bushes, and see red morning bricks of Bronx, and the trees of the Hudson Heights, the good-enough old world of dew and sidewalk spitters goin to work, the crowds of hospital attendants arriving up the gate, Negroes, blond bully ex-Navy goats, tall thin junkies taking secret fixes from the drug cabinets, lounging Porto Rican hepcats who smoke tea after work and just before, who all come high to dig the hospital and help the sick and roll out big wheeled tray-trucks full of good three meals a day (with pay) (and at night they roll up goofballs, 'Take your pick, yellow ones, blue ones, red ones,' sleeping pills, enough to make a man go mad, my ulcer friend takes two a night, I take one every other night, reason for sweat sleeps for me, till I couldnt sleep, and stopped, then started again, and slept ever and ever again in the protection of society and the arms of my God)—

God is that which passes through all, and passes through *as*—

224

Jack Kerouac

And as for those who say that the present history of our world hangs in the balance, and God is an unimportant thing to talk about, I say only the history of yourself, your country, hangs in the balance.

And as for those who say that science has no boundaries, I say that God has no boundaries—And if you say science has boundaries, very well then, God has boundaries (which is the curve of your arms, the curve of the earth, the curve of the womb of the universe).

God is that which passes through all, and passes through as Frank Worthington sitting there in his wheelchair yelling at the ball game (Bobby Thomson at bat in a tense 9th inning),[192] as me in my bed, as the twenty men in the ward and all the extra watchers, as the watching itself, and the TV seen, as the seeing and the seen and the seer, as the empty space between us, in other words, *all*—Frank Worthington who told me he usually spent his time sitting on a doorstep in his Harlem neighborhood, on long sunny afternoons, with in his hand a beer bottle however filled with straight whiskey, which he drinks, digging the city, the people, the *action* in the street, everything, girls going by, children with jump ropes and songs ("Hunchback hopscotch, jump the rope"), the trucks, trade, hepcats on corners, "I dig the *scene*" says Frank "and everybody thinks I'm sipping beer—I'm a tailor by trade," he sits and sews suits—He is a vast natural poet of Harlem ready to blow songs about the morning noon and night of Harlem moon—Could tell you more mauve or *brown* stories about what happened in a bar, on a corner, in a ballroom, in a spare ribs shack on the corner of Lenox and so, and sing histories of characters with cue sticks, diamond rings, black fur collars, funerals, doves, moonshine, murder, broken glass and bits of love on rooftops and his own woeful legerdemain and haunted history family—we all know that—Yelling at the ballgame he is, when Willie Mays catches a hard line drive in right center on the dead run and spins around counterclockwise to come around and whip the throw home, catching the runner dead on the way from third (by 10 feet), wham, wahoo, he lets out the biggest blast of screaming mad American joy you ever heard in any oldtime saloon or yelling field beneath the alltime stars—"*Yes! Yes!* Will-lee *Mays*"—He done did it again!"—"A-gain and a-gain!"—"Whoo! Wow! Hey! Yes! That is *my*

---

192   The allusion here seems to be to Bobby Thomson's "Shot Heard Round the World," a ninth-inning walk-off three-run home run that won the three-game playoff for the Giants over the Brooklyn Dodgers on October 3, 1951.

The Buddhist Years

boy"—"Will-lee *Mays!*"—"Out at thee *plate!*"—and everybody else slapping their knees and chiefly it is such a fabulous play (now famous, that throw)[193] no one who understands baseball sport can fail to see the magnificent crazy act—a hubbub runs thru the hospital.

Yet at ten p.m. as I am wheeling my wheelchair from the basement to the elevator door, here they come, the attendants, rolling a new dead old man on a stretcher with wheels, profiled in shroud, to be dumped in the earth grain—"Ashes to ashes," says the nurse. "Some come in some go out, some come in dont go out, some do both, or neither, or either—I wonder where my Paraldehyde is tonight."

---

193   Kerouac seems to be referring to "The Catch," considered Willie Mays's greatest play, but if so the details of it are not presented accurately here. Mays's spin and throw didn't reach home plate, but it did prevent the runner on first base, Al Rosen, from reaching second, preserving the game for the Giants, which they later won in extra innings. "The Catch" would also be anachronistic, as it occurred on September 29, 1954 during Game 1 of the World Series, whereas the setting of this story is 1951, which was Mays's rookie season.

Avalokitesvara

The other night I had a vision of some kind, of [an] official about to make a speech and suddenly he goes cross-eyed and floats away like cardboard!—It's like Buddha laughing on Mt. Lanka,[194] contented as a lion, pleased, seeing that the fact the world is beautiful is a joke, clapping his hands, like Jimmy Durante,[195] like a giggling maniac Zen Tao lunatic from another planet another world system yowling happily and unhappily (what's the diff?) that everything will suddenly go cross-eyed and float away like cardboard!—It's all fact!—Electricity pours from his ears, his toes are hungled up pleased at his mandalan base, he exudes glee, his wisdom eye's a little cocked, his big head bats out magnetic waves crazy in every direction, suffering serious musical mortals wait with pained expressions for what comes next and suddenly

Bing!

Nothing's there!

Hey beautiful, the fact that you're beautiful is only a joke, mata nu a faca—*A child, a child*, hiding in a corner, paka, infolded in veils, in swirling shroud, and mystery, all tee hee, all earnest, all innocence with shining love, sweeter than birds, pure with pretty gleaming eyes and rosy lips and the crazy little tongue sticking out, all writhing and grimacing with phantasie and understanding and pickly tiddly fleshy little muscles, and eager bonies, and the possibility of fears. Ah dad, and humanity, amid all and among and alive all, swirling O unaware of dusky birds with disillusioned eyes flying nigh, upsidedown birds with small mouths open, birth O, flying nearer, come nearer, O but not now, hey wait, not now God—The child, giggly tiddly chidrers, unknows, yet best knows, Godly all-knows, Lord, the child, the child, it cries

"I SEE YOU...PEEKABOO..."

And when I had that waking dream the other night, the official flying away like cardboard, the whole world flew away, like a root, like legs of sages,

---

194   See fig. 2.

195   Jimmy Durante (1893–1980) was an American comedian, actor, and singer known for his raffish grin, large nose, and gravelly voice.

like basket disappearances, faces mawked everywhere and went crazy and went flurming off into space nobody knows where, I had it—MIND MAD—Because the child knows, soon's he wakes up everything'll go with it, the world will end in a splendid guffaw on Mt. Lanka—And for this midnight knowledge of the jumping diamond I owe it all to Avalokitesvara, Buddha's favorite long name—Who do you think was on that Cross reincarnate? Who else? *You!* YOU AVALOKITESVARA, READER!

> On the sidewalk,
>   a dead baby bird
> For the ants

The story of how I got to discover (re-discover) Avalokitesvara begins in November of 1953 when there you see me enveloped in gloom in my room wearing a Korean prisoner of war cap (they were selling them to painters and bums in Army Navy stores, my mother'd bought it, it was too small for my head, it peaked my crown, jealous as Joe Louis.[196] I walked in my tiny room measuring about twelve jazz notes by twelve with that November hat, wishing to die, because I had just been in love with my Subterranean doll (all noted down in THE SUBTERRANEANS of which chronologically this is the sequel) and I was 31 and when you gets volved and vulva'd pal in love lost at 31 that's when you begin to count the wrinkles in yr belly and soon snow's in your hair and you think "Now I want to die—I will sit in my room and wait to die—" For she'd 'cheated' on me and I was held up in the measureless pain of the sea of Samsara birth-and-death sorrow, done for, like Proust says when a man loses a woman it's always for the same tragic reason—so what'd I care about the romantic trucks of Texas any more, at the moon shining on Bowery spittle, or of red neons of Milner Hotel,[197] and all I see in the mirror is blue loss (angry blue eyes nowhere staring at pain pools, lost my love) and worse, I'd wanted to lose her, we always kid ourselves and say "O I lost my love" after we've netted the plan and—but that's all explained in T[HE] S[UBTERRANEANS] and all love stories. This present new story (brothers and buddies and sisters and sad girls) (?) is a love story *nonpareil* none like it

196   Joe Louis (1914–'81), nicknamed the Brown Bomber, was the world heavyweight boxing champion from 1937–'49. However, it's also possible that Kerouac is referring to Joe Hill Louis (1921–'57), a blues musician whose recordings in the early 1950s included the song "Jealous Man."

197   Formerly the Grand Hotel, built in 1868, the Milner Hotel was in Kerouac's day a cheap place to stay, located at the corner of 31st Steet and Broadway. It was designated as a New York City landmark in 1979 and was added to the National Register of Historic Places in 1983.

because when you fall in love with God you cant miss and that's because you cant miss yr reward and that's because you cant miss existing and O the utter holiness of being, O the utterance of being is holy, O holy night!—Let me rave and clap my hands, this is my book! Critics! take care!

> Voices of critics
>   in the theater lobby —
> A moth on the carpet

I'll hex you with haikus (haikus are little three-line poems)—Nobody from *Time* or *Life* can stop me now, go ahead and take my picture standing on my head, you think that'll stop me from standing on my head? I got my alto horn and I'm gonna leave that horn unblown?

> A whole pussywillow
>   over there,
> Unblown!

Clap! Clap! Here comes Charley Poonyak who lost his dream mind baby in Baltimore! Enough?

(2)

I lived in Richmond Hill Long Island, went to the public library crossing the November railyards to do so, on long boxcar lines shadows of boys listlessly playing at dusk, what'd they care of the sad lonesome 31-year-old love lost awkly down the cinders to his *Daily News*?—I'd stop and stare at the boxcars, hid[e] between them, alongside the couplers, and dream of New Mexico snows then I'd stop myself and say "No, stay in yr room and die—But what'd Thoreau say again?" and I'd go to the library to recapture the delicious bliss I'd had at 18 in wintry New England reading Henry David Thoreau's *Walden* and *Walking* and other books that had made me puff my pipe with contentment and consider future love affairs as being just like Dostoevsky novels 'good for me'—

> T'only means
>   that lark
> Was poor fool

Because because because a kid of 18 sees life as a movie and he's making a movie where nothing touches him, he's in the audience safe in the dark seat

The Buddhist Years

richness, knees on seat front—his eyes to the glittering screen (chewing Mr. Goodbars) that when the cowboy's shot (Burt Lancaster with Italian sleer jaw) *blam*, that's only Burt Lancaster getting shot in a warm show,[198] t's all to the good, and the kid is RIGHT, and you gotta reach 80 to realize it! Be a Chinese Immortal! Ride away on a dragon!

But there cant help being one sad eye among the three eyes of the Laughing Buddha.

(3)

And when you've been defeated in love all the beautiful tight-skirted girls in the library appear as symbols of your slobbishness, they chew gum and just *wait* for you to make an advance, they'll burn you down with that girl gum—So I curse them and look for Thoreau— There he is, varnished covers all about winter spring summer and fall, from his Journals, the stack of which is still unpublished in the basement of the millionaire on Park Avenue and Thirty-Sixth Street (pigeons crud on statues)—Clean-panted Thoreau, spindly bird dreck Thoreau, I take him home under my arm, re-cross the railyard, stop again, now it's cold and still and blue-black, the stars moan huge slivers at me, big givers—Indian givers, who only occasionally give—

I sit on the piles by the LIRR mainline and uncork this evening's quart of port and loft up big drinks to the shimmery night that shines in my eyes like a thousand million diamonds, no comparison with the tinsel star-eyed sidewalks in front of World Premiere Theaters—Embosomed in time is my salvation, then, because I already know about swarming diamonds.

(4)

Now don't blame the big serious face with which I walk back up the railyards, right under the yard lights, nodding saying hello to railroad men with that vague way indicating I'm a railroad man too (though they see the books), up to the tunnel, the little steps down to the street, over on Atlantic Avenue, the long fence, the big Milk Factory redbrick wall and neon, the hopeless corner where I cross the street in wintercoming winds, to the bleak twigs of trees in my front yard (rented two-room apartment with my mother), the outer door I open slowly, the hall, the inner door, pushing it open against my mother's pitiful bed where she lies on a fragrant pillow and you hear

---

198   Burt Lancaster (1913–'94) was one of the top male movie stars from the 1940s to the mid-1960s. He appeared in more than a dozen westerns including *The Unforgiven* and *Gunfight at the O.K. Corral*.

her rosaries rattling (the special blue rosaries with the silver genuine silver cross, on her birthday)—the television is still on to the eleven o'clock news: "Leave it on till the news is over," she says, as on every night, by the time Morgan Beebe's on the hockey scores she's snoring, every time, O laugh, laugh! Sad violins laugh! So I turn off the Chester Morris late show[199] and in the kitchenette heat water for tea and pour it into a little cracked teapot and take that with cup inverted to my bedroomette which measures 8 feet by 5, in which I can pull out the panel of my rolltop desk only when I'm seated, which I do, clicking on little lamp, putting on November Korean hat, turning on the zigzag nonsense of violin concertos on QXR[200] and then (since it just zigonnes) to the colored jazz stations where the piano bobs and the girls sing in late afternoon sheets right from the bed—Fit as the thrush warbler of the Seine for my studies of sober Thoreau, who quotes from some Latin or "Eurus ad auroram, Persidaque, Nabathaque recessit, et radiis juga subdita matutins" (sic)[201] when I see he wants us New England eyes to scan pure dawn, because he says "I want to live as tho every morning the sun rising were a challenge to me" (words [to] that effect)[202] and this leads me to study his rapidly penciled sketches, one written at night when the kids had been sledding and now all in bed, the umpteenth star quiet there—Avalokitesvara bends his compassionate head over these my little preliminary readings, *towards Him*—for then I come (and coming, pass on) to a vague mention about the "Hindoos" (as tho Thoreau was a Salem sea captain archaically spelling names his own rummy way)—*HINDOO* like

---

199   Chester Morris (1901–'70) was an American actor who made several successful films and played the lead character Boston Blackie in fourteen films in the 1940s. In the 1950s and 1960s, television stations' standard fare was to broadcast old movies, often referred to as "The Late Show" and followed by "The Late Late Show."

200   WQXR-FM was and remains a popular classical music radio station serving the New York metropolitan area.

201   The parenthetical "(sic)" is Jack's. The actual quote, from *Walden* ch. 17, reads, "As every season seems best to us in its turn, so the coming in of spring is like the creation of Cosmos out of Chaos and the realization of the Golden Age.—

'Eurus ad Auroram Nabathaeaque regna recessit,
Persidaque, et radiis juga subdita matutinis.'

'The East-Wind withdrew to Aurora and the Nabathean kingdom,
And the Persian, and the ridges placed under the morning rays.'" (244)

202   Kerouac was perhaps thinking of the following quote from *Walden* ch. 2: "Every morning was a cheerful invitation to make my life of equal simplicity, and I may say innocence, with Nature herself. I have been as sincere a worshipper of Aurora as the Greeks" (72).

molasses the heavy New England Malaga[203] reference to something distant, older yet than Jugurtha,[204] *Hindoo*—At the sight of the word HINDOO I see a turban, brown legs crossed, I see Mahatma Gandhi, I make a back mental note to read up on Oriental 'philosophy'—which leads me the following week to select a book from the rack entitled SACRED BOOKS OF THE EAST and come home the same way meandering in the railyards, pausing by the couplers, looking up, up, always up at the stars that before'd shined for me consoling through jail window, madhouse window, porthole, drunken field, telescope, tenement fire escape (under the stars crosslegged facing a girl in a T-shirt on Manhattan rooftop) (flat on my back in the sand with empty bottle) the star the star that shines for me, for thee—home the same way, under the yardlights, nodding to switchmen and car knockers, down the tunnel, the grit of November city streets, the hopeless avenue (long red sad lane for Sunday butterflies), my street again, the knocking trees, the twigs, the five stars among the twigs, the door—my mother in bed, "Leave it on till the news is over" ("Oui Ma")—the tea, my room, the lost hat—I open the book any old how to Asvaghosha's *Life of Buddha* because I'd seen the one sentence: "O painfully deluded man, seeing all coming to naught everywhere and still not moved, and yet is your heart stone?"[205] which unblocks an unmelted stone in my belly, the mystery of it, and another sentence: "As the birds that gather in a tree all day, and at sunset depart, so are the separations of the world!"[206] So I start reading about Prince Sakyamuni who grows up golden haired and favored, his father the Kind King, his mother delicately dead at his birth, his doting Aunt, his lovely young wife, his infant son Rahula, his horses and harem—and how suddenly he gives all this up as empty pain show, rides away at night on his great white horse, into the forest, with his favorite attendant, blond long hair flying, spurs digging, it's like an old dream I see him shining like a diamond riding out the Cinderella walls of the Maharajah's palace, from the embosomed elephant stone of gold he goes

203 Perhaps a reference to Malaga Island in Maine.

204 Jugurtha (b. 160 BCE) was a king of Numidia (in northwest Africa) from 118–105 BCE until captured and executed in Rome a year later.

205 The actual quote, from LOB, reads as follows: "Oh worldly men! how fatally deluded! beholding everywhere the body brought to dust, yet everywhere the more carelessly living; The heart is neither lifeless wood nor stone, and yet it thinks not 'all is vanishing!'" (37).

206 The actual quote, from LOB, reads as follows: "Like as in a wilderness on some high tree all the birds living with their mates assemble in the evening and at dawn disperse, so are the separations of the world" (66).

to dark fern forests and cuts off his hair with a sword, hands sword and horse back to servant Kandaka, makes a solemn speech of firm intention to attain to the knowledge that will save the world from this incessant living and dying routine! "Wow, how?" I think—

And now I know, it's a trick of the mind, not the knowledge alone but the living and the dying too! Ha-ha! Clap hands! Follow me down the misty road. I'll show you!

(5)

Nobody believed me as I made my initial studies. When I came out and explained it to them, my mother first off said "Boo*da*! Stick to yr own religion!" That's true, what's the difference between the matutining of Zenbos and Bumbos and Whicheverbos!

(6)

Because the young Buddhist starts out he's fascinated by the teaching that everything is emptiness which is something he's suspected ever since he was 16 years old (he thinks) but actually since babyhood crib wise, and he goes out and as I did sat there in the railyards contemplating the railroad iron convinced it was marshmallow and so it would serve me right if the world crucified me by 18 hoodlums picking me up and holding me stiff straight out like a battering ram and ramming me straight on into a Pennsylvania Railroad coal hopper, even tho I scream as they rush me along: "But whether my body is wrecked, has nature added anything to nothing or removed anything from nothing?" But a young Buddhist (a virgin Buddhist) becomes an old dry dharma-bone Buddhist and that is to say he becomes not-a-Buddhist, he becomes nothing, he becomes the mailman shouting hello to you at nine o clock in the morning, he becomes like everybody else already was!

He gets drunk with the butchers in the springtime![207]

So you see, there's nothing snobbish about any of this and I'll show you how to remember that you were always like you will be! But the path I went thru was to study and think and came out talking and explaining the Law and

---

207   See DB 174–75, 190, where Ray Smith and Japhy Ryder discuss "The Ten Bulls" or "Ten Ox Herding Pictures," a series of short poems and accompanying drawings used in the Zen tradition to describe the stages of a practitioner's progress toward enlightenment. Having achieved it, the practitioner returns to society, and according to Japhy, "to get drunk with the butchers" is part of the effort to enact wisdom and compassion.

even rushing to bars and addressing long sutras to strangers on stools—this is called the disciple stage.

> Just as plain
>> as the nose
>> on your face
>
> *****

(Marshmallow, *I'd* say)

> *****

(Then)

> *****

But now I see you need endurance to know all is over and everything is alright forever and forever and forever—Buddha was the Hermit Known As Endurance.

> *****

But O the rocky foreheads (and the throbbing veins) of young Buddhists I got to know later on who sat with me in rooms drinking tea, their words as light as the feathers of a Japanese bird but endurance breathing like fog from their wintry mouths—who banged gongs for me to come to breakfast, I took to sleeping outdoors on a bed of grass (in a sleeping bag)—those rocky foreheads didnt fool me, emptiness is *not* emptiness it's rocky foreheads!

(7)

I see the marshmallow soldiers marching ahead in the parade of life, which is like an endless train into an endless graveyard—O all the thoughts that swirled out of my head as I studied head bent over book—Rushing back to the library for the *Surangama Sutra*, for the Chinese Way of Life (Tao), for the Steps of the Law (the *Dhammapada*)[208] (which scared me, it said you had to be as tough as a rhinoceros walking in the jungle mindless of gadflies and snakes and thirst and searing heat, I naturally took it to be a plain demand on the part of the old tough rhino sages to go out to that jungle and *walk*) so that I began planning a trip cross-country to California to begin in earnest

---

208   While the *Dhammapada* is often referred to as the "Path of the Law," Kerouac is here referring to the Introduction to the *Dhammapada* in SBE, one of the first Buddhist texts he studied, which calls it "Footsteps of the Law" (315).

"the life of the wandering bhikkhu" not realizing (as now) that it meant you should tread this vale of darts mindless of the pain (as best you can), there are worthier things to do than gripe—It's an immense comedy every detail of how I planned my 'American Bhikkhuhood,' down to diet, cornmeal and brown sugar, no salt ("Taste the flavorless") and all such nonsense as virgins begin on—Laugh! laugh!

With pack on back, I saw myself going down the California Railroad like a rhinoceros, talking to no one, head lowered modestly like Buddha, at night sleeping in me blanket under a tree after hours of starbright meditation on the emptiness of phenomena, homeless, loveless, outlaw, gentle new walker of the West—But you'll see.

(To big black Composition Book A(2)—Titled "1957 Prose")[209]

---

209   This notebook has not been found.

The Buddhist Years

Two 1957 Fragments

1.

People all know but're afraid to believe that the mind, not the external world, is their refuge, because the external world is in the mind. The mind is peaceful essence so peaceful it yields to dreaming. Thinking about Khrushchev last night and the bomb on the verge of Turkey, and the earth casting its natural shadow on the half moon that the Russians wanta smear with red dye, and all the hysteria about Asiatic flu and missiles, and the atomic depth charges that would render the Mediterranean unfit for fishing, I realized it was exactly like a dream: that is, the characters in the dream dont realize that they're being dreamed by a mind, the mind of peaceful essence, God.

God is dreaming that He is dreaming. When He wakes up, the reality of the peaceful essence will simply obliterate the dream. This thinking is just like God's.

2.

NOTES   Berkeley '57

A rose arbour covers my imagination when I try to think of that porch on Beaulieu Street and especially as I saw it the night in 1940, in the summer, which will mark the end of this story, because though the pure blue sky with its white clouds did float over my kidhood days so purely it was only for to float over this dense crusted psychic sad earth of thoughts and deaths, nothing so pure as impurity—And though my eyes are sad and dim now as I get old, and my interest lags, the burn in my mind's there, it's right smack from that summernight street of 1940 that all of it swirls, in outgoing concentric circles, into the past and the future, when I sat whiteshirted and crying and eighteen on a curbstone across the street from our old cottage and foresaw the in-gone dream the timeless dense SWIRL which is our days and nights on earth I dont understand why anymore'n you do—

As though some Rouault had crisscrossed paints over that porch, in pinks and Chagall blues, and then comes Van Gogh to dot infinities in it, the rose arbour of imagination vines the mystery river (time) of thoughts-made-out which is all I can offer (using words) and so enough of apologies and a little inside mad explanation now—

Because I'm lonesome to rediscover my own mind's interest and swabble it down on paper to be neatly printed by linotypists and give old-agers something to read, cancel your science fiction futures and swapped moon proses, I like my own grand oldfashioned yonk yearning to rediscover the unrediscoverable wobweb mind.

Vibratory concentric rings of light, white, white as a mission of mercy,[210] mark that whiteshirt spot, fan out to all quarters of the uneven past present and gone—

It all swings out from the dead lips of my brother pouting on satin coffin pillow, and other deads, my green faced Uncle Joe coughing also in a rose-arbour hidden vine porch, his blown brown gloom house, dominoes and cuspidors and that shaft of light prophesying for me the later-interest in Proust that made me understand why eyes dim the long spindle yack-stick, push us out over time but space is another yo—Hand wearily to sigh, O yes all's got to be spontaneous.

ONLY INTRO

---

210   See MCB's 1st Chorus, where the last line reads "Mersion of Missy."

The Buddhist Years

Northport Sutra

Just now, in yard, had this dialogue with myself. I'm imagining another fella with me and when I told him all existence was ignorance he said "Ah what the hell you talking about? And why do you keep saying that existence doesnt exist?" So I said "Awright, look at that tree, there are three ways that that tree and all things dont exist but are based on ignorance… That tree is a vision." "What do you mean a vision etc.?" and all such outbursts so I said "There are three ways in which that tree is a vision. First, if I reached inside your head and pulled out your mind how could you know or say that that was a tree?" And he said the funny remark "If you pulled my mind out of my head what would you replace it with, empty space?"…Zenny…"So that you need a mind to perceive the tree, so the tree is a vision of your mind, because if you didnt have a mind to transfer the reflection of the tree as it hits and reflects off the mirror of your eyeballs…your eyeballs themselves dont do the perceiving of the tree. So the tree is a vision. Number two, the tree and all things that exist as we know and 'd been proved by intuiters as well as scientists, is an arrangement of atoms…of phantom atoms. If you had a powerful enuf microscope you would see that these atoms have sub-atoms and the subatoms have subsubatoms etc. on down to sub subs to emptiness and silence. So the tree is a vision. Number three, since the tree is going to return to dust in 200 years it doesnt exist anyway." "Yes it does," he retorts, "it exists in time, right now, and in 200 years I can come back and say 'that tree existed 200 years ago but now its substance is scattered in dust into other trees and bushes.'" Me: "But do we have to wait 200 years to admit that it doesnt exist any more? Why not admit it now, since time is coming anyway, so it already doesnt exist anyhow. Why wait 200 years to admit it?" "So what IS all this world then?" "Ignorance…if we knew and concentrated on the golden eternity of our permanent essence of mind all the time, we would see all things clearly in these three ways all the time and not be fooled by ignorance. The golden eternity is not subject to ignorance, IGNORANCE is. What Buddha saw under bo-tree." "Well, what about screaming atomic wars and screaming people?" "Run THAT thru the same wringer, a collection of phantom atoms screaming, already inexistent in time so why not admit it now, and if I pulled your mind out of your head you wouldnt know about it anyway since it's just a vision in your ignorant mind. So this is the blessedness surely to be believed, that all things come from perfect emptiness and go back to perfect emptiness and are already in perfect emptiness therefore so all is actually well if you stop being ignorant. Ignorance rippled waves of false phenomena across the calm face of universal perfect golden eternity but it didnt really happen anyway." "So what do we do?" "Concentrate on our permanent golden eternal essence of mind, as often times a day as possible, running almost everything thru the wringer of enlightenment, till the recognition of the truth grows in us and so when we are offered further chances for ignorance in the future we reject them with all their suffering and tears, in favor of tranquillity and peace and happiness. For I fainted once (1954) and saw the golden eternity of bliss and happiness and when I "came to" it was more like falling asleep than waking up." "Write that down," he said. "That's as great a discovery as Pasteur's or anybody's." "It actually is, because the man who makes a beautiful table doesnt explain what the use of it is, after all, man dont live by bread alone actually, like it says. It wont be by gabbing that we'll be alone with the golden eternity of God. Must stop thinking of God, though, as a Being or as One…he is neither One nor Infinite, neither he nor she, being nor non-being. God can be the name for the golden eternity but we gotta be careful about ignorance. Anyway, concentrate. Dont be a fool. Oh, yes, too, you'll find that the greatness of Man is his compassion and there is nothing but compassion in the happiness of the golden eternity. I saw it, felt it. I was so happy. I was alone with the golden eternity. I came to, back to this world, and felt like crying. Be sharp, dont be ignorant. See what happens if we all concentrate now. Or, they say, when one man, one living self, concentrates, all the others are saved anyway. God help us. God does help us or we wouldnt know this now."

JACK KEROUAC, Sept. 12, 1958, Northport.

The Buddhist Years

Four Poems

TAO   (Mexico 1957)

Trees don't complain
 because of parasites:
Trees know
 they dont exist for themselves,
 but for eternity:
Same with a man,
 if grums want some of him,
 give:
You cant be greedy of your self
 in infinity,
The world is like a wise man,
 it seems unkind,
But because of the reward
 of eternity
It is really secretly kind
 in the end.

GOD   (Orlando 1957)

The world is a show in God's mind
Because God wanted to think
But since it's only thought
And thought is unthinkable
There really is no show,
Only the golden eternity

I shuddered to think
That God was thinking me
having fun watch my vanity
loving me as he loves all things
 poor lonesome One-God

I love you too
Let's go home
and rejoice
In the freedom of eternity

God, stop thinking
—Come on now, Pap,
stop thinking—

We are God's thoughts
Praise God for his mercy
making us
just a show

THE CHINESE POET   (Northport 1958)

Lightning, boom
—the new moon
No friend—
Do I doubt myself?

On Desolation
I was the alonest man
in the world.

Depended on rocks
for comfort—
Hot milk, honey,
song.

Sleep.
This was two years ago.
Today I'm rich.
A Chinese merchant
once told me:
"_____"

The Buddhist Years

But I said:
"The virtue of virtue
    is not the way"
(The tch of tch
    is not Tao)

He said I would be rich
    and be drunk
    alone and sick
    and wont care.

My red rocks are wet
    from a millionaire rain.
My grapes are oozing
    out of joints.
My larder, so-called,
    is full of milk
    and dates.
What have I got
    to worry about?

Just worry.

Desolation, many a
moon have I seen
in this old tired
Navajo soul—
H o r s e   s h I t—
Ladies of the world,
pull down your shades.

Wonder when I'll be
a real Chinese Poet?

            June 19, '58

UNTITLED   1958

Paradise is the blissful smile
on the babe's dark mouth
when wisdom fails—

Paradise is Thy Guardian Angel—

Remember that nothing ever happened
    except God,
And God is Paradise

This world is the Holy Ghost—
Paradise is inside the Holy Ghost.

Jesus is the son of God
because I saw his torso on the Cross
in a vision on my pillow

And I saw Paradise,
    the Golden Eternity,
The smile of God

Therefore be sure—
This world is an appearance,
render unto it
its own—

And unto Paradise
render faith

You *must* believe;
say:—
"I do believe You, God."

The Buddhist Years

The Virgin Mary is the Mother of All,
we are the Virgin's Child.

The Virgin Mary is Paradise,
God is the Virgin Mary.

Letters to Myself

Letters to Myself   Nov. 21 1960

Dear Jack,

Civilization is rapidly becoming a multiplication of the evil influence of the disturbed. Where once you'd sit in front of a quietly spitting clicking fire of logs, staring with legs crossed in a comfy chair, thinking yr own thots, now you sit in front of the loud screaming agonies of disturbed soap operas. The addition of every new television channel merely multiplies the evil influence of the disturbed. When they talk of funds for "disturbed Children" they are talking about their own evil influence on young hearts of new children.

Every time you sit to read the newspaper you yourself are being disturbed by the disturbedness of others; nasty police drives to fine everybody for traffic violations, nasty fire department drives to push people (even artists I think now) out of "unsafe" lofts (lofts where you might expect an occasional quiet evening of tea and painting), addition of new safety experts to put up signs hiding trees (for our "safety" and at enormous salaries per year at our own expense), sirens wailing on the quiet November horizon warning us of the evil influence of the disturbed out there (a fire, a leaf fire in November, advertised by howling sirens that make dogs howl and children cry), sudden radio station screams about "bulletins" or even silly disturbed songs…I'm using the typewriter now to keep up my "diary" because my hands cant keep up now with what I want to say, used to say in pencil…I'm not going to use any form…I started up, above, using form, that is, the long sentence with the commas…I prefer Celine's dots now…or my own dash, what difference—I have to remind myself now every morning of the enormity of the dreams I've had in my sleep (lately such terrible visions following the most recent and one of the longest beings (binges) I've ever had, which began with Jimmy Benenson insisting I go to New England with him) (for no sensible reason I can imagine) and ending exactly eight fucking days later

The Buddhist Years   245

each day a horror[211]—culminating in the nightmare's death—I'll describe as best I can—But when I woke up this afternoon at four finally healed after two days of horror and self-medicine and yogic exercise in the yard and prayer on my knees it occurred to me, yes, I must go into the woods but not as my mother says to "hide" (*allez t'cachez*) but to remove myself from the evil influence of the disturbed *in* civilization, not civilization itself—Beatniks who visit Cuba and go among the screaming mobs in the hills and come back with glowing hate-America reports are disturbed, because they are after all American citizens and they live in a land where the arts to comfort & poor human convenience have reached their apogee (with however the eventual multiplicity messing up)—I know this makes hard understanding—My mind is muddled because I havent written a line in 10 days—And the reason I havent written a line in ten days is because the evil influences have been pestering me and telepathizing at me and killing me—Where for instance it was I myself who "interviewed" others & asked them questions and gained thereby an interest in life and in the way of an author gathered life-material, now they are interviewing ME constantly because I'm a famous and "rich" author and the bloody King of the Beatniks—I'm going to a cabin in the woods and sit before a quiet fire with a cup of tea and be a contemplative, there's no other way for me and for many other poor people in this world who dont realize whats being done to them by mentally-disturbed experts and "friends" of all kinds the net result of whose concern is synonymous to the sticking of replica dolls with pins in yr bloody fucking name—I aint even started…

NOTES TO MYSELF

Yes, to make things simpler I'll just call it Notes to Myself. And write in little separate paragraphs the little separate reminders etc.

Each house in this naborhood on Earl Ave. has an antenna on the roof; each house is connected to the evil influence that flows electronically from the "artistic" centers of the television industry. The only good thing about TV I can think of are the food ads showing good food pictorially. The rest,

---

211   In his "Later 1960" journal (Berg 57.8 Diary #25), Kerouac wrote, "Went on big dissipate drive with Jim Benenson, to Yale & Old Saybrook, saw John [Clellon Holmes] and [Alan] Harrington— Jim's beautiful girl Alice—goofed a lot—saw Lois [Sorrells] back in N.Y. […] Got smashed at John's, long talks—Woke up in Lois' horrified as usual."

the cowboys, hysterical soap operas & night plays, the sinister newscasters, even some of the old late movies, the sudden screaming commercials about useless articles, even the fanfare over Xmas shopping, the panels discussing "problems" is all evil influence and comes from people who are so DISTURBED that they have to propagate it over the air and fill all the homes of America. For instance the man next door: just now his tethered dog began to scream in pain. He rushed out to see what had happened, stopped the dog's yelling (dog was dreaming?). Coming back he said to his wife's query what's the matter, said "I dont know" and ran immediately back into the house to continue watching TV. (Dog has St. Vitus attack) (he knocked out the dog?)...Anyway I was pacing under the new moon and stars and heard it all. That was the only sound in this populous naborhood. Everybody else is inside and heard nothing because of the blare of their TV sets...I dont understand America any more.

When I get up in the morning to come down tell my mother a few things, maybe dreams (not morning but my usual 2 PM or so) it is with a sinking feeling I walk into the bright sunny livingroom which is booming with television noise and if I want to tell her anything I would have to lower the sound but then she is engrossed in what she's watching...So I say nothing. I take coffee and go out in the yard tremendously depressed AND THIS HAPPENS EVERY DAY. The TV has cut off simple contact. It has deprived me of a place in the house (other than upstairs in my attic) where I can sit and read the paper, for instance, or just sit and think. There isnt a fire to sit in front of. I have to go in the yard or back upstairs. In the yard I hear strange disagreeable noises everywhere: growling trucks, roaring booming jetliners in the air, screams of demented children (they've changed awfully, their screams no longer gleeful)...

Now of course I realize I'm beginning to sound like an old sickmonster Scrooge of the block myself...But somehow the screams of children of old in glee of November dusks had a playful sound—Now it has a hysterical and disturbed sound and this of course comes from the children being subjected to the evil influences flowing across the air through "communications" and especially I say from the fact that they are no longer allowed to walk to school but must be supervised immediately by waiting for the School Bus on the little corner here, and must come back the same way after an entire day

The Buddhist Years

of teacher supervision, and of course the supervision on both ends of that sandwich at home…By television and clubwoman mothers!

My little cat Timmy is my favorite being because of his loyalty, purity of heart, constancy, simplicity…The virtues of Heaven are his, not men's any more. This is why I love my cats and it is not a neurotic attachment so much.

There go the sirens now, announcing SIX O CLOCK, scaring my cat and making him run into the house in fear!

My cat raises its little paw to say hello, it does NOT grin at me with a mouthful of skulltooth death and make me nervous with hypocrite greetings and interruptive behavior and hysterical "enthusiasm."

The reason why I've been reluctant to write a true new novel: (1) I dont want people to know what I'm really thinking, as soon as they find out they will all begin yelling at me again, or pawing at me, for one reason or another, all BAD (with a few exceptions) and (2), the second reason, my visions of late have been so horrible I hesitate to scare people whether good or bad people… Let them find out for themselves what I'm thinking. Shall I tell them?

Shall I tell them I saw a vision of horrible primeval slime in the middle of the earth turning and steaming slowly and then suddenly I saw muddy men pulling awful mud burdens down there with expressions of Dantesque woe so hopeless and sad it almost gave me a heart attack?

Shall I show how I saw the death of the cat in the vision of a Claw in the earth? Or the death of the man in the vision of a Skull Tooth in the earth?

My cat is not full of false optimism. And he doesnt put the cart before the horse by saying that men should praise God for the glories of Thanksgiving Day (meaning decapitated turkeys by the millions). My cat knows that the earth is awful because it is ignorance. And that men tried to make the best of it therefrom by discovering the meat of the turkeys.

The world is real only in imagination. It is a real existence in real imagination. But since it is only imagination then figure that one out for yrself…But in God, in Heaven, in Nirvana, there is no such thing as imagination and therefore Heaven is not imaginary, therefore only Heaven is real…And thats why I praise God.

God manifested imagination, which manifested ignorance, which manifested this horrible birth-and-death situation of existence…In that sense of course therefore I say (or have to say) (still) that God is Everything… But what God manifested, "imagination," is only imaginary, therefore there never was a world at all…We all find that out in blissful astonishment when we lose our imagination as I lost mine when I fainted in 1954…There is yr reality: the astonished blisshood of No Imagining Whatever…So my relation to God cannot be established in any form of imagining and that is why it is truly the "Cloud of Unknowing"…But it was revealed to me in that faint, it was revealed to my memory of that faint, that is, that there is astonished bliss in Heaven when all imagination puts this silly existence astill…& restores us to our primordial (not "our," excuse me) to the primordial condition of eternal bliss…eternal ecstasy…

I put down and eschew this world because it is ignorant of all this. It puts the cart before the horse constantly. It says that God made us because he loved us, as tho we had existed in the beginning co-existent with God (like Neal says with his "co-creator" horseshit vanity)…

In the beginning was nothing, not-imagination…"from the beginning not a thing is"[212]…Then came imagination, which produced ignorance, which then electromagnetically created matter in all its forms and Mother Nature arranged it male and female to go on turning the wheel of Ignorant Grief. But "men" put the cart before the horse by "praising God for the polarity of male & female" (which is precisely the ignorant cause of their grief, their grief of having to realize that one day their bodies which began as little drops of pearly sperm have now to be laid in a muddy grave a huge bulk of awful fat decayed meat enuf to disgust the angels)…

And men refuse to face all this either because of their phony optimism or their ignorant "enthusiasm" (like that awful nauseating vertiginous enthusiasm of college boys) (and girls) and the worst enthusiasm of them all: of show business people (and of phony beatnik poets)…

The enthusiasm of screaming masses of Jap students snakedancing in hate-America parties in the streets of bloodshed: blaming America or anything they can think of instead of BLAMING THEMSELVES… And that I think is what Jesus meant by repenting for our OWN SINS, not accusing others of THEIR sins…We repent (I repent anyway) for the

---

212   The quote is by Hui-Neng (Kerouac also quotes it in verse 47 of SGE) although it does not appear in *The Sutra Spoken by the Sixth Patriarch* in BB, Kerouac's primary source. The closest approximation is where Hui-Neng states that "intrinsically [the world] exists not" (554); see also SOD 405. However, of the many translations of this famous verse available online, there is this one from Zen Master Albert Low (1928–2016): "*Bodhi originally has no tree, / The mirror also has no stand. / From the beginning not a thing is / Where is there room for dust?*"

sin of my own fucking ignorance…I am not going to blame colonialism or capitalism or communism or poverty for my horror or any of the people who can be blamed for the causing of those things: I am going to blame myself, the originator of my own ignorance…for my unhappiness I cannot blame others (it is so silly)…BLAME BIRTH, blame the ignorance of Nature and of birth, for your fucking death…It is birth that causes death as Buddha said and that is why goddamit (and nobody faces Buddhism any more, only Zen) Buddha warned his buddies to look out for Lady Amra and her entourage of courtesans coming across the fields with offerings…Offerings indeed…All looking to be knocked up because of the nature of their own ignorance… And the men just as bad with their poor hardons…hardons of ignorance is what they are…The universe is an ignorant hardon caused by imagination. And from that proceeds the grief, the unimaginable grief, the dimensionless tears and old histories in old caves, the old mud of earth, the old toothy death of old skulls with hair and nails growing out a mile long in the shitty stench of old Peruvian graves and any kinda graves.

Last night I dreamed I saw a funny flying saucer, very large & clear, flying fast across the night sky, round and saucer shaped but with a diamond crown…Then I saw a pale worm flying across higher, a kind of cigar shaped ship of pale white…I saw a satellite pass swiftly…But suddenly as I looked at the moon it leered at me and a little piece of moonball was flung at me and I ran into the house in fear…I realized they had noticed I was noticing them and they drove me away…Does this mean that the flying saucers come from the Leering Moon?

And listen to this: I said to myself "I've seen that flying saucer in my dreams but this time I'm not dreaming, I'm not asleep" (!)…So I was Dreaming that I was Dreaming that I was NOT Dreaming! Or let's see: I was dreaming that I was not dreaming what I had already dreamed, and when I woke up in the dream of this imaginary existence I realized that I was dreaming all this.

There will be no need for the Passion of Christ, in Heaven, says the author of The Cloud of Unknowing. I gather that Christ (whose cross I kept seeing all summer in my nightmares & hangover visions) (in closed eyes, in the woods, in the sky once, all over)[213] is a messenger from No Imagination whatever to come and hint at us, truly thereby the Son of God, who

---

213   See BS ch. 37.

undertook the same imagination we have to bring the hint of Heaven which is bliss of no-imagination…something like that…and I do believe his words were garbled just as much as my own have been by critics…So I dont believe the New Testament any more than I believe what the critics *say* about me.

Dipankara Buddha was a cave man, a Neanderthal, & brought the message of No Imagination to cave men…who didnt listen…and brought us ultimately to this horrible point where civilization is drawing us away from the verity of the Last Things (of birth & death & mud) towards a senseless exploration of other planets in the ignorance of space & imagination… Imagine earthlings bringing all the ignorance outward into space, including their greed & murderousness.

I used to think in my *Diamond Sutra* assurance or at least Golden Eternity assurance therefore that there was no "choice" to make (thereby putting down all of the sutras thinking I had discovered the One Choicelessness of One Unified Field of Ecstasy as reality) but now, as you can see from preceding notes, it has returned to me (from the church too) *You* have to make some sort of choice. In this case: choose the ignorance of the world's imagination, or the enlightenment of God's Non-Imagination, or perish. For me perish. So this is a return to the essential dualism of Catholicism (and of Manichaeism) that I had been trying to put down. But you've got to make a choice, use yr will, to find the Path. And this is also implicit in all religions even the Tao with its cloud-formlessness. Previous to this I drowned myself in drink assured (and drowned in assurance and mistiness) that there was no choice to make in the Not-Two world. In the Universal-Substance-which-is-Divine Substance scheme. For those who dwell in the dimension of sufferish flesh, of imagination thereby, a choice has to be made. In self-reliance, too, simply. If your sleeping bag bursts you must either choose to go on sleeping in floating flying feathers, or get up in the middle of the night and sew it. Will. Will to Self-Reliance. In this world of birth and death I choose the self-reliance of contemplation upon the world's ignorance and eschewing of that, followed by contemplation of Nirvana's perfect sky of Paradise and Eternity…O the way I repeat myself. Now I'm starting to screw up these notes…(must write a little more slowly).

Down to a few details. This week in NY Ginsberg seemed very critical of me. I was sick and when I took a vitamin I heard him say in a low voice to

The Buddhist Years

Howard Shulman in the other room "A vitamin freak."[214] Shulman himself, once wide eyed and enthused to show me how fast he can drive, is now quiet, has just returned from Cuba where he marveled at Castro and his murderous crew of righteous haters and enviers of American middleclass comfort (which they want for themselves by taking it from us rather than studying to work at it for themselves). It seemed I felt hostility from Shulman (a quiet one, tho) but a definite new hostility far from his old admiration of me. And Ginsberg is positively green with hatred of everything and of me too. I argued with them.

I am in the position of being shot at the wall by the revolutionists even before the FBI of the opposition comes to imprison me and shoot me too… Granville Hicks Jones says I am an "individualist"[215] and this at least sho proves it. Conformity my ass. There are two conformities in America now: communist and non-communist conformity. I take to either a nice bucket of shit.

Ah well, enuf for today

---

214   Howard Schulman was, at the time, a twenty-four-year-old beat poet. In 1962 he was the editor of *Pa'lante* a collection of American and Cuban poetry and prose published by the League of Militant Poets. Contributors included Ginsberg, Michael McClure, Leroi Jones, John Wieners, and Paul Blackburn.

215   While a graduate student at Columbia University, Granville Hicks Jones wrote his master's thesis comparing the works of Kerouac, Walt Whitman, and Thomas Wolfe. As a young English professor at the Carnegie Institute of Technology, he sent it to Kerouac c/o Avon Books, the publisher of a number of Kerouac's works, including *Maggie Cassidy* and *Tristessa* as paperback originals.

Bed Thoughts at 3 A.M.

BED THOUGHTS   by
at   Jack Kerouac
3 A.M. January 3, 1962

Therefore the electromagnetic gravitational field exists for the sake of the adoration of the field itself—The angel of light emanates the angels of light infinitely, who assume flesh infinitely for the purpose of the adoration of God the angel of light—They cannot touch i.e. or adore one another (Liebniz's monads)[216] ("orgones" in the air)[217] (swarms that you see) by nature of being light

[drawing of a monad or orgone swarm, i.e., a round cluster of small oval shapes]

—They can only adore Light itself, God—Jesus being part of the Trinity is therefore God Himself & exists for the sake of being adored because all the angels of light assume burdens of flesh for the purpose of suffering & sinning & being forgiven by Jesus God & therefore adoring him—*it*—

Who is it disappears in time? the person, not the angel of light that assumed the personhood—Who are all these babies being born? not "babies"—It's not the person being born, living, or dying that counts, it's the angel of light—the Buddhist in-view of Original True Mind Essence—

The world exists for the adoration of God—The Father wants us to adore the Son (himself) via the Holy Spirit (himself) therefore it's not a drama of angels of light being forced to adore a pampered son—All the "monads" are swarming in bliss—

---

216   The term "monad" is used to refer to a most basic or original substance. As originally conceived by the Pythagoreans, the Monad is the Supreme Being or totality of all things. Later the term was used by philosopher Gottfried Wilhelm Leibniz (1646–1716) and others to refer to elementary particles that make up the universe.

217   For "orgones" see fn. 35 herein.

The Buddhist Years

"All the Monads" is God Itself—

The Tathagata has assumed the Light, or Suchness—All things are Tathagata—

The Buddhist Trinity is Nirmanakaya (assuming the flesh)

Sambhogakaya (assuming the bliss)

Dharmakaya (assuming the light)

* * *

So the reason why life is suffering is for the purpose of the adoration of God—We kneel & kiss the Cross, or pray, or enter Dhyana for the sake of Samadhi & then go forth in Samapatti to other worlds of flesh to adore Tathagata further—What "never happened" is the flesh, Samsara—Light itself is happening, yet it is also not "happening" being transcendental of that word—"Words of Mystery"—Christ being born of a Virgin means he is unborn—resurrected means he is undead—All the angels of light have this revealed to them in their fleshly assumption, a hint for adoration—but it doesn't "work" in the "world" because the suffering must go on for the sake of gratitude to God (for when suffering ends), the sinning must go on for the sake of forgiveness (for when sinning ends), the hating must go on for the sake of adoration (for when the hating ends)—

Pooey, anybody can do it, everybody's doing it—

Who is it disappears in time? not a person—not even an angel—

So rather than being a snake with tail in mouth,[218] or Mother Kali eating herself back,[219] it's really the Light swarming in adoration of itself (its Self)—The dove of the Holy Spirit descending is confirmation—The Holy Ghost adoring the Holy Ghost

period.

Sinners provide Jesus God with a *field*—birth and death Samsara provide Buddha God with a *field* (of Bodhisattvas like the one I saw jump into the sea

---

218   The "snake with tail in mouth" is an ouroboros, an ancient symbol signifying cosmic harmony, eternity, and the cycle of birth and death.

219   In Hinduism, Kali is a supremely powerful and ferocious mother goddess ruling over time, destruction, and death and who is also associated with sexuality and violence. In the *Devi Mahatmyam*, a text written approximately in the Sixth Century, Kali fights a battle against the demon Raktabija, who is able to clone himself from every drop of blood that hits the ground. She defeats him by sucking up much of his blood before it lands and then eating up all the clones. Kerouac's sense of Kali "eating herself back" relates to his sense that birth inevitably leads to death. See S-P 335, where, while he was hallucinating on mescaline, Kali appears before him.

to become a little fish) (after patting other Bodhisattvas in the ass like a coach saying "Go, Team!")—[220]

It's all tied in—Napoleon at Waterloo didnt know this—but the horse did—Who are all these babies being born?

not a one.

Words were not invented to discuss the enigmatic Truth—but here it is,

in words.

You dont have to believe it simply because it's true.

So all things tend to the adoration of God—so know this, Angels of Light, and adore God, not thyselves enflesh't—you cant adore thyselves anyway by nature of being angels of light—Be ye lamps unto thyselves—Dance and flit in the universe, back & forth, all around, ring around the rosie, among the Roses of the Unborn, bing, bang, pop, electromagnetic crackle in the Field—adore God—adore Tathagata—adore Jesus—adore the Name, adore the Name you give it in yr part of the Field—Your fleshly sufferings are not in vain & are not real—For if you cant remember a dream, *what is it* that cant remember the dream? What is it that tries the remembering? Where is the mind struggling to try this remembering? Location, please? Size, please?—Since there are an infinity of Angels of Light there's sense in calling them personal entities only if you can make a census of all their names, an Infinite Census—a Census of Infinite Numbers of Angels of Light—Who can do that but God the Light Itself—(in the infinite census of the angels of light, I am he who has taken the vow of kindness to make life more fun)—(But continuous fun is impossible by nature of flesh to make gratitude less destitute of gratitude)—(So I will be grateful to adore)—Whatever the angel of light assumes after this corpse is dragged away for me, it wont be the corpse of J. Kerouac—It is J. Kerouac writing this, so the trouble is all over—and the angel of light is like the Bodhisattva who suffers without minding it.

---

220   See DB 86–87, where the Negro preacherwoman says, "'the Lawd will take care of you if you re-recognize that you have a *new field*'" and Ray claims that the "'*new field* [is] a new Buddha-field.'"

Sources

MOST OF THE MATERIAL in this collection has been transcribed from the Jack Kerouac Papers archive housed at The Henry W. and Albert A. Berg Collection of English and American Literature, The New York Public Library, Astor, Lenox and Tilden Foundations, with two exceptions: "The Little Sutra" and a portion of version 2 of "A Dream Already Ended" (see below) are part of The Allen Ginsberg Papers archive in Columbia University's Rare Book and Manuscript Library.

"My Sad Sunset Birth": Berg 32.3 Typescript short stories and story fragments. 1941(?).

"The Story Just Begins": Berg 4.21 Typescript fragment, revised. "I The Story Begins." (Earl John Moultrie version of 'On The Road' with notes on "Aspects of the hip") 1949.

"I Was Born at Five in the Afternoon": Berg 48.9 Contained within Holograph notebook "DR (10)." Entry titled "The Pathos of People." May 7, 1954.

Reflections on Birth (from Dharma Notebooks): Berg 49.1 Contained within Holograph notebook "Dharma (A) 1953." & 49.2 Holograph notebook "Dharma (1)." (Begins: "Memory Babe Dec 9, 53.").

"Morning March 12 1922" & "Confessions of the Father": Berg 3.30 Typescript fragments, untitled. And "Confessions of the Father." (Material on earliest memories), 1954.

"The Heart of the World: The Legend of Duluoz": Berg 6.45 Typescript story, revised. "The Heart of the World. The Legend of Duluoz." April 19, 1954.

"The Legend of Three Houses": Berg 24.1–5. Mislabeled as "an early version of On the Road," begun June 22, 1954, it comprises parts of three holograph notebooks and two inserts, one handwritten and one typed. See also Berg 23.6 Typescript "The Tragedy of Old Bull Balloon" (1st chapter of 'Ray Smith Road') (written 1954)."

"The Long Night of Life": Berg 54.1 Holograph notebook, signed by Jack Kerouac on front cover.

The Buddhist Years

"A Dream Already Ended" (Two Versions): Berg 3.26 Typescript fragment, untitled. Version 2 is contained within 48.10 Holograph notebook "DR (12)." Rear cover labeled "J K / V(1). Includes material for "Book of Dreams" and "Book of Visions." There is also a typed portion of version 2 in Columbia University's Allen Ginsberg archive, and I've relied on that version (the handwritten opening note and the first seven paragraphs) up until it ends, at which point the handwritten version continues.

"The Universe is empty…": Berg 3.32 Typescript, revised. 1954?

Dharma Fragments & Ascetic Plans for the Future: Berg 3.23 Holograph and typescript notes, fragments, and sketch & 3.25 Holograph and typescript fragments, notes and quotations.

"The City and the Path": Berg 18.7 Typescript, revised. April 21, 1955.

"On the Path": Berg 18.9 Holograph draft "On the Path, Aug. 19, 1955, Mexico City."

"The Blessedness Surely To Be Believed" (Two Versions): Berg 51.1 Holograph notebook Rocky Mt. Dec. 27 1955. The rear of the notebook is titled "Mary" and contains forty-five-page holograph draft that is part of *Maggie Cassidy*.

"Beat Generation": Berg 19.2 Holograph draft 1957.

"Avalokitesvara": Berg 56.5 Contained within Diary #5. Holograph diary "Berk / 1957." June 6, 1957 - June 17 1957.

Two 1957 Fragments: Berg 19.14 Holograph notes, untitled. 1957. & Fragment 2 contained within 56.5 (see "Avalokitesvara" above).

"Northport Sutra": Berg 19.47 Typescript Sutra, signed. (1 leaf).

Four Poems:

"Tao": Berg 56.6 Contained within Diary #6. Holograph diary "Mexico 1957 Summer."

"God": Berg 56.7 Contained within Diary #7. Holograph diary "Autumn '57 / Orlando."

"The Chinese Poet": Berg 56.11 Contained within Diary #11. Holograph diary "Northport / Sketches (1) / Summer '58."

Untitled "Paradise is the blissful smile": Berg 19.52 Holograph poem and prose fragment. "Visions of Paradise." Poem on verso. 1958.

"Letters to Myself": Berg. 12.9 Photocopied typed letter, unsigned. November 21, 1960 (5 leaves).

"Bed Thoughts at 3 A.M.": Berg 46.2 Typescript, revised. January 3, 1962.

* * *

"My Sad Sunset Birth" previously appeared in Issue 5 (Fall 1995) of *Dharma Beat* under the title "My Mad Sunset Birth."

"Modified Ascetic Life," the first page of "Ascetic Plans for the Future," previously appeared in *Big Sky Mind: Buddhism and the Beat Generation*, ed. by Carole Tonkinson. Riverhead Books, 1995.

Acknowledgments

THE PROJECT OF COMPILING this book would not have been possible without the assistance and encouragement of Jim Sampas, Literary Executor of the Estate of Jack Kerouac, as well as Sylvia Cunha, Director of Marketing and Development for the Estate of Jack Kerouac and Co-Founder of Sal Paradise Press. Special thanks to Jean-Christophe Cloutier, Associate Professor of English and Comparative Literature at the University of Pennsylvania, who kindly translated the passages herein written by Jack in New England French-Canadian patois. Professor Cloutier translated Kerouac's original French writings in *The Unknown Kerouac*, and is the editor of *La vie est d'hommage* (Éditions du Boréal, 2016), a volume that gathers all of Kerouac's major French writings in their original untranslated glory.

Special thanks also to John Shen-Sampas, Maria Perritano, Mary-Claire Paicopolis, Dorothy Sampas, Tony Sampas, Nancy Bump, George Sampas, Lawrence Sampas, Betty Sampas, Rachel Reisman, Joel Reisman, Gemma Sampas, Chloe Sampas, Simon Warner, Paul Marion, Matthew Kaplan, Dave Metzler, Mike Downie, Kurt Hemmer, Erin Hemmer, Johnny Surprenant, Robert Allen, Sonya Kolowrat, Edward Edwards, M. C. Taylor, David Greenberg, J. C. Cloutier, Lois Sorrells, Sebastian Beckwith, John A. Hennessey, John D. Hennessey, Jeffrey Horblit, Sheila Quinlin, Mike Gambino, Pat Crowley, Rich Harnois, Joseph Cohen, George Tobia, Jr., Burns & Levenson, Dave Ouelette, Dave Perry, Ronna Jonson, Alicia Blue, Brian Ross, Tim Hunt, Ray Farrell, Eliza Hindmarch, Brian Coombes, John Battsek, Ebs Burnough, Armen Madikians, Michael Kagan, Laura Coxson, Range Media, Ventureland, Big Night Media, Happy Valley, Ethos Genetics, Colin Gordon, Michael Reardon, Jessica VanDeWalle, Tim Larson, Zach Wise, Dan Nelson, Gregg Weiss, Heather Lovett, Robyn Pierce, Sean Corrigan, and Scott Heigelmann.

Thanks to Dave Moore, author of *The Kerouac Companion: A Guide to the Duluoz Legend and other related works,* which was an invaluable resource in my compiling the notes included in this volume and from which, with his permission,

I liberally borrowed. Dave, as always, was my go-to person for all Kerouac-related questions. And thanks to Jean Vertefeuille and George Hall, whose kind support on this project in giving me a place to stay in New York was critically important in allowing me to spend many weeks deep-diving at the Berg. And to Holly George Warren, my fellow diver, for her encouragement and support.

I also received great support from the administration and staff at the Harker School in San Jose, California, where I am fortunate to teach. I'm especially grateful to Brian Yager, Jennifer Gargano, Paul Barsky, Pam Dickinson, Pauline Paskali, Clifford Hull, Christopher Hurshman, Diane Main, and all of my English Department colleagues.

Thanks to everyone working at the Berg Collection for help and encouragement, especially Emma Davidson, Julie Carlson, and Simi Best.

At UMass Lowell, special thanks to Tony Sampas, archivist and special projects manager at the Center for Lowell History, as well as Professor Michael Millner.

And most importantly at home, to my wife, Michelle, daughter, Maddy, our dogs, Buddy and Brooke, and our bearded dragon, Zayda.

Images and Figures

Figure 1: Gerard and Caroline (Nin) Kerouac. Photo taken around the time of Jack's birth.

Figure 2: This drawing in Jack's notebook coincided with his writing "Avalokitesvara" in May 1957.

MODIFIED ASCETIC LIFE
For Temporary & American Responsibilities
FOLLOWED BY FINAL AUSTERITIES

1. No chasing after women any more — no hankering
   to lust & create sorrow & multiply desires & raise

2. No more drunkenness on alcohol, no more
   "sipping" — no sickening of healthy body, or
   temporary numbing of body blanking mind

1954   3. No false social life — no 'friendships',
        except associations in temporary movement

4. (No more work) ~~either too~~ ~~reverse~~

1955 ·   ~~breaks to buy~~ ~~shook in SF~~ ~~Ma~~
          ~~& money for carbون truck (temporary)~~
          ~~vehicle for Hitching America)~~ ~~buildy~~
          ~~huts in Calif. & Mexico (temporary)~~

5. No more rich or /and expensive foods —
   elementary diet of salt pork, beans,
   bread, greens, peanuts, ~~butter~~ figs, coffee,
   (& later grow everything & pick acorns),
   pinyon nuts, cacti fruit mssrch)

6. Finally (after 5-volumed LIFE) no
   more writing for communication & after
   SKETCH books of wilds no more writing
1960   or I art-ego of any kind, finally
        no I-self, or Name; no shaving of beard

1970   7. No possessions finally, but wilderness Robe, no hut,
           no mirror, begging at houses of village
        8. No communication with rest of world or family
        9. Dhyana & contemplation ecstasy
2000   10. nirvana & willed death beyond death

Figure 4

ELEMENTS OF THE BASIC DECEIT [Poor] × [?]

1. Search for Nest Place +	1. Search for Love + 1. Ma
a. Mexico ———	a. Indian whores, with No
b. California ———	b. #, "with " Yes
c. No. Carolina ———	c. None, "with" Yes
d. Lowell ———	d. None, "with" ———
f. N.Y. L.I. ———	f. N.Y. girls, "with" Yes
g. Woods ———	g. None (except McKee (woods)) + NO
	Disadvantages
2. Means of Saving Stake	a. No sleep, no Eastern work, or unease Texas
a. Railroad	b. Bribes, work, war, men
b. Seaman	c. No money, art compromise
c. Writing	d. Not enough $
d. Others	
	3. Fears Specifically
3. Fears	a. Mexico — Alien scorpion land, fever, no more-joy meaning
a. Changemending	b. California — No sex, overculture, dry reason, expensive, thin
b. No patience or stamina	c. N.C. — No sex, strange snake land, southerness, dullness, overculture, notoriety
c. Inability to work well	d. Lowell — Drearisten, cold, notoriety, expensive
d. Art Ego anxiety	f. N.Y.L.I. — Overcrowded, expensive, cold, sinister, washing, thesis
e. Loneliness	g. Woods — Inexperience, poison plants
f. Basic Insanity	
g. Cowardice	
h. Appetites rule	

Figure 5

Articles in Small World Bag

1. Camp Kit (cooking)
2. $1.25 Peruvian jack knife
3. Bible, Shakespeare, Dante, Thoreau, Buddha, Latin, Finnegans Wake, maybe blue
4. Cord-voys, 2 Levis, 1 slack pants, swim shorts
5. Two flannel shirts, red & green, old, black & white
6. Socks – workshirts (2)
7. Underwear – tops
8. Sweatcoat (torn), tie
9. 3 sport shirts, red, gray, tan + tie
10. New shoes, workshoes (old shoes)
11. Plenty pencils (3), lead, notebooks (few), papers+pens, thin paper, clamps
12. Pipe, pipe cleaners
13. Mirror
14. Lantern, bulbs
15. Razors, both
16. Workstones
17. H Brush
18. 2 caps (dunnit + RR)
19. Tooth smokes (3)
20. Slippers

WOODS

21. Raincoat
22. Medical Kit (ideal)
   - Victorn
   - iodine
   - Bandaids
   - Anacin
   - Noxzema
   - sulfadiazene
   - Penicillin pills
   - Anti blistatmines
   - Benaris } In Mexico
   - Goofballs } no presc.
   - Codeine tabs
   - Castor + drersin
   - Water pills (hidaleone)
   - Serum snakebite
23. Hotplate
24. Railroad watch
25. Old pictures
26. Machete
27. Lamp, bulb, wire, ext.
28. Matches (big box)
29. Alkaline yellow soap (wash poison ivy)
30. Ginger for emetic (in woods)
31. Sleeping bag

WOODS: axe, spade, hoe, nails, fish hooks, line, matches · (raincoat), camp stove, shell or flint, sugar, ballpoint, vitamins · boots, seeds (all), Bull Durham, candles, flint, camp cook kit · Medical Kit, Harmonica (big), Rope + string, sleeping bag, Blankets (?), Mags, glasses

WITH TRUCK: Sweetmeat, sugar, spices + needles, rice, Epsom, needle, Castor + Salad oil, cider or salt, clothes jars + containers

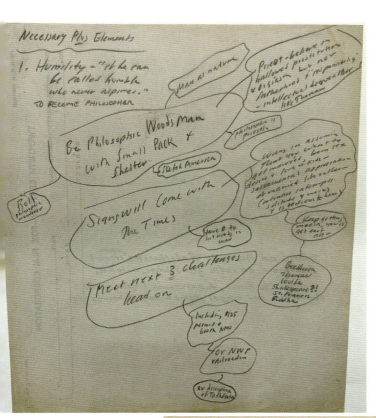

Figure 6

Figure 7

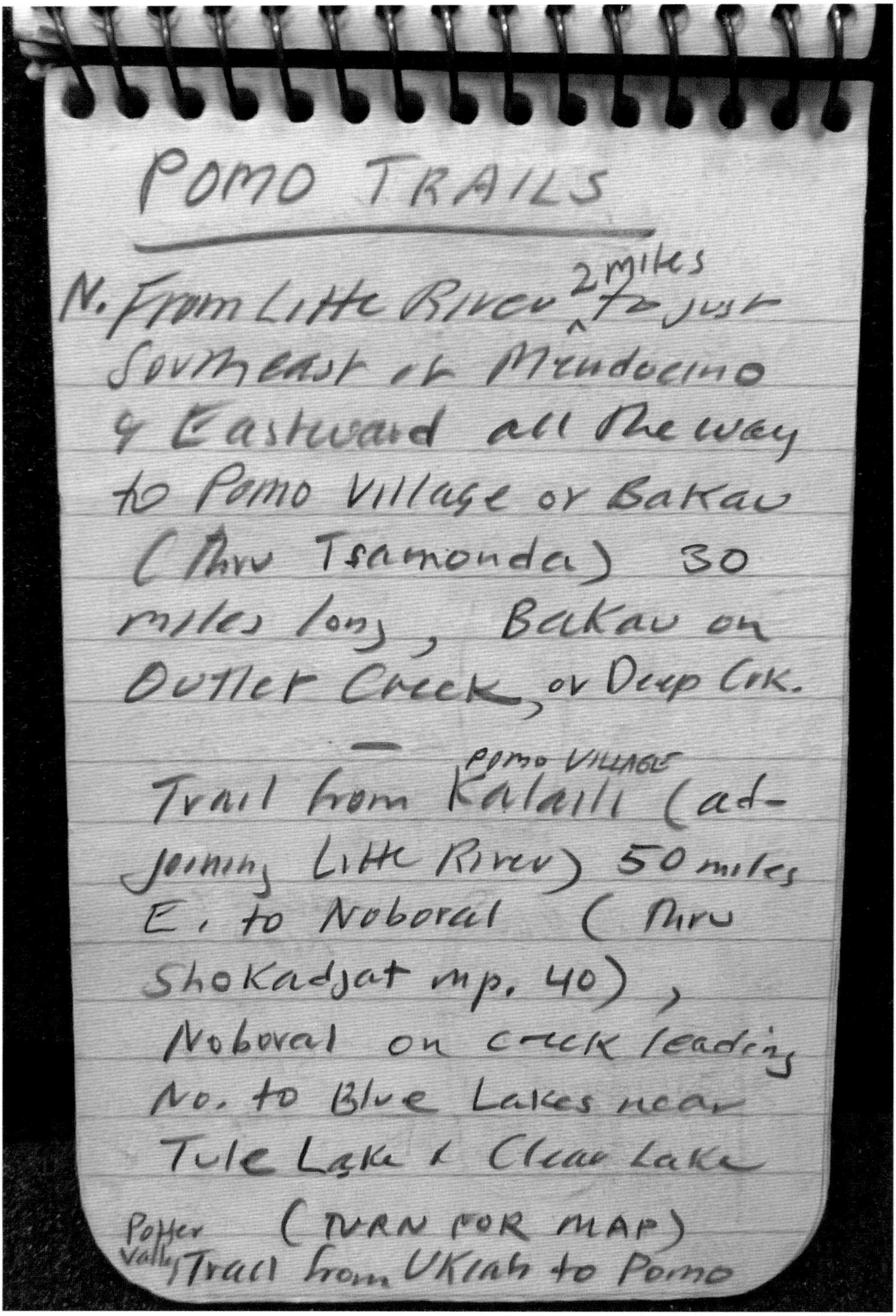

POMO TRAILS

N. From Little River 2 miles to just
Southeast of Mendocino
& Eastward all the way
to Pomo Village or Bakau
(thru Tsamonda) 30
miles long, Bakau on
Outlet Creek, or Deep Crk.

—

Trail from Kalaili (ad-
joining Little River) POMO VILLAGE 50 miles
E. to Noboral (thru
Shokadjat mp. 40),
Noboral on creek leading
No. to Blue Lakes near
Tule Lake & Clear Lake

Potter
Valley (TURN FOR MAP)
Trail from Ukiah to Pomo

Figures 8 & 9: Journal pages (directions and map) showing Jack contemplating becoming a hermit, engaging in subsistence living in Northern California. December 1953.

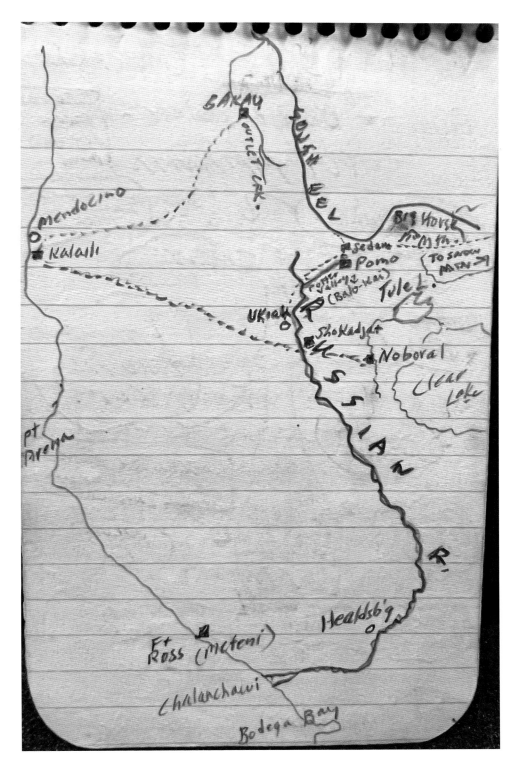

Figure 9

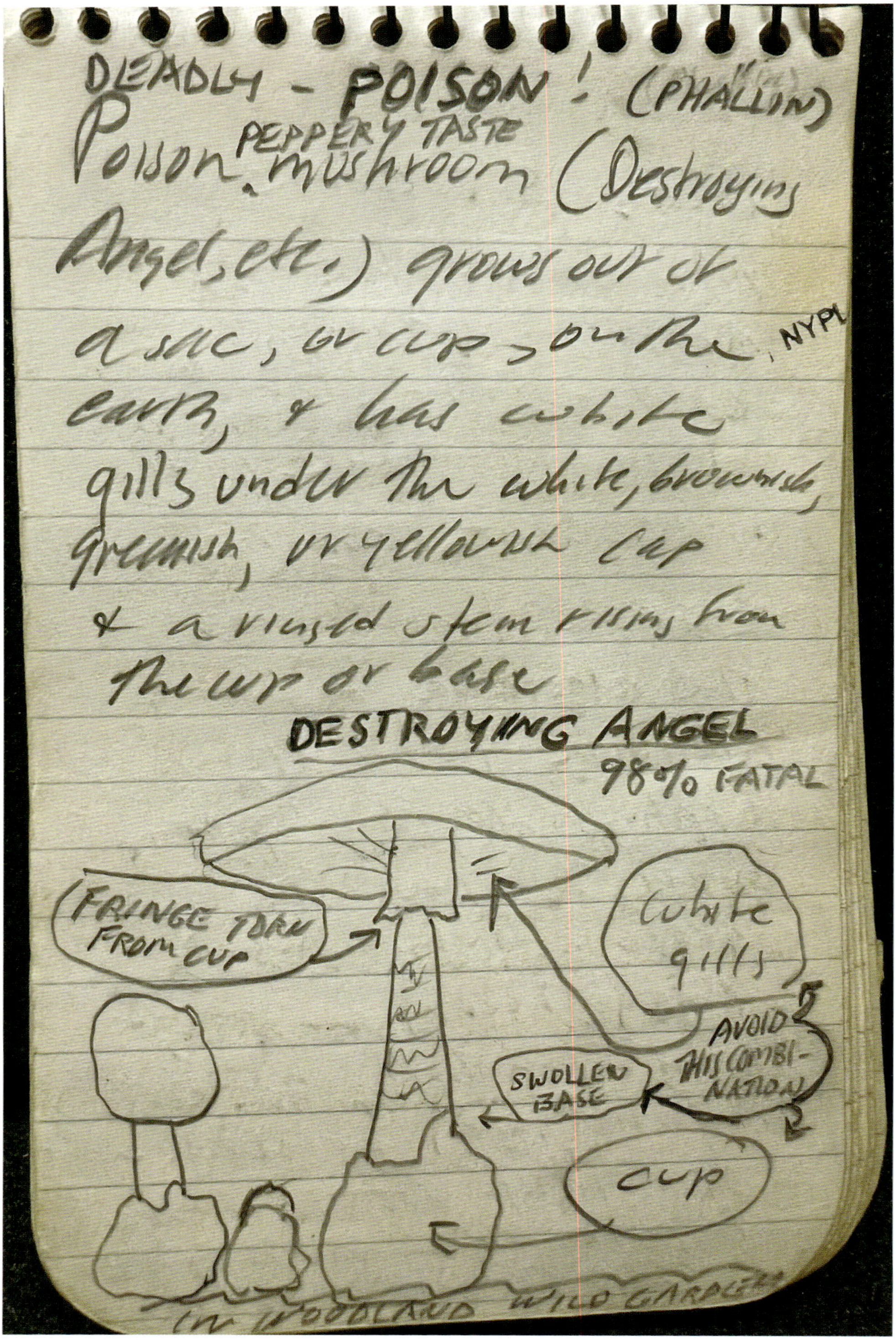

DEADLY - **POISON**! (PHALLIN)
Poison PEPPERY TASTE mushroom (Destroying
Angel, etc.) grows out of
a sac, or cup, on the , NYPL
earth, + has white
gills under the white, brownish,
greenish, or yellowish cap
+ a ringed stem rising from
the cup or base

DESTROYING ANGEL
98% FATAL

(FRINGE TORN FROM CUP)

white gills

AVOID THIS COMBI-NATION

SWOLLEN BASE

cup

IN WOODLAND WILD GARDEN

Figures 10–15: Journal pages showing Jack's fears and effort to educate himself as he continued to contemplate subsistence living.

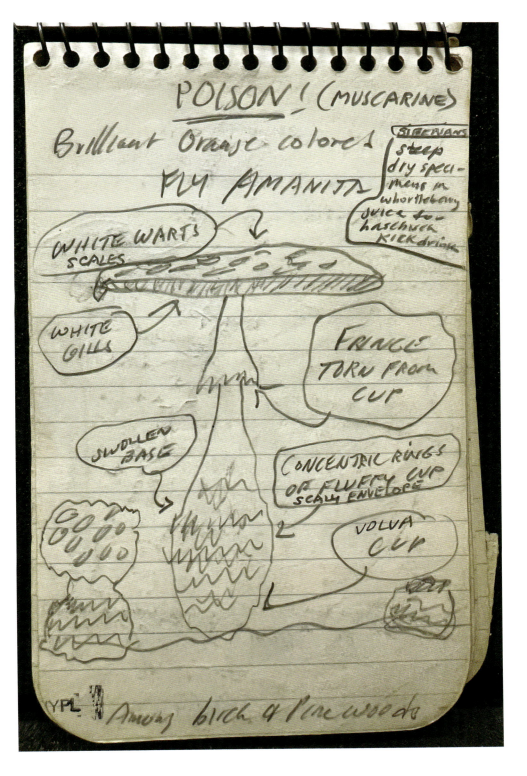

Figure 11

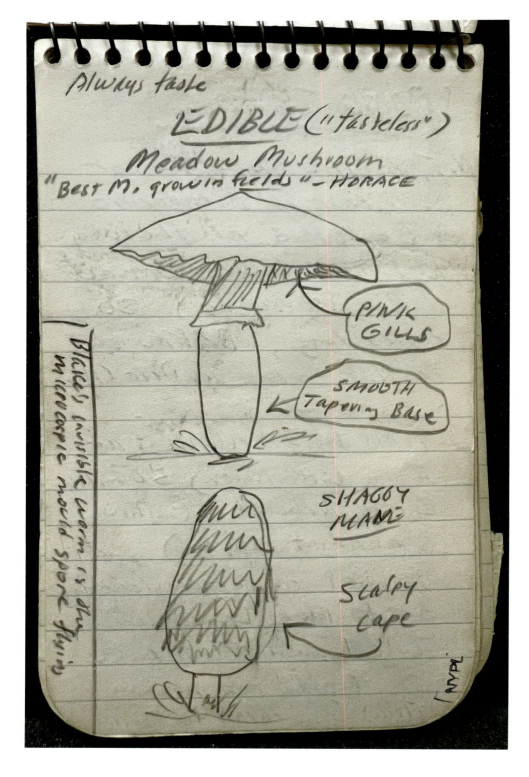

Figure 12

Figure 13

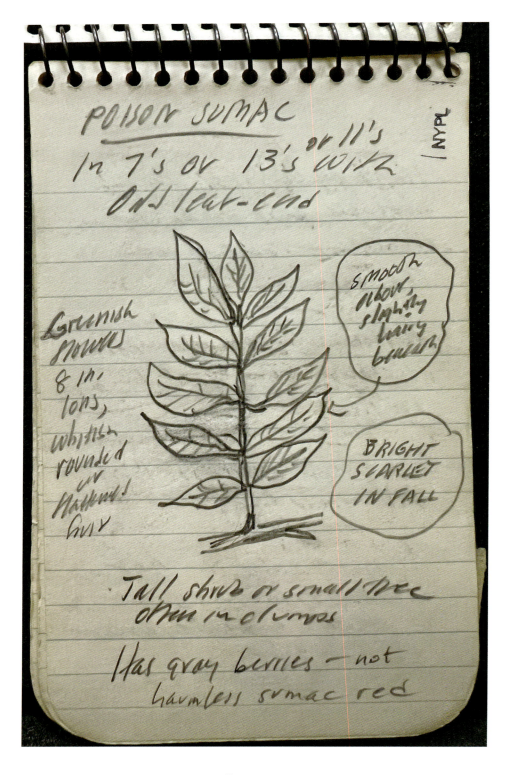

Figure 14

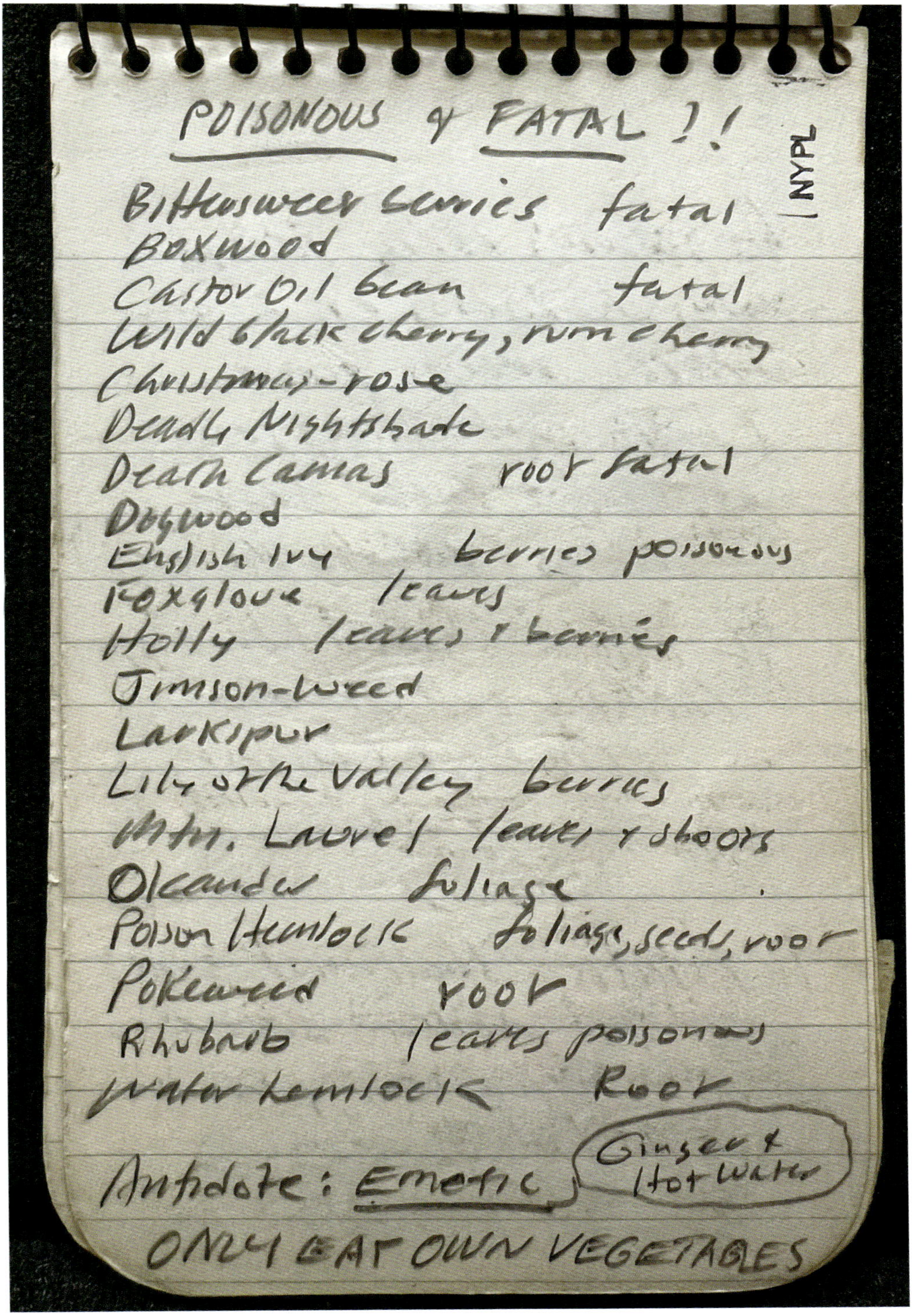

POISONOUS & FATAL ?!

|NYPL

Bittersweet berries   fatal
Boxwood
Castor Oil bean   fatal
Wild black cherry, rum cherry
Christmas-rose
Deadly Nightshade
Death Camas   root fatal
Dogwood
English Ivy   berries poisonous
Foxglove   leaves
Holly   leaves & berries
Jimson-weed
Larkspur
Lily of the Valley   berries
Mtn. Laurel   leaves & shoots
Oleander   foliage
Poison Hemlock   foliage, seeds, root
Pokeweed   root
Rhubarb   leaves poisonous
Water Hemlock   Root

Antidote: Emetic ⟨Ginseu & Hot water⟩

ONLY EAT OWN VEGETABLES

Figure 15

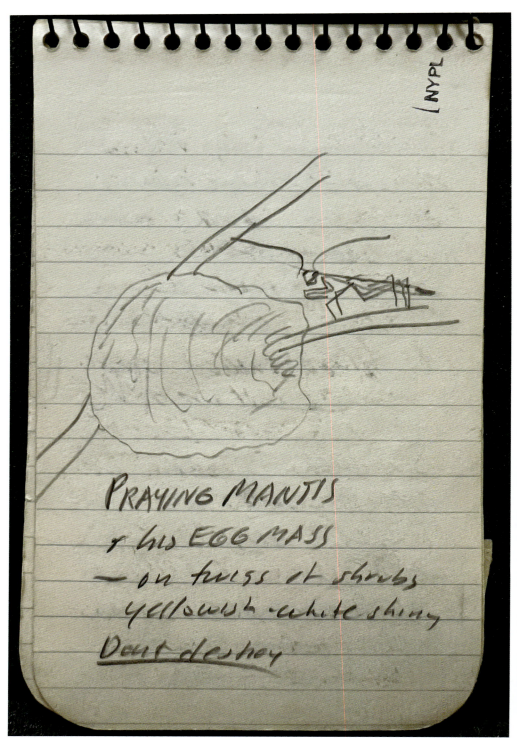

Figure 16: Journal page (immediately following those in figs. 10–15) showing Jack's concern not to harm sentient beings.

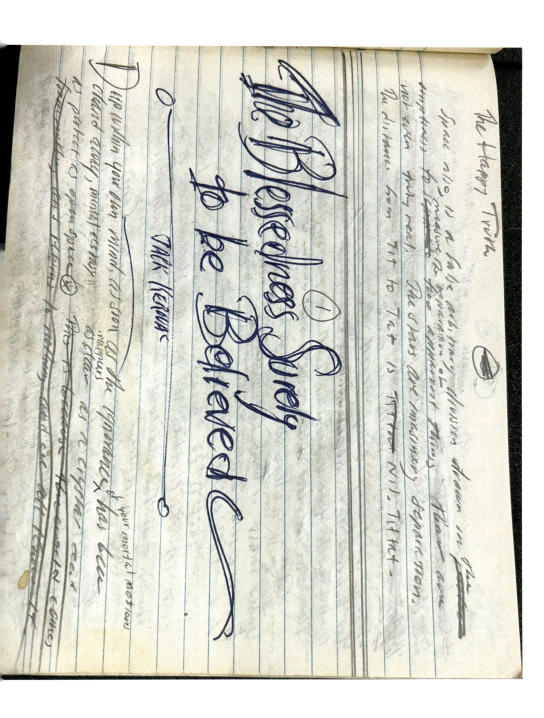

Figure 17: This page contains the last paragraph of "The Blessedness Truly to Be Believed" version 1 and the beginning of version 2.

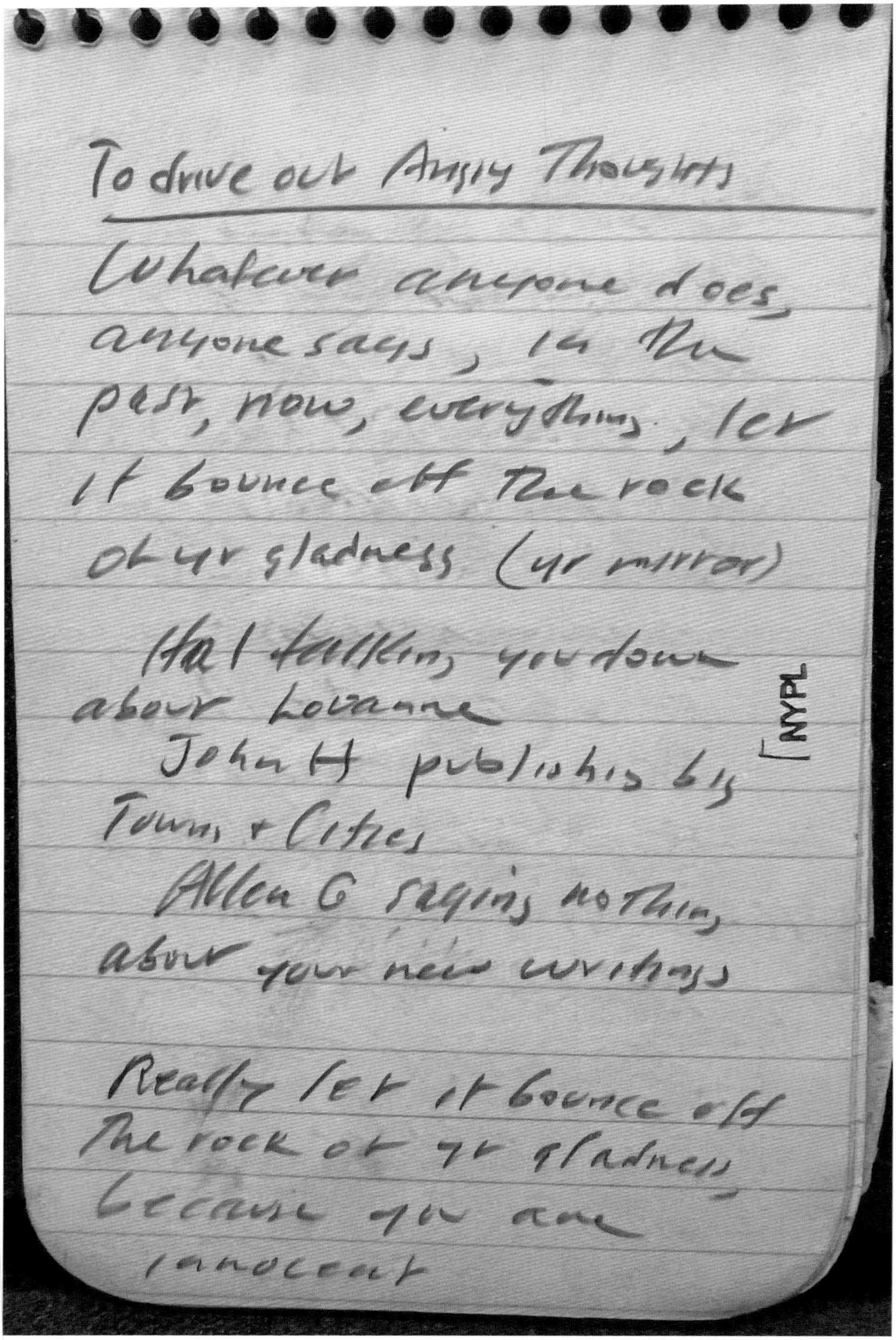

To drive out Angry Thoughts

Whatever anyone does,
anyone says, in the
past, now, everything, let
it bounce off the rock
ot yr gladness (yr mirror)

Hal talking you down
about Loraine
    John H publishig his
Town & Cities
    Allen G saying nothing
about your new writings

Really let it bounce off
the rock ot yr gladness
because you are
    innocent

*Figure 18: Page from the same notebook (December 1953) showing Jack's spiritual resolve.
References are to Hal Chase, Luanne Henderson, John Clellon Holmes, and Allen Ginsberg.*